SleepWell:

Adult Medicine

Vol. 1

SleepWell:

Adult Medicine

Vol. 1

Edited by:

Benjamin Clyburn, MD
Assistant Professor of Medicine
Internal Medicine Residency Program Director
Medical University of South Carolina
Charleston, South Carolina

George J. Taylor, MD
Professor of Medicine
Medical University of South Carolina
Charleston, South Carolina

Blackwell
Publishing

© 2003 by Blackwell Science
a Blackwell Publishing company

Blackwell Publishing, Inc., 350 Main Street, Malden, Massachusetts 02148-5018, USA
Blackwell Science Ltd, Osney Mead, Oxford OX2 0EL, UK
Blackwell Science Asia Pty Ltd, 550 Swanston Street, Carlton South, Victoria 3053, Australia
Blackwell Verlag GmbH, Kurfürstendamm 57, 10707 Berlin, Germany

02 03 04 05 5 4 3 2 1

ISBN: 0-632-04662-7

Library of Congress Cataloging-in-Publication Data

Sleepwell. Volume 1, Adult medicine / edited by Benjamin Clyburn, George J. Taylor.
    p.   ;   cm
    ISBN 0-632-04662-7 (pbk.)
    1. Internal medicine—Examinations, questions, etc.   2. Physicians—Licenses—United Staes—Examinations—Study guides.
    I. Clyburn, Benjamin.   II. Taylor, George Jesse.   III. Title: Adult medicine.
        [DNLM: 1. Internal Medicine—Examination Questions.   2. Cardiology—Examination Questions.   WB 18.2 S632 2002]
    RC58.S57 2002
    616¹.076–dc21

2002009534

A catalogue record for this title is available from the British Library

Acquisitions: Beverly Copland
Development: Angela Gagliano
Production: Debra Lally
Cover design: Leslie Haimes
Interior design: Mary McKeon
Typesetter: TechBooks in York, Pennsylvania
Printed and bound by Sheridan Books in Ann Arbor, MI

For further information on Blackwell Publishing, visit our website:
www.blackwellscience.com

• Contents

• Contributors

J. David Bohler, DVM, MD
Gastroenterology Fellow
Medical University of South Carolina
Charleston, South Carolina

Benjamin Clyburn, MD
Assistant Professor of Medicine
Internal Medicine Residency Program Director
Medical University of South Carolina
Charleston, South Carolina

Kevin M. Dineen, MD
Pulmonary/Critical Care Fellow
Medical University of South Carolina
Charleston, South Carolina

Glenn C. Douglas, MD
Rheumatology Fellow
Medical University of South Carolina
Charleston, South Carolina

Sam G. Dozier, MD
Clinical Instructor
Medical University of South Carolina
Charleston, South Carolina

Keith A. Frick, MD
Rheumatology Fellow
Medical University of South Carolina
Charleston, South Carolina

Anne M. Hauet, MD
Cardiology Fellow
Medical University of South Carolina
Charleston, South Carolina

J. Terrill Huggins, MD
Pulmonary/Critical Care Fellow
Medical University of South Carolina
Charleston, South Carolina

William A. Jackson, Jr., MD
Cardiology Fellow
Medical University of South Carolina
Charleston, South Carolina

Gretchen M. Labarowski, MD
Hematology/Oncology Fellow
Medical University of South Carolina
Charleston, South Carolina

Robert M. Malanuk, MD
Cardiology Fellow
Medical University of South Carolina
Charleston, South Carolina

Greg Moffitt, MD
Endocrine Fellow
University of Louisville
Louisville, Kentucky
Endocrine Department
Medical University of South Carolina
Charleston, South Carolina

Eni Okonofua, MBBS
Clinical Instructor
Medical University of South Carolina
Charleston, South Carolina

Pamela Pride, MD
Assistant Professor
Medical University of South Carolina
Attending Physician, Department of Medicine
Medical University Hospital
Charleston, South Carolina

Patrick F. Reilly, MD
Gastroenterology Fellow
Medical University of South Carolina
Charleston, South Carolina

David A. Sabol, MD
Gastroenterology Fellow
Medical University of South Carolina
Charleston, South Carolina

A. Thomas Siachos, MD
Cardiology Fellow
Medical University of South Carolina
Charleston, South Carolina

Michael A. Smith, MD
Fellow, Academic Generalist Program
Department of Medicine
Medical University of South Carolina
Charleston, South Carolina

Jeremy Soule, MD
Endocrinology Fellow
Medical University of South Carolina
Charleston, South Carolina

J. Lacy Sturdivant, MD
Cardiology Fellow
Medical University of South Carolina
Charleston, South Carolina

William Ward, MD
Nephrology Fellow
Medical University of South Carolina
Charleston, South Carolina

Jessica Wells, MD
Internal Medical Resident
Medical University of South Carolina
Charleston, South Carolina

David E. Wood, MD
Cardiology Fellow
Medical University of South Carolina
Charleston, South Carolina

• Reviewers

Joe Caron, MD
Chief Resident
Wausau Family Practice Residency Program
Wausau, Wisconsin

Chris Caraang, MD
3rd Year Resident
University of California, Los Angeles—San Fernando Valley
Los Angeles, California

Jennifer Heidmann, MD
Resident, Primary Care Internal Medicine
University of California, San Francisco
San Francisco, California

Brian F. Morris, MD
Resident
Ball Memorial Hospital
Muncie, Indiana

Nancy Pandhi, MD
Resident
Shenandoah Valley Family Practice Residency Program
Winchester, Virginia

John Bryan Waits, MD
Family Practice Resident
In His Image Family Practice Residency
Tulsa, Oklahoma

Sanford F. White, MD, MPH
Resident
Utah Valley Family Practice Residency
Provo, Utah

• Preface

The *SleepWell Review* series is a **review for the National Board examinations,** compiled for students and residents taking parts 2 and 3 as well as international medical graduates. It is also **suitable for recertification exams in family medicine and state licensure exams.**

In the three volumes, we have attempted to cover all of the topics that you will encounter on the exams. The series differs from many practice tests, as we provide a brief discussion of the questions and answers. The emphasis is on "brief," and we do not pretend that the discussions provide a thorough review—you do not have time for that. Rather, the short explanations will remind you of the concept(s) that the board examiner wants you to know. Understand that clinical issue and you will be able to handle related questions.

Many of you will use this review as a study guide as you begin preparing for the boards. For the brave soul who decides not to study, it would be a suitable one-shot review. For most of you, we suggest using it just before the exam. After studying for months, you are burned out and cannot memorize another table or list of facts. So what do you do in the last week? Here is our best advice: go to the gym every day, get to bed early, and breeze through these sample questions with their short explanations. **Use these books** as your last study exercise, and **you will sleep well the night before the boards.**

We welcome feedback and suggestions you may have on this book or any in the new *SleepWell Review* series. Send to blue@blacksci.com.

• Section 1

Cardiology

Anne M. Hauet, MD

William A. Jackson, Jr., MD

Robert M. Malanuk, MD

A. Thomas Siachos, MD

J. Lacy Sturdivant, MD

George J. Taylor, MD

David E. Wood, MD

● CASE PRESENTATION

A 43-year-old woman is seen in the emergency department complaining of a 6-week history of episodic, squeezing chest discomfort, usually lasting for 10 to 15 minutes and accompanied by shortness of breath. The pain tends to occur at night and awakens her from sleep. She also reports that she had no difficulty playing tennis with her daughter and has not experienced exertional pain. Her only risk factor for coronary artery disease is smoking. While relating this history, she experiences chest pain. An ECG shows 4-mm ST elevation in leads V_1 to V_6 and reciprocal changes in the inferior leads. After she receives nitroglycerin sublingually, her pain resolves and the ECG normalizes.

1. What is the cause of the patient's chest pain?
   A. Acute anterior myocardial infarction
   B. Acute inferior myocardial infarction
   C. Coronary vasospasm
   D. Pericarditis

2. Proper initial therapy in this patient could include the following:
   A. Amlodipine 5 mg PO
   B. Nitroglycerin
   C. Verapamil 10 mg IV
   D. Intravenous metoprolol
   E. A, B, and C

3. The patient had coronary angiography, which showed a 50% stenosis in the proximal portion of the left anterior descending coronary artery. The best therapy is:
   A. Angioplasty
   B. Bypass surgery
   C. Diltiazem plus aspirin
   D. Metoprolol and aspirin

4. Conditions that may precipitate coronary vasospasm include:
   A. Cocaine use
   B. Hyperventilation
   C. Pheochromocytoma
   D. Hypermagnesemia
   E. A, B, and C

● COMMENT

Variant angina • The history suggests Prinzmetal's variant angina secondary to coronary vasospasm, and ST segment elevation during pain is the usual finding. Spasm may develop at the site of an atherosclerotic plaque but may also occur in normal-appearing coronary arteries. Patients with variant angina typically have angina occurring at rest, with no relation to exercise or emotional distress. The prevalence is unknown, and the condition is more common in women.

Treatment • Although the exact mechanism of coronary vasospasm is unknown, it is probably related to dysfunctional endothelium. The final step is increased intracellular calcium in arterial smooth muscle. The mainstay of therapy remains calcium channel blockers, which inhibit the influx of calcium. The use of nitrates may also be needed. Because of the potential for unopposed alpha-adrenergic stimulation—aggravating vasospasm—beta-blockers should be avoided in patients with variant angina. In fact, it is not uncommon to see coronary spasm in patients recently started on beta-blockers for hypertension.

Vasospasm is a medical condition and not a surgical one. Spastic arteries tend to be touchy and may develop intense spasm at the time of surgical manipulation. Postoperative ST segment elevation, arrhythmias, and infarction may follow. Revascularization is considered only if there is a tight atherosclerotic lesion.

Even the use of aspirin should be approached with caution as aspirin inhibits the production of prostacyclin, a coronary vasodilator, and thus may aggravate spasm. In this patient, however, most would use daily low-dose aspirin because of borderline coronary atherosclerosis.

Precipitating factors • Cocaine inhibits the reuptake of norepinephrine by sympathetic nerve endings, which leads to vasoconstriction. It is a common cause of myocardial infarction in those with normal-appearing coronary arteries. Autopsy studies of patients with pheochromocytoma often show patchy areas of myocardial necrosis, presumed secondary to coronary vasospasm.

Vasospasm requires the availability of calcium ions. Hydrogen ions compete with calcium ions; vasoconstriction may occur if the hydrogen ion concentration falls, as with hyperventilation (respiratory alkalosis). Magnesium lowers the available calcium ion concentration, and correction of hypomagnesemia may reverse spasm in a patient with resistant variant angina.

Answers • 1-C 2-E 3-C 4-E

● CASE PRESENTATION

A 71-year-old man is in clinic with progressively worsening shortness of breath over the past several days. His activity has been limited over the past day or two because of episodes of marked dyspnea that resolve with rest. He describes mild chest tightness and anxiety with these episodes. There is a long history of hypertension, and he has regularly failed to take prescribed medicines. On physical exam he seems comfortable, but has blood pressure of 195/90mm Hg, heart rate of 92/min, and respirations of 16 breaths/min. He has a forceful apical impulse in the midclavicular line and a grade 2 systolic murmur without radiation to the carotid arteries. S_1 and S_2 are normal with a prominent S_4 gallop. There is no jugular venous distension, but there is hepatojugular reflux (abdominojugular reflux). His lung fields have bilateral crackles up to the midlung zones. He has no ankle edema. An electrocardiogram (ECG) is shown in Figure 1 (next page).

1. Your next step in management should be:
   A. Urgent coronary angiography
   B. Signal averaged ECG
   C. Thallium scan
   D. Beginning of diuretics, angiotensin-converting enzyme (ACE) inhibitors, and continuation of daily aspirin
   E. Ventilation and perfusion scan of the lungs

2. During the evaluation an echocardiogram is performed; it shows a normal ejection fraction and normal wall motion. What is the most likely cause of the patient's symptoms?
   A. Aortic valve stenosis
   B. Pulmonary embolus
   C. Chronic, uncontrolled hypertension
   D. Pneumonia
   E. Coronary artery disease

3. The S_4 gallop on physical exam:
   A. Results from the emptying of blood into a "stiff" ventricle during atrial contraction
   B. Is no surprise given the ECG findings
   C. Occurs immediately before S_1
   D. Is diagnostic of systolic left ventricular dysfunction
   E. A, B, and C

4. Which of the following is true regarding therapy?
   A. ACE inhibitors are most effective for regression of left ventricular hypertrophy.
   B. Reducing preload with diuretics and nitrates improves pulmonary congestion.
   C. Reducing blood pressure has an immediate and lasting effect.
   D. Controlling the heart rate with beta-blockers or calcium channel blockers will improve exercise tolerance.
   E. All of the above

● COMMENT

Congestive heart failure (CHF) and diastolic ventricular dysfunction • It is clear from the history and physical exam findings that the patient has congestive heart failure. His symptoms require immediate treatment. An echocardiogram is a good early diagnostic step as it provides a precise estimation of ventricular function and excludes occult valvular heart disease. Coronary angiography would be appropriate if there were a clinical history indicating unstable angina, or if echocardiography showed regional wall motion abnormalities. Otherwise, screening for coronary artery disease (CAD) with perfusion scanning is adequate (and most patients with new CHF are screened for CAD), but it is not a medical emergency. The signal-averaged ECG is a test to identify those at high risk for ventricular arrhythmias.

The definition of diastolic CHF is simple: clinical heart failure plus normal left ventricular (LV) ejection fraction. Hypertensive heart disease is a common cause. It is seen much more frequently in elderly patients, and especially older women. The prognosis with diastolic heart failure is better than with systolic CHF (as a rule, low LV ejection fraction means bad prognosis!).

Atrial contraction • Because patients with diastolic dysfunction are "preload-dependent," atrial contraction and its contribution to diastolic filling are critical. In addition to showing LV hypertrophy (high QRS voltage in V_2, lateral T wave inversion), the ECG in Figure 1 reveals left atrial abnormality (biphasic P wave in V_1); the left atrium is working hard to fill the stiff ventricle. This is also reflected in the physical exam; the S_4 gallop is produced by atrial contraction against the stiff LV. A loss of atrial contraction could drop cardiac output by as much as 25%, so it is important to maintain sinus rhythm.

Therapy for diastolic dysfunction • Because of the increase in left ventricular diastolic pressure, there is increased pressure in the left atrium and pulmonary vasculature, causing pulmonary congestion and dyspnea. You must relieve congestion with diuretics and/or nitrates. Reducing blood pressure or afterload will improve relaxation through regression of LVH. The most effective agents at reversing LVH are ACE inhibitors, but all antihypertensive agents work. Slowing heart rate increases the amount of time in diastole, thus increasing ventricular filling and cardiac output. Maintaining a normal sinus rhythm is of paramount importance, as is prevention of ischemia.

Answers • 1-D 2-C 3-E 4-E

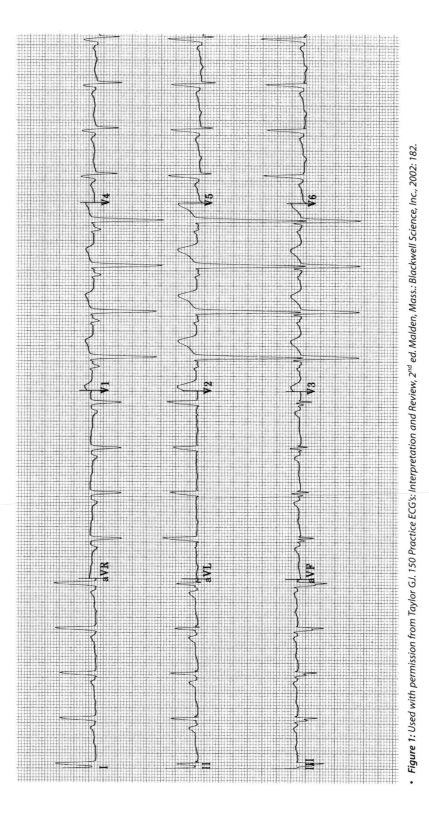

• **Figure 1:** *Used with permission from Taylor GJ. 150 Practice ECG's: Interpretation and Review, 2nd ed. Malden, Mass.: Blackwell Science, Inc., 2002: 182.*

● CASE PRESENTATION

A 47-year-old man enters the emergency room with squeezing midchest pain that began 1 hour ago. He also has had profuse sweating and severe nausea with two episodes of emesis. There is no positional component and no change with deep inspiration. Other history is positive for hypertension and heavy tobacco use. On exam, he is diaphoretic and appears to be in severe distress. Heart rate is 109 beats/min and blood pressure is 174/90. There are no obvious murmurs or rubs. Lung fields are clear. An electrocardiogram (ECG) done on arrival is shown in Figure 2.

1. Which of these laboratory values is most likely to be elevated at the time of presentation in the above patient?

   A. Troponin I
   B. Creatinine kinase
   C. Both of the above
   D. Neither of the above

2. Which of the following would be appropriate in the period immediately after presentation?

   A. Aspirin
   B. Beta-blockers
   C. Morphine
   D. Epinephrine
   E. A, B, and C

3. Which of the following are contraindications to administration of intravenous thrombolytic therapy?

   A. Major surgery or trauma 6 weeks ago
   B. Intracerebral neoplasm
   C. Suspected aortic dissection
   D. History of a cerebrovascular accident
   E. All of the above

4. Which of the following occurs first in the development of myocardial infarction?

   A. Platelet adhesion and activation
   B. Activation of factor VII
   C. Conversion of fibrinogen to fibrin
   D. Activation of plasmin
   E. Release of antithrombin III

5. The diagnosis of acute myocardial infarction and decision to use thrombolytic therapy should be based on which of the following clinical tools?

   A. Electrocardiogram
   B. Physical exam
   C. History
   D. Chest x-ray
   E. A, B, and C

● COMMENT

Pathophysiology of MI • The patient is having an acute anterior myocardial infarction (MI). The usual initiating events are the spontaneous rupture of the thin fibrous cap that overlies coronary artery plaque, exposure of underlying collagen, and activation of platelets. Other elements of the coagulation cascade follow.

The decision to use thrombolytic therapy • The physical exam plays a role in the decision to use thrombolytic therapy primarily to exclude recent trauma (a bump on the head may be a contraindication). History and the electrocardiogram (ECG) showing ST segment elevation establish the diagnosis, and these are the only diagnostic tests needed to apply thrombolytic therapy. Blood tests and a chest x-ray unnecessarily delay therapy. You would wait for an x-ray if the history suggested aortic dissection rather than MI, but in that case you would also want a more definitive test (computed tomography [CT] scan or transesophageal echo). Cardiac enzymes including creatinine kinase and troponin do not become abnormal until 3 to 5 hours after the onset of MI.

Establishing prognosis at the onset of MI • The physical exam does help establish prognosis, as rales or pulmonary edema indicate large, high-risk MI. Other indicators of poor prognosis are age above 70, previous history of MI, atrial fibrillation, anterior infarction, hypotension, sinus tachycardia, female gender, and diabetes mellitus. Long-term prognosis is related to left ventricular function and the amount of residual myocardium that is ischemic and at risk for future injury.

Initial treatment of MI • In the emergency room, treat the patient with aspirin, morphine, and oxygen. You may try nitroglycerin for the patient with recent onset chest pain. If you are not going to use thrombolytic therapy, intravenous beta-blockade has been found to improve survival with acute MI with ST segment elevation. The other alternative to coronary thrombolysis is immediate angioplasty.

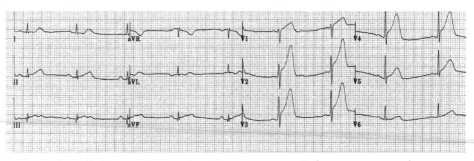

• **Figure 2:** Used with permission from Taylor GJ. 150 Practice ECG's: Interpretation and Review, 2nd ed. Malden, Mass.: Blackwell Science, Inc., 2002: 60.

Answers • 1-D 2-E 3-E 4-A 5-E

● CASE PRESENTATION

A previously healthy 20-year-old man enters your clinic after having a syncopal event while jogging with a friend. He denies any chest pain or shortness of breath and on auscultation has a prominent precordial impulse, an S_4 gallop, and a dynamic systolic ejection murmur that intensifies with standing and Valsalva maneuver and decreases with the handgrip maneuver.

1. Your next step would be to:
   A. Reassure the patient and inform him that it is likely that dehydration led to his episode.
   B. Order an exercise stress test to exclude the possibility of underlying coronary disease.
   C. Order an echocardiogram.
   D. Order cardiac magnetic resonance imaging (MRI).

2. Which of the following may control symptoms in patients with hypertrophic cardiomyopathy?
   A. Disopyramide
   B. Amlodipine
   C. Metoprolol
   D. A and C
   E. A, B, and C

3. The risk of sudden death in patients with hypertrophic obstructive cardiomyopathy has been associated with:
   A. Hypotensive response during exercise testing
   B. Septal hypertrophy of 3 cm or more
   C. Family history of sudden death in two or more first-degree relatives
   D. High outflow tract gradient
   E. A, B, and C
   F. All of the above

4. Which of these invasive procedures has been used to help those patients' symptoms that are refractory to medications?
   A. Purcutaneous alcohol septal ablation
   B. Surgical myomectomy
   C. Pacemaker placement
   D. Aortic valvular replacement
   E. A, B, and C

● COMMENT

Hypertrophic cardiomyopathy • The history and physical exam are most consistent with hypertrophic cardiomyopathy (HCM), formerly called idiopathic hypertrophic subaortic stenosis (IHSS). This is a potential cause of sudden death in young athletes. It is an autosomal dominant trait. Physical findings may include a fourth heart sound and, characteristically, a changeable murmur, which intensifies with Valsalva's maneuver or with standing after squatting. The subvalvular gradient results from overcrowding of the outflow tract by the septum as well as anterior movement of the mitral valve leaflet into the outflow tract during systole. High-velocity blood flow across a narrowed space creates a Venturi effect that pulls the leaflet toward the septum, recognized as systolic anterior motion (SAM) of the mitral valve on echocardiography. The outflow tract becomes more crowded, and the gradient and murmur increase with lower left ventricular (LV) volumes (as occurs during the Valsalva maneuver and when the patient stands after squatting). The echocardiogram clearly demonstrates HCM and the Doppler study measures the outflow tract gradient.

HCM patients have variable symptoms and may complain of dyspnea, chest discomfort, presyncope, syncope, fatigue, and palpitations, with symptoms often induced by exertion, dehydration, and sudden changes in body posture. Outflow tract obstruction is but one of four mechanisms that contribute to symptoms. The others are diastolic dysfunction, myocardial ischemia, and arrhythmias.

Treatment of HCM • Drugs that depress ventricular contractility (verapamil, beta-blockers, and disopyramide) cause ventricular dilatation, widening of the outflow tract, and reduction of flow velocity, which minimizes the degree of SAM. These drugs also help diastolic filling by slowing heart rate. Digitalis should not be administered because it may increase contractility and the degree of outflow obstruction.

Risk of sudden death • Asymptomatic or mildly symptomatic patients may die suddenly, and the annual mortality risk is 4% to 6%. Risk factors for sudden cardiac death are septal wall thickness greater than 3 cm, an abnormal response to exercise testing, and a family history of sudden death (first-degree relatives should have screening echocardiograms). The degree of outflow tract obstruction has not been shown to correlate with the risk of death; nor has reducing the gradient with surgery or medical therapy been shown to lower the risk.

Invasive therapies • A small number of HCM patients have persistent symptoms that are refractory to medical therapy. Previously surgical resection of the septum was done. More recently, "septal ablation" is performed by injecting alcohol through a catheter positioned in a septal artery. An occasional patient may benefit from pacemaker therapy (the paced QRS has a left bundle branch block pattern with delayed septal activation and decrease in the outflow tract gradient). As the aortic valve is normal, valve replacement surgery is of no value.

● CASE PRESENTATION

A 55-year-old Hispanic man complains of slowly increasing fatigue, malaise, and dyspnea on exertion for the past 5 to 6 months. With the dyspnea he has had cough with occasional blood-streaked sputum. He also notes the new onset of palpitations. He denies chest pain, dizziness, or presyncope. He likewise denies recent fever or chills and on further questioning indicates a history of rheumatic fever as a child.

Physical exam reveals an irregularly irregular rhythm with a low-pitched, diastolic "rumbling" murmur best heard at the cardiac apex. The position and quality of the apical impulse are normal, and there is no gallop.

1. The patient most likely has:
   A. Mitral regurgitation
   B. Aortic stenosis
   C. Mitral stenosis
   D. Aortic regurgitation
   E. Unstable angina

2. The palpitations and irregular rhythm that the patient is describing are frequently seen in patients with this valvular disorder. The rhythm described is most likely:
   A. Frequent premature ventricular contractions
   B. Atrioventricular (AV) nodal re-entry tachycardia
   C. Atrial fibrillation
   D. Ventricular tachycardia
   E. Ventricular fibrillation

3. Which of these statements regarding the valvular problem described is *true*?
   A. Rheumatic fever is the cause.
   B. There is left atrial overload, with relative sparing of the left ventricle.
   C. Notching of the P wave in leads II and III, and AVF or a biphasic P wave in lead V_1 are common (for those in sinus rhythm).
   D. There is a state of increased left ventricular afterload, which eventually causes LV failure.
   E. A, B, and C

4. In addition to the diastolic murmur heard in this patient, which of these findings is diagnostic?
   A. A holosystolic murmur heard best at the right upper sternal border
   B. An opening "snap" just after S_2
   C. Bilateral carotid bruits
   D. A pulsatile liver and elevated neck veins

5. Which of the following is an indication for repair or replacement of the valve?
   A. No symptoms but a tight valve
   B. Recurrent rheumatic fever
   C. Left atrial enlargement on the echocardiogram
   D. Moderate to severe symptoms

● COMMENT

Rheumatic heart disease • This patient has mitral stenosis (MS). For practical purposes, mitral stenosis can be equated with rheumatic heart disease (congenital MS has been described but is extremely rare). The disease is much more common in less developed countries and is now an uncommon illness in the West because of aggressive treatment of streptococcal infections.

Pathophysiology of MS • With progressive scarring, calcification, and decreased mobility of the mitral valve, left atrial overload develops. Left ventricular (LV) preload is low (MS impedes LV filling and thus "spares" the LV), even though vascular volume is high. The patient has pulmonary congestion (cough, dyspnea on exertion, winter bronchitis, and even hemoptysis), but there are no signs of LV failure (i.e., gallop or displaced apical impulse). In addition, physical exam reveals the presence of the pathognomonic opening snap (OS) and low-pitched diastolic murmur ("rumble").

ECG and clinical course • With time, in most patients left atrial enlargement develops, manifested by the P mitrale pattern (notched P wave in inferior leads or biphasic P wave in V_1). The typical arrhythmia of left atrial enlargement is atrial fibrillation. The patient's irregular pulse and palpitations suggest atrial fibrillation as the cardiac rhythm. Asymptomatic patients in normal sinus rhythm require only antibiotic prophylaxis for infective endocarditis. For mild symptoms, diuretics lower left atrial pressure and usually relieve pulmonary symptoms. Surgical treatment is recommended for moderate to severe symptoms (usually with a tight valve), systemic embolism as a result of atrial fibrillation, or severe pulmonary hypertension. Exercise-related symptoms are the usual indication. Remember that the LV is protected by the mitral stenosis, and surgery is not required prophylactically to protect it.

Answers • 1-C 2-C 3-E 4-B 5-D

● CASE PRESENTATION

An 80-year-old man reports several episodes of dizziness over the last few days, including one episode of syncope. He denies any chest pain or shortness of breath associated with these episodes. He has no history of cardiac disease. He takes an aspirin each day. His primary care physician has recommended a Holter monitor. A rhythm strip during an episode of dizziness is shown (Figure 3).

1. The rhythm strip reveals:
   A. Atrial fibrillation
   B. Atrial flutter
   C. Sinus pause
   D. Junctional escape rhythm
   E. Complete heart block

2. What is the appropriate next step?
   A. Left heart catheterization
   B. Permanent pacemaker
   C. Stress thallium test
   D. Beta-blocker
   E. No further treatment needed

3. Which of the following does *not* require a pacemaker?
   A. First-degree heart block
   B. Second-degree heart block (Mobitz) type I
   C. Second-degree heart block type II
   D. Complete heart block
   E. A and B

4. If the Holter monitor shows sinus rhythm with a 2-second pause, what treatment would you recommend?
   A. No further treatment, observation only
   B. Permanent pacemaker
   C. Stress thallium test
   D. Beta-blocker
   E. Electrophysiology (EP) study

● COMMENT

Indications for pacemaker therapy • The rhythm strip illustrates complete heart block. P waves march through the QRS complexes, indicating atrioventricular dissociation. Furthermore, the atrial ryhthm is faster than the ventricular escape rhythm. The next step would be placement of a permanent pacemaker for this patient.

The usual clinical indication for permanent pacemaker therapy is a symptomatic bradyarrhythmia (Table 1). Complete heart block is a condition of elderly patients, with block of conduction below the atrioventricular (AV) node. They usually have ventricular conduction abnormalities (bundle-branch block) on a pre–heart block ECG. A degenerative process of the cardiac nerves, not coronary artery disease, is the usual cause.

Other manifestations of infranodal block (Mobitz II block) are also indications for pacing. On the other hand, first-degree heart block and Mobitz 1 second-degree block (Wenckebach block) do not require pacing. These patients usually have a narrow QRS on ECG indicating that the site of block is the AV node.

Sick sinus syndrome is another common indication for pacing. An atrial tachyarrhythmia or atrial fibrillation requires drug therapy to prevent tachycardia, and the drugs aggravate bradyarrhythmia. Pacing is indicated so that the patient can tolerate necessary drug therapy.

In asymptomatic patients with a sinus pause less than 4 seconds in duration, only observation is needed. A sinus pause of just 2 seconds rarely causes symptoms.

TABLE 1 • Most Common ECG Indications for Permanent Pacemaker
1. Complete heart block (usually have wide QRS, indicating infranodal disease)
2. Mobitz II second-degree heart block (usually have wide QRS)
3. Sinus arrest (usually $\geq$ 4 seconds)
4. Sick sinus syndrome (rate slowing drugs needed to control tachyarrhythmia and pacer needed to prevent bradycardia)

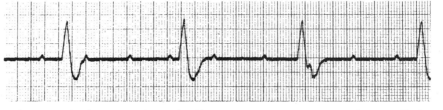

• *Figure 3: Used with permission from Taylor GJ. 150 Practice ECG's: Interpretation and Review, 2nd ed. Malden, Mass.: Blackwell Science, Inc., 2002: 19.*

● CASE PRESENTATION

A 25-year-old woman with no prior history of cardiac disease was at dinner when she noticed the sudden onset of palpitations and dizziness. She reports the episode lasted for 30 minutes and subsided spontaneously. The electrocardiogram (ECG) the next day is shown in Figure 4.

1. The ECG reveals:
   A. Atrial fibrillation
   B. Atrial flutter
   C. Wolff-Parkinson-White syndrome
   D. Multifocal atrial tachycardia
   E. Ventricular tachycardia

2. The appropriate next step is:
   A. Reassurance
   B. Stress thallium scan
   C. Electrophysiology (EP) study
   D. Tilt table test
   E. Left heart catheterization

3. Which of the following is contraindicated in Wolff-Parkinson-White (WPW) syndrome?
   A. Procainamide
   B. Atrioventricular (AV) nodal blocking drugs
   C. Angiotensin converting enzyme (ACE) inhibitors
   D. Diuretics

4. What is the definitive treatment for WPW?
   A. Calcium channel blockers to block AV nodal conduction
   B. Catheter ablation of the bypass tract
   C. Digoxin
   D. Valsalva maneuver
   E. Carotid massage

● COMMENT

Pre-excitation syndromes • The Wolff-Parkinson-White syndrome is intermittent supraventricular tachycardia (SVT) in a patient with a short PR interval (<0.12 second) and a delta wave (note leads I and the V leads). The SVT involves a re-entrant circuit that includes the AV node and an accessory pathway. Early conduction through this pathway "pre-excites" the ventricle, causing the delta wave.

What to advise this patient is open to discussion (there is no clear answer). When there is no prior history, most would elect to reassure and observe a patient who has had a first episode of SVT. Frequent or bothersome symptoms may prompt electrophysiologic testing to identify the accessory pathway. Once the pathway is located, catheter ablation can be performed, providing a permanent cure for 95%. Most now agree that ablation is preferable to lifelong drug therapy (especially as medicines are not very effective). There is no role for exercise stress testing, tilt table testing, or left heart catheterization when the diagnosis of pre-excitation is apparent (coronary artery disease does not cause it).

Blocking the AV node with digoxin and verapamil is contraindicated in Wolff-Parkinson-White syndrome patients because this can promote antegrade accessory pathway conduction. Adenosine, beta-blockers, and vagal maneuvers may help slow the rate and are occasionally used with caution. However, any drug or maneuver that blocks AV conduction should be avoided when there is atrial fibrillation, as blocking the AV node can promote unusually rapid conduction through the accessory pathway. Degeneration of these fast rhythms to ventricular tachycardia is possible.

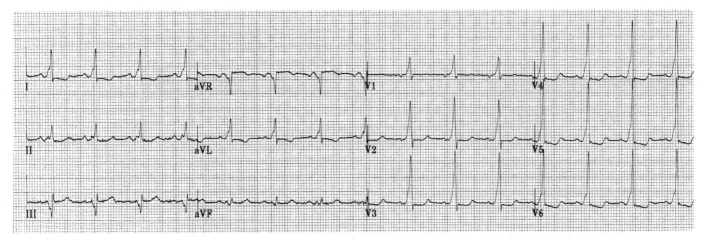

• **Figure 4:** Used with permission from Taylor GJ. 150 Practice ECG's: Interpretation and Review, 2nd ed. Malden, Mass.: Blackwell Science, Inc., 2002: 102.

Answers • 1-C   2-A or C   3-B   4-B

● CASE PRESENTATION

A 42-year-old patient with known idiopathic dilated cardiomy-opathy (ejection factor = 20%) has had stable class II heart failure symptoms. He reports 1 week of worsening dyspnea, paroxysmal nocturnal dyspnea, abdominal fullness, and lower extremity edema, for which he has been taking increased doses of his di-uretic. Symptoms began shortly after the patient sustained an acute ankle injury and started taking ibuprofen. His medications also include digoxin, a diuretic, an angiotensin converting enzyme (ACE) inhibitor, and warfarin. On exam, he is normotensive with a pulse of 96/min and is afebrile. His lung fields have crackles two-thirds of the way up bilaterally. His cardiovascular exam shows JVP at 20 cm, S_3 gallop, a soft systolic murmur, and a laterally displaced PMI. The chest x-ray confirms pulmonary edema. The ECG shows sinus rhythm and is unchanged when compared with previous ECGs. Lab results are notable for creatinine 2.5 mg/dL (baseline 1.7 mg/dL), INR 3.8, and normal troponin.

1. The next step should be:

   A. Intravenous (IV) heparin bolus with initiation of heparin infu-sion and immediate V/Q scan
   B. Emergency echocardiogram to assess left ventricular (LV) function
   C. Stopping of ACEI and warfarin, starting of diuresis with IV diuretics, starting therapy with hydralazine and isosorbide dinitrate
   D. Diuresis, oxygen therapy, holding warfarin, and monitoring INR; continuation of ACEI therapy; discontinuation of ibuprofen
   E. Transplantation evaluation

2. The pulmonary findings on exam in this patient:

   A. Would further indicate a cardiac cause if a unilateral left-sided effusion is identified
   B. Are consistent with cardiac rales if they occur in late inspiration
   C. Are indistinguishable from pulmonary fibrosis
   D. Would not be cardiac if there were associated wheezing
   E. Would be more obvious if the patient had advanced chronic obstructive pulmonary disease (COPD) as the associated barrel-shaped chest would better amplify the rales

3. The following statements about cardiac output are true:

   A. Diuretics, by decreasing preload, cause the ventricular function curve to shift up and to the left.
   B. Reducing afterload with the addition of an ACEI shifts the Frank-Starling curve down and to the right, improving ventric-ular function.
   C. Determinants of cardiac output are heart rate, preload, after-load, and contractility.
   D. A and B
   E. All of the above

4. Which of the following is true of ACEIs?

   A. They inhibit formation of angiotensin II
   B. They retard the degradation of circulating bradykinin
   C. They can be used safely in combination with a beta-blocking agent
   D. They are contraindicated in patients with bilateral renal artery stenosis
   E. All of the above

● COMMENT

Precipitation of heart failure with nonsteroidal anti-inflammatory drugs • This man shows acute decompensation of stable heart failure. He has pulmonary edema with a stable blood pressure and cardiac rhythm. You already know he has left ventricular dysfunction, and another echocardiogram will add little. Attention needs to be fo-cused on clinical stabilization and identifying what precipitated his recent decline. In a patient with significant heart failure and baseline renal insufficiency, the likely culprit is the ibuprofen as the patient would be dependent on renal production of prostaglandins. Pul-monary embolus does not usually cause worsening of heart failure over a period of many days, and the patient has been adequately an-ticoagulated. The increased creatinine is secondary to the ibuprofen; therefore, discontinuing the ACEI is not necessary unless renal func-tion does not improve. In that case, a switch to hydralazine and nitrates would be appropriate.

Pleural effusion • Heart failure is the most common cause of pleu-ral effusion. When it is unilateral, it is usually right-sided. An isolated left-sided pleural effusion suggests a noncardiac cause. Inexperienced peo-ple describe "wet" as opposed to the "dry" rales, but the quality of fine crackles is the same with heart failure and pulmonary fibrosis. The tim-ing of rales helps. With interstitial edema (mild heart failure), the rales are end-inspiratory, and with fibrosis they are paninspiratory. Wheez-ing is a sign of airway obstruction and can occur with pulmonary congestion. Rales are often inaudible in those with emphysema, and a chest x-ray is needed to exclude congestion.

Effects of treatment on the ventricular function curve • Diuret-ics are used in the treatment of congestive heart failure to improve symptoms of pulmonary congestion. They actually decrease preload and therefore stroke volume. Shifting the Frank-Starling curve up and to the left by increasing contractility or reducing afterload improves the stroke volume. Cardiac output is increased as well, as it is the prod-uct of stroke volume and heart rate.

ACE inhibition • An ACEI impairs the production of the potent vasoconstrictor angiotensin II. As the feedback inhibition stimulus is lost, renin production is *increased*. ACEIs are contraindicated in renal artery stenosis since reduction in systemic arterial pressure may lead to renal hypoperfusion.

Answers • 1-D   2-B   3-C   4-E

● CASE PRESENTATION

A 62-year-old woman scheduled for carotid surgery is referred for preoperative surgical clearance. She had myocardial infarction 3 years ago and is treated for hypertension and hyperlipidemia. She is physically active, swimming at her local pool four times per week without difficulty. She has no chest discomfort or dyspnea. On physical exam the blood pressure is 134/82, and heart rate is 64/min. Her lungs are clear. She has an S_4 gallop and a grade 2 systolic murmur at the apex. Her neck veins are not distended, but she does have a right carotid bruit. Her peripheral arterial pulsations are palpable but diminished. She has no ankle edema. ECG reveals sinus rhythm with inferior Q waves and probable left ventricular hypertrophy.

1. On the basis of these findings, which of the following is true?
   A. She is at the highest risk for cardiac complications.
   B. Vascular surgery does not predispose this patient to any higher risk than nonvascular surgery.
   C. Stress testing will allow further risk stratification.
   D. If stress testing reveals no evidence of myocardial ischemia, the patient has essentially zero risk for cardiac complications.

2. The patient has perfusion imaging, which reveals an inferolateral scar but no ischemia and an ejection fraction of 46. Perioperative management should include:
   A. Preoperative coronary angiography and revascularization
   B. Beta-blockers
   C. Pulmonary artery pressure monitoring
   D. All the above
   E. None of the above

3. A patient with a remote history of myocardial infarction and left ventricular hypertrophy (intermediate risk for cardiac complications) should have screening for active ischemia before
   A. Femoral bypass surgery
   B. Carpal tunnel surgery
   C. Inguinal hernia repair
   D. A nose job
   E. A, B, and C

4. Which of these physical findings indicates an increased risk with anesthesia and surgery?
   A. Carotid bruit
   B. Distant breath sounds, prolonged expiration, and wheezing
   C. An S_3 gallop
   D. All of the above

● COMMENT

Preoperative risk assessment • Based on clinical variables, patients can be classified as at low, intermediate, or high risk for cardiac complication during or after a surgical procedure. To determine risk, the patient's age, general medical condition, and history of myocardial ischemia, aortic stenosis, arrhythmia, or heart failure are evaluated. Patients at high risk have a rate of cardiac complications that exceeds 15%. Such patients should have medical therapy optimized, surgery cancelled or modified, and consideration given to coronary revascularization. A patient determined to be at low risk may proceed to surgery with a risk of less than 3% for cardiac complications.

The majority of patients—including this one—fall into an intermediate risk group and should have stress testing with imaging. With a stress perfusion scan that shows no ischemia, the risk of MI or death is less than 3% and no further cardiac evaluation is necessary (there is no such thing as zero risk). The risk of cardiac complications associated with surgery is variable, depending on the type of surgery; vascular and orthopedic surgery have the highest risk. Practice guidelines call for screening of intermediate-risk patients who are having vascular surgery.

Perioperative management • The risk of cardiac complications is lower after coronary revascularization. But the indication for revascularization is independent of the need for noncardiac surgery, and is based on the patient's cardiac condition. Our stable patient has no cardiac symptoms that require further work-up.

Prophylactic use of beta-blockers during noncardiac surgery reduces the risk of cardiac complications (the indication is any prior history of coronary artery disease [CAD] or two risk factors). Patients with impaired left ventricular (LV) systolic function should have careful fluid and electrolyte management to prevent fluid overload after surgery. If the patient has valvular heart disease, antibiotic prophylaxis should be given for oral surgery, gastrointestinal surgery, genitourinary surgery, or surgery involving an infected site.

Other risks of surgery • Do not forget to consider other medical conditions that increase the risk of general surgery. With diabetes there is a higher rate of wound complications. Carotid bruit has been identified as a risk factor for perioperative stroke. An abnormal chest exam raises the possibility of respiratory failure and prolonged ventilator dependence. And an S_3 gallop indicates a higher risk of perioperative heart failure or death. Any of these must be considered when weighing the risks and benefits of any operation.

● CASE PRESENTATION

A 63-year-old woman has been hospitalized for 3 days after having a relatively uncomplicated inferior myocardial infarction (MI). On morning rounds you notice that the patient is now breathing quite rapidly and appears to be in significant distress. The patient is taking 32 breaths/min; heart rate is 120 beats/min, and blood pressure is 104/62. Jugular venous pressure is high, and there are rales halfway up the chest bilaterally. There is a new 3/6 pansystolic murmur at the apex that radiates across the precordium and into the patient's axilla. The ECG is unchanged with the exception of the new finding of sinus tachycardia.

1. Which of the following are possible explanations for the patient's decline in respiratory status?

   A. Acute rupture of the interventricular septum
   B. Right ventricular infarction
   C. Acute rupture of a papillary muscle and mitral regurgitation
   D. Acute rupture of the right ventricular free wall
   E. A and C

2. The risk of myocardial rupture is increased by:

   A. Prior use of corticosteroids
   B. Early institution of thrombolytic therapy
   C. A long history of angina before MI
   D. Non-Q-wave infarction

3. Diagnostic tests that may help identify the cause of the murmur include:

   A. Echocardiogram
   B. Thallium scan
   C. Coronary angiogram
   D. All of the above

4. Myocardial rupture

   A. Usually occurs within 1 day of the onset of MI
   B. Is a common cause of death after MI
   C. Can be predicted from the patient's clinical course
   D. Can be anticipated with early cardiac catheterization

● COMMENT

New murmur after MI • A new murmur may indicate either acute mitral regurgitation (papillary muscle rupture) or ventricular septal defect (VSD, rupture of the septum). Both cause a loud systolic murmur, and it is hard to distinguish between them on exam. Occasionally a patient with VSD has a palpable thrill, and the degree of pulmonary edema tends to be worse with acute MR (the chest x-ray does not differentiate between them).

There is usually uncertainty about the diagnosis. The echo-Doppler study is the diagnostic test of choice. Pulmonary artery catheterization allows measurement of higher oxygen saturation in the pulmonary artery than in the right atrium in the case of septal defect (an oxygen "step-up" with left-right shunting), and a tall V wave on the wedge pressure tracing in the case of acute mitral regurgitation. Complete (right and left heart) cardiac catheterization allows definite diagnosis, and surgical correction includes coronary bypass. But tests that look at just the coronary circulation, such as thallium scan and coronary angiogram, do not identify the cause of new murmur after MI.

Myocardial rupture—of the free wall of the ventricle or the interventricular septum—after MI is more common in elderly women. Steroid therapy and late thrombolytic therapy (more than 12 hours from the onset of MI) both increase the risk of rupture. Rupture may occur with a small, first MI. Patients with a long history of coronary disease tend to have more collateral circulation, possibly lowering the risk of rupture. It usually occurs 5 to 10 days after the acute MI, at a time when the necrotic myocardium is mushy. There is no way to anticipate it with diagnostic studies, and it is a possible cause of death in the patient who has been discharged after a small, uncomplicated MI. Interestingly, rupture of the free wall of the ventricle is relatively common, following arrhythmias and heart failure as the most common causes of death after MI.

● CASE PRESENTATION

A 50-year-old man with no history of coronary artery disease (CAD) and no other risk factors for CAD has the following lipid panel: total cholesterol 350 mg/dL, low-density lipoprotein (LDL) 280 mg/dL, very low-density lipoprotein (VLDL) of 35 mg/dL, HDL of 45 mg/dL, and triglycerides of 150 mg/dL. After dietary therapy his repeat LDL is 195 mg/dL.

1. What is the best treatment for this patient?
   A. Continue dietary therapy with addition of vitamin E 400 units and folate 1 mg/day.
   B. Begin 3-hydroxy-3-methylglutaryl-coenzyme A (HMG-CoA) reductase inhibitor.
   C. Start niacin at 200 mg three times a day and increase as tolerated.
   D. Start gemfibrozil 600 mg twice a day.

2. Risk factors for CAD include:
   A. Cigarette smoking
   B. High blood pressure
   C. Family history of CAD
   D. Presence of atrial fibrillation
   E. A, B, and C

3. Which of the following can be expected to increase this patient's HDL levels?
   A. Exercise
   B. Gemfibrozil 600 mg twice a day
   C. Niacin 1 gm twice a day
   D. Beta-blockers
   E. A, B, and C

4. The patient's lipid profile is most consistent with:
   A. Familial hypercholesterolemia
   B. Type III dyslipidemia
   C. Familial combined dyslipidemia
   D. Familial chylomicronemia

● COMMENT

Treatment guidelines • The National Cholesterol Education Program (NCEP) current guidelines recommend that dietary therapy be initiated for all patients with a LDL greater than 160 mg/dL who are without evidence of coronary artery disease and have fewer than two risk factors. If dietary therapy fails to lower the LDL to less than 135 mg/dL, then drug therapy should be initiated for primary prevention. Patients without vascular disease who have two or more risk factors should be started on dietary therapy if the LDL is greater than 130 mg/dL, and started on drug therapy if the LDL remains above that level.

An HMG-CoA reductase inhibitor (statin) was chosen because of its potent effects on lowering LDL and its low side effect profile. The statins are competitive inhibitors of a key enzyme involved in the cholesterol biosynthetic pathway in the liver. The liver senses the decreased supply of cholesterol and extracts LDL from the circulation by making more hepatocyte LDL receptors. The net effect is a reduction in circulating LDL. High-dose niacin works, and it is not a wrong choice. It is difficult to use because of side effects, and most would agree with using a reductase inhibitor first.

Since these NCEP guidelines were published, it has become clear that we should use statins to lower LDL below 100 mg/dL for anyone with vascular disease (secondary prevention). Just how low the LDL should be pushed is an ongoing debate.

Risk factors • Major risk factors for CAD include hypertension, dyslipidemia, diabetes mellitus, cigarette smoking, family history, male sex, and advanced age. Risk factor modification remains the cornerstone of treatment for all atherosclerotic conditions. Atrial fibrillation may be a complication of myocardial infarction, but it is frequently encountered in patients with normal coronary arteries and is not a risk factor for CAD.

HDL cholesterol • HDL is the lipoprotein responsible for reverse transport, the removal of excess cholesterol from the periphery. A low HDL is a predictor of increased CAD independent of all other risk factors. Factors that cause or correlate with *low* HDL level are cigarette smoking, lack of exercise, obesity, androgenic steroids, diabetes, beta-blockers, and hypertrigyleceridemia. Exercise, estrogens, and red wine consumption can increase HDL. Niacin has the greatest ability to raise HDL by as much as 30%. Gemfibrozil raises it about 12%; the statins have only minimal effects.

Familial hypercholesterolemia (FHC) • FHC is an autosomal dominant disorder that results in the production of abnormal or ineffective hepatic LDL receptors. This results in high LDL, with normal HDL and triglyceride levels. Heterozygotes have approximately 50% ineffective receptors and are fairly common (1:500 in the U.S. population). Homozygous patients die prematurely in their second decade with premature atherosclerosis. Of note, the use of statins in homozygotes is ineffective because of total dysfunction of all LDL receptors. The physical exam is remarkable for corneal arcus and tendonous xanthoma. The other disorders listed involve the presence of abnormal triglyceride metabolism, the levels of which were normal in this patient. (Note: FHC is probably the only inherited lipid disorder you will encounter on this board exam.)

Answers • 1-B 2-E 3-E 4-A

● CASE PRESENTATION

A 77-year-old man has had chest pain with exertion over the past 6 to 9 months. He has also been experiencing lightheadedness, and he passed out while mowing his grass with a push mower last week. He denies pain at rest but states that his susbsternal pain with radiation to the left shoulder occurs with a moderate level of exertion. He has noticed a decline in stamina over the past year.

On exam, a harsh 4/6 midsystolic murmur loudest at the right upper sternal border is noted. The murmur radiates to both carotids, but the carotid upstroke is both delayed and diminished in intensity. You are unable to hear the second heart sound at the right upper sternal border. There is a forceful apical impulse in the midclavicular line and an S_4 gallop. Electrocardiogram (ECG) shows left ventricular hypertrophy with strain and left atrial enlargement.

1. The patient has:
   A. Mitral stenosis
   B. Mitral valve prolapse with regurgitation
   C. Aortic stenosis
   D. Severe aortic regurgitation

2. Which of the following facts about his valvular disorder is true?
   A. It is the most common valvular lesion that requires surgery in old people.
   B. The appearance of symptoms is the usual indication for surgery.
   C. Valve replacement (rather than repair or valvuloplasty) is usually required.
   D. The murmur may be audible at the apex with a different quality (pitch).
   E. All of the above

3. The patient's physical findings reflect
   A. An immobile valve
   B. Left ventricular hypertrophy
   C. Delayed emptying of the left ventricle (LV)
   D. All of the above

4. Which of the following symptoms of this valvular lesion indicates the highest mortality rate?
   A. Palpitations
   B. Congestive heart failure
   C. Chest pain
   D. Syncope

5. An indication for surgical correction of this valvular disorder is:
   A. Symptoms
   B. Left ventricular hypertrophy
   C. An increasing pressure gradient across the valve detected by serial echocardiograms
   D. A need for inguinal hernia repair in the absence of symptoms
   E. All of the above

● COMMENT

Calcific aortic stenosis in the elderly • The patient has classic signs and symptoms of severe aortic stenosis (AS). This is the usual cause of left ventricular outflow obstruction, and the most common valve lesion requiring surgery (in the United States). In younger patients, a congenitally bicuspid aortic valve is the usual cause. In those patients older than age 70, degenerative changes of a tricuspid aortic valve are responsible. By the same token, other types of left ventricular obstruction must be ruled out before making a diagnosis of AS (i.e., subvalvular or supravalvular obstruction, hypertrophic obstructive cardiomyopathy).

Men outnumber women 4:1. Rheumatic disease never causes isolated aortic valve disease. Those with rheumatic heart disease always have mitral stenosis, and when they have aortic valve disease, the usual lesion is aortic regurgitation.

Examination • Physical exam usually reveals a harsh crescendo-decrescendo systolic murmur loudest at the right upper sternal border. The second heart sound becomes softer and eventually disappears with severe AS as the calcified valve becomes immobile. There may be an S_4 gallop and prominent apical impulse (left ventricular hypertrophy). As the murmur moves from the base of the heart to the apex, the pitch may change so that it has a musical quality (Gallavardin phenomenon). Delayed LV emptying causes a delay in upstroke of the carotid pulse.

Symptoms, natural history, and surgical correction • The three classically described symptoms of severe aortic stenosis are angina, syncope, and congestive heart failure (CHF). In the absence of symptoms, the survival rate is normal. However, once symptoms of angina, syncope, or CHF develops, the survival curve drastically plummets. Average survival is 5 years after development of chest pain, 3 years after an episode of syncope, and 2 years with CHF. Surgery is indicated when any of these symptoms develops, and may it be safely delayed until there are symptoms.

The heavily calcified valve requires surgical replacement. Repair is not possible. Closed balloon valvuloplasty has lost favor because of poor results and a high rate of recurrence of stenosis.

About half the patients with AS and angina also have coronary artery disease, and bypass surgery is often done with aortic valve replacement. AS increases the risk of noncardiac surgery. However, aortic valve replacement is not indicated for an asymptomatic patient in order to have another procedure. (That is true of other heart disease as well. The decision for heart surgery is independent of the need for the other operation.)

Answers • 1-C   2-E   3-D   4-B   5-A

● CASE PRESENTATION

A 50-year-old man has an annual physical exam. He denies any cardiac history and has no symptoms. On exam you hear a fixed split S_2 and a soft systolic ejection murmur at the left sternal border. Electrocardiogram (ECG) reveals an incomplete right bundle-branch block and normal QRS axis. Chest x-ray reveals a prominent pulmonary artery and engorged pulmonary vessels.

1. What is your diagnosis?
   A. Pulmonary stenosis
   B. Ventricular septal defect (VSD)
   C. Patent ductus arteriosus
   D. Atrial septal defect (ASD)
   E. Eisenmenger's syndrome

2. What other tests may help make the diagnosis?
   A. Right heart catheterization
   B. Echocardiogram with Doppler imaging
   C. Coronary angiogram
   D. A and B

3. Given our patient's findings, which type of congenital heart defect is most likely?
   A. Primum ASD
   B. Secundum ASD
   C. Location not possible without more data

4. Which of the following require antibiotic prophylaxis for subacute bacterial endocarditis?
   A. Primum ASD
   B. Secundum ASD
   C. VSD
   D. All of the above

● COMMENT

Atrial septal defect (ASD) • The classic finding of ASD on physical exam is a "fixed split" second heart sound. Associated findings include a systolic flow murmur across the pulmonary valve and possibly a right ventricular lift. All of the physical exam findings are right-sided because the defect causes volume overload of the right side of the heart.

Diagnosis • The diagnosis may be certain with these physical findings. The ECG always shows incomplete right bundle-branch block (the ECG sign of right ventricular volume overload). Chest x-ray shows an enlarged pulmonary artery and "pulmonary plethora," a fairly specific finding (note that with a 2:1 shunt, the lungs have twice as much blood flow as the systemic circulation). Echocardiography can usually identify a hole in the atrial septum and shows right ventricular enlargement. Right heart catheterization may quantitate the shunt by showing higher oxygen saturation in the right atrium than in the systemic veins. Coronary angiography is not needed to confirm the diagnosis.

Ostium secundum versus primum ASD • Secundum ASD is more common (85%), and patients often survive to adulthood without symptoms. This condition is usually found on routine exam.

Ostium primum defects are a form of endocardial cushion abnormality, and there may be associated mitral or tricuspid regurgitation. This defect alters intraventricular conduction, and left anterior fascicular block is usually present (extreme left axis deviation).

Isolated ASD does not require antibiotic prophylaxis for subacute bacterial endocarditis. It is recommended for those with primum defect and associated mitral or tricuspid regurgitation. High-pressure congenital defects that have more of a jet effect are indications for prophylaxis (VSD, patent ductus arteriosus, and the more complex congenital lesions).

● CASE PRESENTATION

A 54-year-old man had acute inferior myocardial infarction (MI) 6 days ago. He did not have reperfusion therapy. There has been no recurrence of chest pain with ambulation, and he has had no arrhythmias.

1. Which of these are long-term predictors of poor prognosis in post-MI patients?

   A. Increased ventricular ectopic activity before hospital discharge
   B. Ability to walk just 8 minutes on a standard stress test
   C. Left ventricular ejection fraction below 40%
   D. Ventricular tachycardia during the acute phase of MI
   E. A and C

2. Short runs of ventricular tachycardia in the immediate post-MI period should be treated with lidocaine.

   A. True
   B. False

3. Which of these tests offer prognostic information for patients for survivors of MI?

   A. Echocardiogram
   B. Stress perfusion imaging
   C. Treadmill exercise testing
   D. Telemetry in the initial 6 hours of MI
   E. A, B, and C

4. Which of these are indications for treatment with angiotensin converting enzyme inhibitors?

   A. Recent myocardial infarction
   B. Coronary artery disease
   C. Diabetes
   D. Dilated cardiomyopathy
   E. All of the above

● COMMENT

Prognosis after MI • The long-term risk after MI is determined by 1) left ventricular systolic function and 2) residual ischemia. Late hospital phase ventricular arrhythmias are markers of poor ventricular function and thus indicate poor prognosis. On the other hand, ventricular arrhythmias in the first 24 hours of MI, including ventricular tachycardia or fibrillation, may occur with even small MI. As they do not indicate poor ventricular function, they are not markers of poor long-term prognosis.

The timing of ventricular arrhythmias with MI • Ventricular arrhythmias at the onset of MI, including premature ventricular beats, indicate a higher risk for ventricular tachycardia or fibrillation. Lidocaine is used to prevent this. There is no indication for lidocaine prophylaxis for patients who have no ectopy.

Late hospital phase and chronic arrhythmias are treated with beta-blockers. If they are severe, electrophysiologic study and implantable defibrillator therapy may be needed. Note that patients with normal left ventricular function are at low risk for severe ventricular arrhythmias.

Risk stratification after MI • Testing should include assessment of left ventricular function (echocardiography, radionuclide angiogram, or cardiac catheterization), and testing for active ischemia (stress testing with or without imaging studies or cardiac catheterization). In standard protocols, an ability to walk at least 7 minutes on the treadmill indicates a good prognosis. Ambulatory monitoring may be added when there is poor ventricular function or arrhythmia on telemetry.

Drug therapy that improves survival rate • Beta-blockade improves prognosis after MI. All patients with arterial vascular disease, including those post MI, benefit from angiotensin converting enzyme (ACE) inhibition, aspirin, and LDL-lowering therapy. In general, those with diabetes are treated as though they have atherosclerosis (secondary prevention), as drug therapy improves survival rate. ACE inhibition also retards progression of diabetic nephropathy.

Answers • 1-E 2-A 3-E 4-E

● CASE PRESENTATION

A 45-year-old man has a 4-month history of substernal chest pain that is characterized as a squeezing sensation precipitated by fast walking. The discomfort subsides when he rests and does not occur when he walks at a slower pace. He has smoked one pack of cigarettes a day for 25 years and his father died of a myocardial infarction at age 52. He denies a history of hypertension and diabetes and has never had a lipid analysis performed. His blood pressure is 155/90 and pulse 82/min. His lungs are clear and cardiac exam result is normal. His electrocardiogram (ECG) is normal. You suspect angina and start him on a beta-blocker, aspirin 81 mg/day, and sublingual nitroglycerin.

1. From this list, what is your next diagnostic test?
   A. Computed tomographic cardiac calcium score
   B. Stress ECG
   C. Dipyridamole (Persantine) stress thallium
   D. Heart catheterization

2. He has a stress test and walks 8 minutes on the treadmill. The test is stopped because of fatigue and after achievement of a heart rate of 160/min. The stress ECG shows 2-mm ST depression in the inferolateral leads. There is no angina during the test. You now recommend that he:
   A. Be admitted to the hospital for urgent heart catheterization
   B. Have an echocardiogram
   C. Begin long-acting nitrate therapy in addition to the beta-blocker
   D. Undergo elective heart catheterization

3. He reports improved exercise tolerance with the addition of nitrate therapy to his medical regimen. His left heart catheterization reveals a 95% proximal stenosis in the left anterior descending artery with no evidence of obstructive disease in the other arteries. You then recommend that he:
   A. Start on atorvastatin 80 mg/day and continue on current medical therapy
   B. Undergo angioplasty of the stenosis with adjunctive use of Reopro (abciximab)
   C. Have heart surgery
   D. Undergo angioplasty and stent placement

4. Two months after undergoing angioplasty he returns with recurrent chest pain. There have been a few episodes. It feels like angina and occurred while he carried groceries upstairs. Nitroglycerin gave him relief. You recommend that he:
   A. Have a repeat exercise treadmill test in your office that day
   B. Undergo repeat heart catheterization
   C. Continue with current medications and start Motrin
   D. Undergo dipyridamole thallium stress testing

● COMMENT

Work-up of angina • By the usual clinical definition, the patient has chronic stable angina pectoris (angina present for more than 2 months, occurring only with exertion, and with a stable pattern). In such cases, evaluating the patient with a stress ECG is reasonable. Many would do a perfusion scan as well, but probably with exercise rather than dipyridamole for a young man who is able to exercise (note that the scan adds $1500 to the cost of the work-up). On the other hand, it would also be reasonable to recommend angiography for a young person with new-onset angina, even though symptoms are stable.

Those with unstable angina (e.g., onset of pain <2 months ago, angina at rest, long episodes, new ECG changes, or an accelerating pattern of angina) should have angiography.

Evaluating the treadmill study result • The goal of exercise testing is to provoke ischemia so that both symptoms and the ECG can be evaluated. The myocardial region farthest from the epicardial coronary artery is the subendocardium, and ST segment depression is the pattern of subendocardial ischemia. The sensitivity and specificity of the stress ECG are about 75%, and adding the perfusion scan increases them to 90%.

Our patient had ST depression. His good exercise tolerance—more than 7 minutes on the treadmill—places him in a good prognostic group. Clinical trials have found that survival rate with medical therapy is as good as that of revascularization with stable angina and two-vessel CAD. However, without knowing his coronary anatomy, most would recommend angiography for a 45-year-old man with new angina and a positive screening result.

Treatment of angina • Drugs that improve survival in patients with CAD are aspirin, statins (LDL < 100), angiotensin converting inhibitors, and beta-blockers for those with history of myocardial infarction. Nitrates and calcium blockers may help control symptoms but convey no survival rate benefit.

On the side of revascularization for this patient is its effectiveness for a stenosis in this location. Bypass surgery is better for left main CAD, and for multivessel CAD in patients with diabetes. The downside of angioplasty plus stenting is the 15% chance of restenosis of the stented artery (it is higher with balloon angioplasty alone).

Restenosis after angioplasty • The recurrence of angina within 7 months of angioplasty indicates restenosis. The angina is usually identical to previous symptoms. The next step is repeat angiography. Consider stress testing if the nature of the symptoms is uncertain. Angioplasty with or without stenting injures the arterial wall. It heals by forming scar. For some, scarring is excessive, encroaches upon the lumen of the artery, and causes angina. This restenosis may be repaired with another angioplasty procedure but on occasion requires bypass surgery.

Answers • 1-B 2-D 3-D 4-B

● CASE PRESENTATION

A 68-year-old man with a history of hypertension, diabetes, and urinary retention awoke feeling short of breath, lightheaded, and nauseated. Emergency room (ER) personnel recorded a blood pressure of 60 mm Hg and administered IV fluids and oxygen therapy. In the ER, the blood pressure was 60 mm Hg, heart rate 120/min, temperature 102 F, and respiratory rate 30 breaths/min. There were coarse rales bilaterally and inaudible heart sounds. Electrocardiogram (ECG) showed sinus tachycardia. A Foley catheter drained 20 mL of dark urine. In the intensive care unit (ICU) a Swan-Ganz catheter was placed: pulmonary capillary wedge pressure was 28 mm Hg, and the cardiac output was 1.8 L/min. Right atrial mean pressure was 10 mm Hg.

1. The most likely cause of this man's hypotension is:
   A. Left ventricular dysfunction
   B. Right ventricular infarction
   C. Gram-negative sepsis
   D. Gastrointestinal bleeding
   E. Pulmonary emboli

2. An echocardiogram shows global hypokinesis with an ejection fraction (EF) under 20. Which of the following agents has been shown to reduce mortality rate in patients with congestive heart failure?
   A. Digitalis
   B. Furosemide
   C. Enalapril
   D. Procainamide
   E. Aspirin

3. The *incorrect* pairing of ancillary tests to determine the cause of heart failure in this patient includes:
   A. Angiotensin converting enzyme (ACE) level with sarcoidosis
   B. Serum copper levels with hemochromatosis
   C. Viral titers and blood cultures with infectious myocarditis
   D. Thyroid function tests with hypo- or hyperthyroidism
   E. All of the above are correct

4. Regarding ACE inhibitor therapy in patients with congestive heart failure (CHF):
   A. It is indicated for symptomatic heart failure patients only.
   B. Patients with baseline hyponatremia are more prone to orthostatic hypotension when starting an ACE inhibitor.
   C. It improves symptoms but not survival rate in patients with CHF.
   D. It is safe for use in pregnant patients.
   E. It may cause a chronic cough that does not improve with discontinuation of the drug.

● COMMENT

Hemodynamic monitoring • The clinical presentation is consistent with pulmonary edema. Given the history of hypertension and diabetes the likely cause is cardiogenic rather than noncardiac pulmonary edema. This is confirmed by an elevated pulmonary capillary wedge pressure plus low cardiac output, which indicate left ventricular failure. Cardiac tamponade is excluded by a right atrial pressure that is lower than left atrial—pulmonary wedge—pressure (equalization of right and left heart diastolic pressures is the classic finding of tamponade). The cardiac output is high with septic shock. The remainder of the choices would cause a decrease in left ventricular filling pressure. Myocarditis is a possible diagnosis given the relatively normal ECG finding and fever.

Treatment of heart failure • There have been a number of trials that have demonstrated improved survival rate with afterload reduction. Although most of the early studies were done with captopril and enalapril, this appears to be a class effect. Beta-blockade and aldosterone inhibition with spironolactone also improve survival rate. The other agents typically used in the treatment of heart failure have not been shown to increase survival. Antiarrhythmics such as procainamide have no role in the therapy of heart failure.

Cause of cardiomyopathy • All of the choices are known causes of systolic heart failure. Serum iron and ferritin levels are used to test for hemochromatosis. Copper levels screen for Wilson's disease, which is not a known cause of heart failure. Note that patients with sarcoidosis typically have an elevated level of ACE.

ACE inhibitor therapy • ACE inhibitor therapy is indicated for all patients with an EF less than 40 even if they are asymptomatic. ACE inhibition improves survival in patients with severe congestive heart failure (CHF) and retards progression of heart failure in patients with less severe disease. ACE inhibition decreases the amount of the potent vasoconstrictor angiotensin II, decreases aldosterone secretion, and down-regulates the sympathetic nervous system. Patients with low serum sodium are particularly sensitive to ACE inhibitors and may have postural hypotension. ACE inhibitors are contraindicated in pregnancy because of significant fetal morbidity rate. The ACE inhibitor–induced cough is idiosyncratic but is relieved by discontinuation of the drug. An angiotensin II receptor blocker may be used in these patients. (The recent HOPE trial also found a survival rate benefit for all with atherosclerotic vascular disease, regardless of left ventricular [LV] function; there is a direct beneficial effect of ACE inhibitors on the arterial wall.)

● CASE PRESENTATION

A 23-year-old man is visiting family members when he enters the emergency department with shortness of breath. He has noticed that his toes have become blue and he has some swelling in both ankles. His past medical history is significant for a heart murmur. On examination, his blood pressure is 113/52 and his pulse is 96/min and regular. His cardiac exam is significant for a 2/6 systolic ejection murmur and a 2/6 diastolic murmur at the left upper sternal border, prominent pulsation at the left lower sternal border, and a loud second heart sound. Splitting of S₂ is audible at the right and left bases. His lung fields are clear and he has cyanosis of his toes and feet with clubbing of the toes but not fingers. His hands and face are pink. His initial evaluation is significant for lung fields that appear oligemic on x-ray and a hematocrit of 67%.

1. The following may be expected on his ECG:
   A. Sinus rhythm
   B. Right axis deviation
   C. Tall P wave in leads II, III, and aVF
   D. Q waves
   E. A, B, and C

2. Possible causes of the condition described include:
   A. Peripheral vascular disease
   B. Patent ductus arteriosus (PDA)
   C. Ventricular septal defect (VSD)
   D. Transposition of the great vessels
   E. B, C, and D

3. What other physical exam findings might be expected?
   A. Bilateral basilar pulmonary crackles
   B. A laterally displaced apical cardiac impulse
   C. Delayed upstroke of the carotid pulsation
   D. Pulsatile liver

4. Which complications might you expect in this patient?
   A. Endocarditis
   B. Paradoxical embolus
   C. Iron deficiency with microcytosis
   D. 85% Mortality rate in 5 years
   E. A, B, and C

● COMMENT

Physical exam and ECG in Eisenmenger's syndrome • Adults who are cyanotic and have congenital heart disease with pulmonary hypertension and right-to-left shunting have Eisenmenger's syndrome. It begins in childhood with a large left-to-right shunt that causes pulmonary hypertension. When the pulmonary artery pressure is high enough, the shunt "reverses," and movement of blood from the right to left side of the heart produces cyanosis. The key to the patient's presentation described is differential cyanosis or cyanosis and clubbing of only the patient's toes, caused by patent ductus arteriosus. VSD and transposition of the great vessels are also frequent causes of Eisenmenger's syndrome, but there are cyanosis and clubbing of fingers as well as toes. (This is a tough case; Eisenmenger's syndrome may be on the boards, but not with differential cyanosis.)

The ECG findings in Eisenmenger's syndrome would indicate right atrial and ventricular hypertrophy with right axis deviation, large R wave in V₁, deep S waves in lead I and V₆, and a large, upright P wave in leads II and III and aVF (right atrial enlargement).

These patients may develop right heart failure with lower extremity edema, hepatomegaly, pulsatile liver, right ventricular lift, and elevated jugular venous pressure. With pulmonary hypertension, a prominent second heart sound or P₂ may be heard at the left upper sternal border, and P₂ may be heard to the right of the sternum as well as the left (normally it is too soft to be heard on the right, so splitting of the second sound is heard only over the pulmonic area). The systolic murmur is likely due to tricuspid regurgitation but may be due to increased flow through the pulmonic valve. The diastolic murmur is likely due to pulmonic valve insufficiency. The murmur of a PDA with left-to-right shunting is continuous and harsh, but the murmur may soften with reversal of the shunt.

Management and prognosis • Because of hypoxemia, patients with Eisenmenger's syndrome have an elevated hematocrit. When the hematocrit gets too high, there is hyperviscocity with lethargy, headache, visual disturbances, dizziness, fatigue, and irritability. These are indications for phlebotomy to take the hematocrit below 65%.

Because of constant stimulation of the marrow to generate red cells, it outruns its iron stores. Though not anemic, the red cell indices may be microcytic. Microcytic red cells are stiffer than normal and contribute to hyperviscosity. To prevent microcytosis, they often need supplemental iron therapy (it seems a paradox: both iron therapy and intermittent phlebotomy).

Prophylactic antibiotics are indicated for invasive procedures. Survival rate is 80% at 10 years, 77% at 15 years, and 42% at 25 years. Right heart failure, syncope, and hypoxemia portend a worse prognosis. Causes of death include paradoxical embolus and stroke, brain abscess, endocarditis, heart failure, and ventricular fibrillation. In addition, mortality rate is high with surgical procedures and pregnancy. Once Eisenmenger's syndrome is evident, surgical correction of the congenital defect is not possible.

Answers • 1-E 2-B 3-D 4-E

● CASE PRESENTATION

A 60-year-old woman has palpitations and "heart racing" for 2 weeks. She has a history of hypertension for 20 years controlled with diuretic therapy alone. On exam she has a resting tachycardia of 120 beats/min with an irregular pulse. A rhythm strip is provided (Figure 5).

1. The electrocardiogram (ECG) indicates:
    A. Sinus tachycardia
    B. Atrial flutter
    C. Atrial fibrillation with rapid ventricular response
    D. Multifocal atrial tachycardia
    E. Normal sinus rhythm

2. The least likely cause of this arrhythmia is
    A. Hypertension
    B. Thyrotoxicosis
    C. Valvular heart disease
    D. Stress
    E. Binge drinking

3. Which of the following are options for slowing this patient's heart rate?
    A. Digoxin
    B. Verapamil
    C. Beta-blockers
    D. Amlodipine
    E. A, B, and C

4. You perform an echocardiogram that reveals an ejection fraction of 35% with normal left atrial size and no evidence of thrombus. Which of the following drugs is indicated at this time?
    A. Warfarin sodium (Coumadin)
    B. Amiodarone
    C. Lidocaine
    D. None of the above
    E. A and B

● COMMENT

Atrial fibrillation (AF) •   The ECG demonstrates AF with rapid ventricular response. AF is the most common arrhythmia encountered. Common causes include hypertension, thyrotoxicosis, valvular heart disease, Wolff-Parkinson-White syndrome, and binge alcohol consumption (holiday heart). There is no clear relationship to stress (although patients often make this claim).

Rate control •   The first step in treatment is rate control, followed by conversion to normal sinus rhythm. Drugs that block the atrioventricular (AV) node and control the ventricular rate include digoxin, beta-blockers, calcium channel blockers (verapamil or diltiazem, but not the dihydropyridines). Digoxin may be less effective than beta-blockers and calcium channel blockers but is a good choice for patients with heart failure. Beta-blockers are indicated in the postoperative period, after an acute myocardial infarction, for chronic congestive heart failure (CHF) and hyperthyroidism. Note that amiodarone is a class III antiarrhythmic but also has beta-blocker and calcium channel blocking properties. (Did you read amlodipine in that question but think amiodarone? Be careful!)

Cardioversion •   This patient has been in AF for a couple of weeks and therefore should be on warfarin for at least 4 weeks before cardioversion. With depressed systolic function, amiodarone is the agent of choice for maintaining sinus rhythm after conversion. With normal left ventricular (LV) function other antiarrhythmic agents can be used. After cardioversion, warfarin is continued for another 6 weeks, as there is a continued risk of peripheral embolism. An alternative approach for patients with more than 2 days of AF is to perform a transesophageal echocardiogram before cardioversion, searching for evidence of a thrombus. If no thrombus is found, perform the cardioversion and treat with warfarin for 6 weeks after conversion.

Emergency cardioversion •   A patient with hemodynamic compromise (shock or pulmonary edema) or unstable angina that is the result of new-onset rapid AF should have immediate cardioversion. Such cases are medical emergencies, and you do not have time to fuss with rate-lowering drugs.

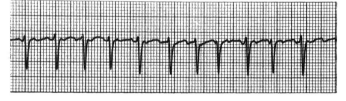

• **Figure 5:** Used with permission from Taylor GJ. *150 Practice ECG's: Interpretation and Review,* 2nd ed. Malden, Mass.: Blackwell Science, Inc., 2002: 25.

Answers •   1-C   2-D   3-E   4-A

● CASE PRESENTATION

A 48-year-old construction worker has dyspnea on exertion and fatigue. He notes that his stamina has markedly decreased over the past several months. He denies any medical problems except a history of hypertension for which he takes a low-dose beta-blocker. He denies chest pain, presyncope, or loss of consciousness. He is a 25-pack-year smoker but does not drink alcohol or use drugs.

On exam, pulse is 88/min, blood pressure 140/45. The apical impulse is displaced laterally and is diffuse and hyperdynamic. There is a decrescendo and blowing diastolic murmur heard along the left sternal border. Peripheral pulses are bounding, and nailbed pulsations are noted. Chest x-ray shows an enlarged cardiac silhouette but no evidence of pulmonary edema.

1. This patient most likely has which valve disorder?
   A. Aortic stenosis
   B. Aortic regurgitation
   C. Mitral valve prolapse
   D. Pulmonic regurgitation

2. Which of the following may cause it?
   A. Endocarditis
   B. Marfan's syndrome
   C. Rheumatic heart disease
   D. Tertiary syphilis
   E. All of the above

3. Which of the following indicates that it is severe (hemodynamically significant)?
   A. Wide pulse pressure
   B. A grade 3 murmur
   C. Normal left ventricular size but left atrial enlargement on the echocardiogram
   D. All of the above

4. Which of these statements best describes treatment of this valvular disorder?
   A. Digoxin, diuretics, and afterload reduction are contraindicated.
   B. Bacterial endocarditis prophylaxis is not necessary.
   C. Intervene surgically before irreversible LV dysfunction has occurred.
   D. Risk of poor outcome increases with LV end-systolic diameter below 50 mm Hg.

5. In the acute form of this valvular disorder, which of the following might be expected?
   A. Concomitant endocarditis is present.
   B. A murmur may be soft or even absent.
   C. Severe pulmonary congestion is often present because of acute volume overload of the left ventricle.
   D. All of the above are true.

● COMMENT

Aortic regurgitation (AR) • AR may occur with endocarditis, disease of the aortic root (Marfan's syndrome or chronic hypertension), and rheumatic diseases. It may accompany rheumatic heart disease but not in this case as this patient does not have mitral stenosis (all who have rheumatic heart disease have mitral stenosis). Regurgitation of blood into the left ventricle (LV) increases the filling pressure. This diastolic volume overload causes decompensation. In acute AR (commonly seen in acute endocarditis, trauma, or dissection), increased LV end-diastolic volume and pressure, and increased left atrial (LA) pressure result in acute pulmonary edema.

Examination • Physical findings include a decrescendo, blowing diastolic murmur best heard along the left sternal border. When it is best heard to the right of the sternum, the patient has a dilated aortic root (possibly Marfan's syndrome). The apical impulse (which is diffuse and hyperdynamic) is displaced in chronic AR.

Patients with hemodynamically significant AR have peripheral vasodilatation and wide pulse pressure. The intensity of the murmur is not a reliable guide to severity.

Management • The most important principle is to intervene with surgery *before* irreversible LV dysfunction has taken place. Patients may do well for many years with moderately severe AR. Drug therapy, especially afterload reduction, may delay progression of disease. Valve replacement is usually needed before symptoms develop, and always with acute AR.

The echocardiogram shows LV enlargement. Asymptomatic patients with evidence for even mild systolic function should have surgery. Monitor the LV ejection fraction and dimensions of the LV with yearly echocardiograms, and send the patient to surgery if ejection fraction falls or the end-systolic dimension is *greater than* 5 cm, or an end-diastolic dimension is above 7 cm.

Acute AR • The most common cause is acute endocarditis in intravenous drug users. Gonococcemia is a possible cause as well and is associated with a fine, erythematous rash. As AR develops abruptly, the LV does not have time to dilate. The small LV is exposed to a huge volume of blood, and LV diastolic pressure is high. There may be little difference between LV and aortic diastolic pressure, and when this is the case, the murmur can be soft or absent. Consider acute AR in the young drug user with acute hemodynamic collapse, pulmonary edema, and a soft or absent murmur (that would be a great board question!).

Answers • 1-B 2-E 3-A 4-C 5-D

● CASE PRESENTATION

A 72-year-old man enters the emergency department after more than 12 hours of substernal chest discomfort described as being similar to indigestion. It radiates down the left arm and is associated with mild shortness of breath. There is no history of hypertension, diabetes, or tobacco use. He is being treated for hyperlipidemia and has a strong family history of coronary artery disease. On exam, vital signs are normal, the chest is clear, and there is a soft systolic "flow murmer" present at the upper left sternal border. The electrocardiogram (ECG) is reproduced below (Figure 6). Blood work reveals a mildly elevated total creatine kinase (CK) with abnormal MB isozyme fraction. Troponin I level is elevated as well.

1. The absence of Q waves on an ECG rules out the possibility of transmural myocardial infarction (MI).
   A. True
   B. False

2. The short-term prognosis is good because:
   A. He does not have rales.
   B. This is a non-Q-wave MI.
   C. He does not have resting tachycardia.
   D. A and C
   E. A, B, and C

3. His long-term prognosis is less certain because:
   A. He is at risk for reinfarction.
   B. There is a chance heart failure and cardiogenic shock will develop.
   C. He may have severe ventricular arrhythmias.
   D. All of the above

4. Treatment should include:
   A. Antiplatelet therapy and heparin
   B. Thrombolytic therapy
   C. Coronary angiography before hospital discharge
   D. A and C
   E. A, B, and C

● COMMENT

Non-Q-wave MI • The designation of non-Q-wave MI is based on ECG findings, but the absence of Q waves does not always exclude transmural injury. The lateral wall of the left ventricle may be "electrocardiographically silent," with just T wave changes when there is transmural injury. Nevertheless, in this case with symmetrical T wave inversion in anterior leads and just minimal elevation of cardiac enzyme levels, the diagnosis of non-Q, or "nontransmural," MI is fairly certain.

Most with non-Q MI have a small amount of injury, so short-term prognosis is good. There is little chance of left ventricular (LV) failure, and with good LV function, little risk of serious ventricular arrhythmias after initial recovery. However, those with non-Q MI usually have tightly stenosed and unstable coronary arteries that are at risk for occlusion in the near future. You may call this "reinfarction," but it may be better to consider it "completion of the MI." It is for that reason that coronary angiography is recommended.

The infarct artery is stenosed but not occluded with non-Q MI. Clinical trials have found no advantage of thrombolytic therapy over antiplatelet therapy and heparin.

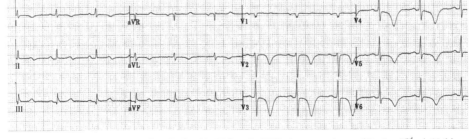

• **Figure 6:** Used with permission from Taylor GJ. 150 Practice ECG's: Interpretation and Review, 2nd ed. Malden, Mass.: Blackwell Science, Inc., 2002: 57.

● CASE PRESENTATION

A patient is referred to you for evaluation of persistent lower extremity edema by her chiropractor, who is treating her for chronic low back pain. She is a 58-year-old woman being treated for hypertension by her primary care doctor. In addition, she has had mild dyspnea with excessive exertion for several months. There are no symptoms at rest and no chest pain. Echocardiography is done to evaluate left ventricular (LV) function. Ejection fraction is 30% and the left ventricle is dilated.

1. This patient's symptoms are consistent with the following classification:
   A. New York Heart Association (NYHA) class 0
   B. NYHA class I
   C. NYHA class II
   D. NYHA class III
   E. NYHA class IV

2. Which of the following is true regarding her therapy?
   A. An angiotensin-converting enzyme inhibitor does not need to be started because her symptoms are not present at rest.
   B. Beta-blockers, because they decrease heart rate and therefore cardiac output, are contraindicated in this patient.
   C. Because digoxin has been shown to increase survival, it should be started immediately.
   D. An aldosterone antagonist (spironolactone) is started for its strong diuretic effect.
   E. None of the above

3. You start your patient on appropriate therapy including digoxin. She returns feeling lightheaded and nauseated and has diarrhea. Her electrocardiogram (ECG) shows complete atrioventricular (AV) block with a junctional escape rhythm. The following statement is correct:
   A. If the patient's digoxin level is in the normal therapeutic range it can be continued at the current dose.
   B. Hemodialysis is done for digoxin toxicity if the patient does not respond to conventional therapy.
   C. Electrolyte abnormalities that occur with digoxin toxicity are the result of cellular shifts and should not be aggressively managed.
   D. Digoxin-specific antiserum (Digibind) can be administered IV to reverse life-threatening digoxin toxicity.
   E. Antacids, Dilantin (phenytoin), and thyroxine would increase the likelihood of increased digoxin levels.

4. The chiropractor calls 3 months later to tell you that a surgeon is going to operate on this patient's back and wants to know whether it is safe to proceed. The patient has felt better on your therapy. You tell him:
   A. You will need to check another echocardiogram first to see whether the ejection factor (EF) has changed.
   B. A stress test needs to be done to evaluate for possible ischemia.
   C. There is no need to delay the surgery.
   D. Surgery for low back pain is largely unsuccessful.

● COMMENT

Functional classification • The NYHA classification is an assessment of a patient's functional status with heart disease. There is no class 0. Class I is no symptoms (but known disease, in this case left ventricular dysfunction). Class II indicates symptoms with strenuous exercise. Class III indicates symptoms with light exertion (one trial defined this as walking less than a block at a normal pace), and Class IV indicates symptoms at rest. This classification is used in the majority of published studies on the treatment of heart failure.

Drug therapy for heart failure • ACEIs are started for all patients with LV dysfunction, even those who are asymptomatic. Beta-blockers have long been considered dangerous for use in patients with congestive heart failure. But recent studies have shown that inhibition of sympathetic stimulation using beta-blockade improves survival rate for those with mild or advanced heart failure. Beta-blocker, either metoprolol or carvedilol, must be started at low dose, with the dose slowly raised over a period of months. Digoxin, although shown to improve symptoms and decrease hospitalization, does not improve survival. Spironolactone, an aldosterone antagonist, is a weak diuretic but may prevent aldosterone-mediated myocardial fibrosis and is prescribed routinely for heart failure. Spironolactone is potassium sparing and increases magnesium.

Digitalis toxicity • The patient's symptoms suggest digitalis toxicity (think of it also with anorexia and visual changes). Digoxin has a very narrow therapeutic window. This patient is obviously toxic and the digoxin should be stopped regardless of the level. Hemodialysis is not effective because of the large volume of distribution of digoxin. Digoxin immune Fab (Digibind) is a digoxin-specific Fab fragment that has a rapid onset of action, a large volume of distribution, and rapid clearance and is used to clear digoxin. Patients often have associated hypokalemia and hypomagnesemia; levels must be replaced. The drugs listed in choice E decrease levels of digoxin. Amiodarone, verapamil, macrolides, and spironolactone (Aldactone) are drugs that increase the levels of digoxin.

Preoperative evaluation • OK, a fuzzy question with a couple of answers that are possible. A part of the evaluation of new congestive heart failure is screening for coronary artery disease. If there are no suggestive symptoms or Q waves on the ECG, screening with a stress perfusion scan is adequate. If this was done as a part of the initial evaluation it does not need to be repeated. If not, it should be done preoperatively. The risk of surgery and anesthesia is higher in patients with heart failure. Preoperatively, the patient should be at dry weight, and electrolytes should be normal. After surgery, monitor fluids and electrolytes.

Answers • 1-C   2-E   3-D   4-B or C

● CASE PRESENTATION

A 40-year-old woman enters the emergency room for evaluation of dizziness. Over the past 2 days she has been experiencing 8 to 10 episodes of diarrhea per day. There is a history of hypertension controlled with a thiazide diuretic, and of hay fever treated with antihistamines. Vital signs reveal normal blood pressure and heart rate, but the patient becomes hypotensive with standing. The cardiac monitor strip is shown (Figure 7). Her serum potassium was 3.0 mEq/L and magnesium was 1.4 mEq/L prior to the event.

1. What does this tracing represent?
   A. Ventricular fibrillation
   B. Sinus arrest
   C. Torsades de pointes (ventricular tachycardia)
   D. Artifact

2. What is the initial treatment?
   A. Intravenous fluids
   B. Magnesium
   C. Calcium gluconate
   D. Lidocaine
   E. Cardioversion

3. What is the most likely cause of her arrhythmia?
   A. Ischemia
   B. Hypokalemia and hypomagnesemia
   C. Overdose of tricyclic antidepressants
   D. Hypercalcemia
   E. Volume depletion

4. Which is a predisposing factor(s) in this case?
   A. Diuretic therapy
   B. Antihistamines
   C. Recent history of diarrhea
   D. All of the above

● COMMENT

Torsade de Pointes • Torsade de pointes ventricular tachycardia occurs when ventricular repolarization is delayed. The axis of the QRS complexes changes, with variation described as "twisting of the points." Anything that prolongs the QT interval may cause it, including medications (antiarrhythmic drugs, tricyclic antidepressants, phenothiazines, or their derivatives, including antihistamines) and electrolyte disturbances (especially hypokalemia and hypomagnesemia). Though uncommon, it may complicate bradycardia after a myocardial infarction.

Treatment • The best treatment to shorten the QT interval and prevent recurrence is IV magnesium. Other treatment options include overdrive pacing or isoproterenol hydrochloride (to increase the heart rate). However, in this patient, who has had syncope and is having the arrhythmia, DC cardioversion is the first step.

In this case, torsade was precipitated by the combination of thiazide diuretics, diarrhea-causing hypokalemia, and antihistamines. With resolution, a follow-up ECG is needed to exclude congenital prolongation of the QT interval and a risk for recurrent torsades.

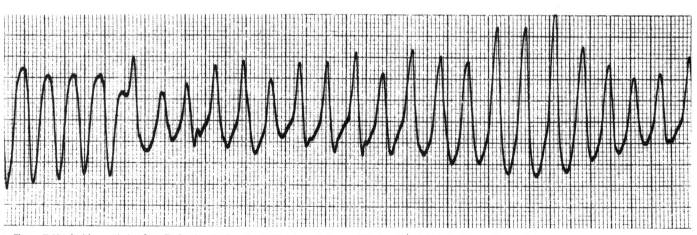

• *Figure 7: Used with permission from Taylor GJ. 150 Practice ECG's: Interpretation and Review, 2nd ed. Malden, Mass.: Blackwell Science, Inc., 2002: 114.*

Answers • 1-C   2-E   3-B   4-D

● CASE PRESENTATION

A 56-year-old woman enters a local emergency room (ER) with a history of crushing substernal chest discomfort for the past 6 hours. The electrocardiogram (ECG) shows ST segment elevation in the inferolateral leads. Physical exam reveals the presence of a harsh, holosystolic murmur at the cardiac apex that radiates to the axilla. There is no S_3, but there is an S_4 gallop. She has rales and worsening dyspnea.

1. She has:
   A. Mitral regurgitation (MR) that is chronic and unrelated to the chest pain
   B. MR caused by papillary muscle ischemia or rupture
   C. MR caused by rheumatic heart disease
   D. MR caused by mitral valve prolapse

2. The most common cause of chronic mitral regurgitation is:
   A. Papillary muscle ischemia
   B. Rheumatic heart disease
   C. Mitral valve prolapse
   D. Mitral stenosis
   E. Dilated cardiomyopathy with mitral annular dilatation

3. Which of the following statements about MR is true?
   A. In acute MR the left atrial size is normal; however, in chronic MR the left atrium and ventricle (LA and LV) are dilated.
   B. Chronic MR causes a large V wave and high wedge pressure on Swan-Ganz catheter readings.
   C. Abrupt-onset pulmonary edema is common with chronic MR but not with acute MR.

4. Which of these statements regarding timing of surgery and prognosis is true?
   A. Acute pulmonary edema necessitates urgent surgery.
   B. Any fall in left ventricular ejection fraction (LVEF) or a rise in LV end-systolic size is an indication for surgery for MR, even in the absence of symptoms.
   C. Prognosis is good after surgical repair of ischemic MR, because dramatic symptoms usually force intervention before there is permanent damage.
   D. All of the above

● COMMENT

Cause of mitral regurgitation (MR) • Acute MR may be seen in the context of acute myocardial infarction (MI) with papillary muscle dysfunction or rupture. It is commonly seen with relatively minor heart attack. The most common cause of isolated, chronic MR is mitral valve prolapse (middle-aged men are at highest risk). Another cause of acute MR is rupture of a cordae.

Pathophysiology • In acute MR, there is no time for the left atrium and ventricle to dilate. There is acute volume overload of the small LV that causes an S_4 gallop (rather than the S_3 gallop seen with chronic MR and a large dilated ventricle). Since the LA also remains small with acute MR, the pressure of ventricular contraction is transmitted to the lungs and is seen as a V wave on the pulmonary artery wedge tracing (this finding is diagnostic for acute MR). In addition, acute pulmonary edema, which can be life-threatening, usually develops. Pulmonary edema is an indication for urgent surgery in the setting of acute MR. Prognosis is good with prompt treatment and surgical repair if the MI is a small one.

In contrast, the LA and LV are dilated by the chronic MR. There may be an S_3 gallop (rapid filling of a big, flabby heart), and little of the ventricular pressure is transmitted through the dilated, flabby LA which absorbs the pressure wave. The pulmonary wedge pressure may be normal in the absence of pulmonary edema. Congestion and other symptoms of congestive heart failure (CHF) usually develop much more slowly in chronic MR.

Timing of surgery with chronic MR • The best predictors of outcome are LVEF and LV end-systolic size. LV afterload is low with chronic MR, since the LV can eject blood into both the aorta and a relatively low-pressure LA. With low afterload, LVEF should be above normal. In fact, you can be fooled into believing the LV is all right just because EF is in the normal range. When the valve is repaired, afterload will be higher, and LVEF may fall after surgery.

When evaluating the asymptomatic patient, realize that ejection fraction near 50% may be a sign of advanced LV injury and bad prognosis. Surgery is usually recommended when the LV end-systolic dimension reaches 4.5 cm or the LVEF falls below 60%. Asymptomatic patients need serial echocardiograms to follow these measurements.

Answers • 1-B   2-C   3-A   4-D

● CASE PRESENTATION

A 58-year-old woman enters the emergency department with a 45-minute history of crushing substernal chest pain radiating into her jaw and associated with severe nausea. There is a long history of hypertension and tobacco abuse. Additionally, the patient was recently diagnosed with diabetes mellitus. Blood pressure is 80/50 and pulse is 50/min and irregular. Skin is cool and clammy. Lungs are clear. There are no murmurs, rubs, or gallops. The electrocardiogram (ECG) shows sinus bradycardia with second-degree heart block, Mobitz I, and ST segment elevation in the inferior leads with reciprocal ST segment depression anteriorly. All blood test results are pending.

1. The combination of hypotension and inferior ST segment elevation raises the possibility of:

   A. Anterior MI
   B. Septal MI
   C. RV infarction
   D. Pericarditis and cardiac tamponade
   E. RA infarction

2. Which diagnostic tests would help to confirm this diagnosis?

   A. Radionuclide angiogram (MUGA scan)
   B. Echocardiogram
   C. ECG with V leads from the right chest
   D. Signal averaged ECG
   E. A, B, and C

3. The most effective initial treatment for the patient's hypotension is:

   A. Dopamine
   B. IV fluid bolus
   C. Isoproterenol
   D. Dobutamine
   E. Milrinone

4. Heart block with acute inferior MI:

   A. Reflects increased vagal tone (the Bezold-Jarisch reflex)
   B. May result from atrioventricular (AV) node ischemia
   C. Seldom requires permanent pacemaker therapy
   D. All of the above

● COMMENT

Right ventricular infarction syndrome • Hypotension with inferior MI suggests right ventricular (RV) infarction. The RV is fed by proximal branches from the right coronary artery. Proximal occlusion of this vessel may cause RV failure. Hypotension results from failure of the RV to push blood to the left side of the heart. The initial treatment of RV infarct–related hypotension is intravenous saline (essentially treating the RV as a passive chamber, pushing blood through it by raising venous pressure). Those with RV infarction may also have left ventricle (LV) failure and require catecholamine support; but the first step is volume expansion.

The echocardiogram shows RV dysfunction. In addition, a V lead in the V_4 position but on the right side of the chest (V_4R) shows ST segment elevation (in addition to the ST elevation in inferior leads). Perfusion imaging does not reliably demonstrate an RV abnormality, but a radionuclide angiogram can assess RV function. The signal-averaged ECG tests susceptibility to ventricular arrhythmias and is of no benefit.

Heart block with inferior MI • Heart block is common and reflects increased vagal tone (the Bezold–Jarish reflex) and/or AV node ischemia (the right coronary artery supplies the node). It is usually transient. The QRS duration is usually normal, an indication that the site of block is the AV node. With infranodal block the QRS is wide. (The exception to this rule is AV nodal block in an occasional patient with pre-existing bundle-branch block.)

● CASE PRESENTATION

A 50-year-old man complains of chest heaviness on exertion that began 2 weeks earlier. Once it occurred after eating dinner while he was watching television, and it lasted for 20 minutes. He states that the pain is present now and he is very anxious because his father died of a heart attack at the age of 52. Other risk factors for coronary disease include smoking cigarettes and hypertension. His blood pressure is 125/80 and the pulse is 85 beats/min. His electrocardiogram (ECG) shows 2-mm ST segment depression in V_2 to V_5.

1. On physical exam you would expect to hear:
   A. Fixed split S_2
   B. An S_4 gallop
   C. Grade 2 diastolic murmur over the left sternal border
   D. Pulse deficit between the left arm and leg

2. The patient is likely suffering from:
   A. A severe episode of stable angina related to his heightened emotional state
   B. Recent change in a coronary artery plaque leading to tighter stenosis
   C. Acute total coronary occlusion or "red thrombus"
   D. Spontaneous arterial dissection

3. After the patient receives an aspirin and nitroglycerin, his pain resolves and the ECG normalizes. Later, he has recurrent pain with similar ECG findings. His first set of lab results also shows an elevated troponin T. You now should:
   A. Give tissue plasminogen activator (tPA)
   B. Increase his nitroglycerin
   C. Order immediate echocardiogram to rule out the presence of acute pericarditis
   D. Start the patient on a IIb/IIIa antagonist.

4. You decide to treat the patient with low-molecular-weight heparin instead of unfractionated heparin because of the following:
   A. Ease of administration
   B. Better bioavailability
   C. Less platelet activation
   D. Ability to measure the degree of anticoagulation properly
   E. A, B, and C

● COMMENT

Physical findings during myocardial ischemia (MI) • During an episode of angina listen for a new or louder mitral regurgitant murmur (transient papillary muscle dysfunction) and for an S_4 gallop. When the myocardium becomes ischemic, there is an increase in left ventricular wall stiffness. The atrium contracting against the stiff LV produces the S_4 gallop. The history does not suggest an aortic dissection, which can involve the aortic valve, producing acute aortic regurgitation. Fixed splitting of the second heart sound is a finding in patients with an atrial septal defect.

Pathophysiologic features of angina • It is useful to think of stable and unstable angina as different clinical syndromes, because the pathophysiologic features and prognosis are different. Both syndromes result from stenosis of the coronary artery. With stable angina, the plaque surface is stable and the stenosis does not vary. Angina is initiated when the work load of the heart increases, which is proportional to the heart rate and systolic blood pressure.

The initiating event in unstable angina—this patient's illness—is a drop in blood supply rather than increased demand. This is caused by a change in the coronary artery plaque. The plaque is unstable, with ulceration, fresh thrombus, and possibly spasm. There is usually antegrade flow. In acute myocardial infarction with ST segment elevation, angiography shows complete occlusion with no antegrade flow.

Treatment of unstable coronary syndromes (unstable angina and non-Q-wave MI) • An increased troponin level indicates a high risk for coronary occlusion and transmural MI; other markers of high risk are prolonged pain (>20 minutes) at rest, ST changes greater than 1 mm, and any sign of heart failure. The use of thrombolytic therapy is of no benefit for patients with unstable angina or non-Q-wave myocardial infarction. It is reserved for MI with ST elevation. High risk patients (especially those with a rise in troponin or creatine kinase-MB [CK-MB]) are treated with IIb/IIIa inhibitor therapy, beta-blockers, intravenous nitrates, and early angiography.

Low-molecular-weight heparin (LMWH) • Several trials have demonstrated superior efficacy of LMWH over unfractionated heparin. The LMWHs include enoxaparin, dalteparin, and nadroparin and are administered subcutaneously. There is no laboratory test for measuring the degree of anticoagulation. This can be a problem when deciding whether it is safe to do invasive procedures, such as cardiac catheterization.

Answers • 1-B   2-B   3-D   4-E

● CASE PRESENTATION

A 56-year-old woman enters your office with new complaints of dyspnea on exertion, orthopnea, pedal edema, and fatigue. She has a history of hypertension. She was a one pack per day smoker until 18 months ago, when she was told she had high cholesterol and would have to quit. She does not have angina. Her only medicine is a diuretic. On exam, her blood pressure is 150/90 and pulse is 108/min and regular. Her cardiovascular exam shows an increased jugular venous pressure (JVP), normal S_1 and S_2, and a summation gallop. Her lung fields are clear, and the electrocardiogram (ECG) shows sinus tachycardia.

1. The next step in management should be:
   A. Starting an angiotensin converting enzyme (ACE) inhibitor and beta-blocker and increasing her diuretics
   B. An echocardiogram
   C. Coronary angiography
   D. Serial cardiac enzyme tests over the next 24 hours
   E. Referral to a nutritionist for a strict weight loss plan

2. The patient is found to have low left ventricular (LV) ejection fraction, normal LV wall thickness, and no evidence for diastolic dysfunction. An unlikely cause of her heart failure is:
   A. Hypertension
   B. Coronary artery disease
   C. Tachycardia induced heart failure
   D. Prior viral myocarditis
   E. A and B

3. The finding of an S_3 gallop in this patient:
   A. Indicates an elevation of LV end-diastolic pressure
   B. Occurs right before the S_1 heart sound
   C. Is consistent with a low cardiac output state and a dilated ventricle
   D. Is a good prognostic sign in a patient with dilated cardiomyopathy
   E. All of the above

4. The emergency room physician phones you later that week to tell you that this patient was in the ER reporting chest pain earlier in the day and now has T wave inversion on the ECG. Appropriate management would be the following:
   A. Admit to the hospital; give aspirin, IV nitroglycerin, IV heparin, and a beta-blocker; and schedule coronary angiography.
   B. Order an emergent stress thallium test.
   C. Give the patient a prescription for long-acting nitrates and low-dose aspirin and have her follow up with you first thing in the morning.
   D. Perform emergency coronary angiography and restoration of coronary blood flow.

● COMMENT

Ventricular function and congestive heart failure (CHF) • The symptoms and physical exam are indicative of congestive heart failure, and you need to determine whether it is caused by systolic or diastolic dysfunction. An echocardiogram to evaluate structure and function is the next step in her management. Findings such as a regional wall motion abnormality may lead to a stress test or coronary angiography, but in this patient with no history of angina, a noninvasive test is done first. A good argument can be made for starting treatment, as both systolic and diastolic CHF may be treated with ACE inhibitors, beta-blockers, and diuretics; it would be important to relieve symptoms in a seriously ill person (probably with admission to hospital). The definition of diastolic dysfunction is CHF plus normal LV systolic function.

Cause of heart failure • Hypertension is a well-known cause of LV hypertrophy (increased LV wall thickness) and diastolic dysfunction. The other choices, however, are all associated with systolic heart failure. Tachycardia-induced failure is a newly recognized entity most commonly seen in patients with supraventricular tachycardia (admittedly, this woman's sinus tachycardia may not be severe enough to cause LV failure).

Gallops • A gallop is a low-pitched sound heard best at the apex with the bell of the stethoscope. The S_3 gallop is heard just after the S_2, early in diastole. It results from unusually rapid filling of a distended, flabby ventricle. It is a marker of poor prognosis with heart failure, and especially with ischemic cardiomyopathy. The S_4 gallop is heard prior to the S_1 at end-diastole and is caused by the atrium contracting and pushing blood against a stiff ventricle. The ventricular end-diastolic pressure is high, and it may occur with left ventricular hypertrophy (LVH), ischemia, and infiltrative diseases. An S_4 is not heard in a patient with atrial fibrillation because of loss of the atrial kick.

In a patient with a rapid pulse, it may not be possible to tell whether the gallop is closer to S_1 or S_2. We refer to the gallop—extra sound—as a "summation gallop."

Managing angina • With development of chest pain and new ECG changes, the diagnosis is unstable angina or non-Q MI. Appropriate therapy would be an aspirin, heparin therapy if there are no contraindications, and nitroglycerin. Admission to a telemetry unit and evaluation for myocardial injury with serial enzymes and ECGs are needed. Emergency angiography is indicated when there is ST elevation with continued chest pain (acute transmural infarction). A stress test is not done when a patient has unstable angina, pain within the last day, and new ECG changes. Sending the patient home is not an option.

• Section 2

Internal Medicine

J. David Bohler, DVM, MD

Benjamin Clyburn, MD

Kevin M. Dineen, MD

Glenn C. Douglas, MD

Sam G. Dozier, MD

Keith A. Frick, MD

J. Terrill Huggins, MD

Gretchen M. Labarowski, MD

Greg Moffitt, MD

Eni Okonofua, MBBS

Pamela Pride, MD

Patrick F. Reilly, MD

David A. Sabol, MD

Michael A. Smith, MD

Jeremy Soule, MD

William Ward, MD

Jessica Wells, MD

● CASE PRESENTATION

A 25-year-old black woman enters the emergency room with chest pain. She describes the pain as sharp and located primarily on the left side of her chest with no radiation. She notes it hurts worse when she takes a deep breath. Her fiancé says that her face has been flushed since returning from a trip to Florida to visit her parents. They had to cut short their trip because of some pains she was having in her ankles and wrists. She has been well otherwise and only takes oral contraceptive pills. On physical exam you notice a fever of 100.8 F. She has an erythematous rash over her cheeks. Her lungs are remarkable for diminished breath sounds in the left base. She has some tenderness of her wrists and ankles, but no effusions.

1. Given the patient's history and physical examination, the most likely diagnosis is:
   A. Rheumatoid arthritis
   B. Reiter's syndrome (reactive arthritis)
   C. Pneumonia
   D. Pulmonary embolus
   E. Systemic lupus erythematosus

2. You obtain a chest x-ray and see a small amount of blunting in the costrophrenic angle consistent with a pleural effusion. You suspect the cause is:
   A. Pneumonia
   B. Infarction
   C. Serositis
   D. Malignancy
   E. Tuberculosis

3. Routine laboratory testing is ordered. Which of the following is least likely to help in the diagnosis and/or treatment of this patient?
   A. Antinuclear antibody (ANA)
   B. Urinalysis
   C. Cultures for *Neisseria gonorrhea*
   D. Platelet count
   E. Hemoglobin

4. Her lab results reveal white blood cell (WBC) count of 2.2, hematocrit of 28, and platelet count of 15,000/mm^3. Her basic metabolic panel is remarkable for a creatinine of 3.4 mEq/L. A urinalysis reveals 37 red blood cell count (RBCs), 24 WBCs, and 3+ protein. Which of the following therapies would be most appropriate at this time?
   A. Initiation of corticosteroid therapy
   B. 7-day treatment with oral antibiotics
   C. Alternating therapy with acetaminophen (Tylenol) and ibuprofen
   D. Referral to a dermatologist
   E. Oral anticoagulation therapy

● COMMENT

Clinical presentation of SLE (SLE) • SLE is an autoimmune disease with numerous presentations characterized by intermittent exacerbations and remissions. The typical patient is a woman (8:1 female predominance) between the ages of 15 and 45 years, although those of any age may be affected. The variability of clinical manifestations can make diagnosis difficult. The recognition of a constellation of clinical and laboratory findings helps the clinician make the diagnosis. The American College of Rheumatology criteria are useful in making the diagnosis. Any patient having 4 of the 11 following criteria is said to have SLE: malar rash, discoid rash, photosensitivity, oral ulcerations, arthritis, serositis, renal disease, hematologic abnormalities, neurologic abnormalities, immunologic abnormalities, ANAs.

The skin manifestations of SLE are variable and are among the most common presenting complaints. The malar, or butterfly, rash is an erythematous macular rash that extends over the bridge of the nose onto both cheeks, sparing the nasolabial folds. Photosensitive rashes occur on sun-exposed areas and possess similar characteristics to the malar rash. Subacute LE rash tends to be serpiginous or annular with central scaling. Discoid LE begins as erythematous papules that evolve into larger lesions with central areas of epithelial thinning and atrophy and follicular plugging. The most affected skin areas include the scalp, neck, and extensor surfaces of the arms.

Arthritis is common in SLE patients. It is a nonerosive arthritis involving peripheral joints characterized by tenderness, swelling, or effusion. Oral ulcerations are another manifestation of SLE. These occur either in the oral pharynx or in the nares and tend to be painless. Serositis often presents as pleuritic chest pain, occasionally with a rub or pleural effusion. The pericardium may be involved as well, resulting in electrocardiogram (ECG) changes, a rub, or an effusion. Neurologic abnormalities can range from seizures to psychosis.

Laboratory abnormalities in SLE • ANAs are the hallmark of SLE. Although the finding is not specific, 99% of SLE patients have a positive ANA result. Antibodies to double-stranded deoxyribonucleic acid (DNA) and to the Smith antigen are more specific for SLE. Other laboratory abnormalities of lupus include leukopenia, hemolytic anemia, and thrombocytopenia. Persistent proteinuria (>0.5 g/day) and active urine sediment with RBCs and cellular casts can indicate nephritis, a serious complication of the disease.

Treatment • Aggressive therapy is often indicated when the disease is complicated by severe lupus nephritis, autoimmune hemolytic anemia, autoimmune thrombocytopenia with low platelet counts (<20,000/mm^3), and central nervous system (CNS) lupus with severe manifestations. Vasculitis and serositis may also necessitate aggressive corticosteroid therapy. Other agents used in the treatment of severe manifestations, particularly nephritis, include cytotoxic agents such as cyclophosphamide and azathioprine.

Answers • 1-E 2-C 3-C 4-A

● CASE PRESENTATION

A 65-year-old African-American woman reports a several-month history of progressively worsening left hip pain, bilateral knee pain, and hand stiffness. Her pain is dull, constant, and aching in nature and is exacerbated by activity such as walking. Her pain improves with rest. She states she feels stiff in the morning and takes 15 to 20 minutes to "loosen up." She denies swelling, prior trauma, fever, or weight loss. Despite her pain she stays active, walking about 1 mile/day, but states that the pain has slowed her pace recently. Her social and family history is noncontributory. Her physical exam discloses normal vital signs, no rash, bony enlargement of the distal interphalangeal (DIP) joints of her hands, tenderness over bilateral carpometocarpal joints, crepitus on extension of her knees, and no erythema or warmth in her joints. The remainder of her exam is unremarkable.

1. What is the likely diagnosis?
   A. Rheumatoid arthritis
   B. Gout
   C. Osteoarthritis
   D. Polymyalgia rheumatica
   E. Psoriatic arthritis

2. Which test will offer the most assistance in diagnosing your patient?
   A. Serum uric acid level
   B. Creatine kinase (CK) level
   C. Rheumatoid factor
   D. X-rays of affected joints
   E. Sedimentation rate

3. What is your next step?
   A. Initiate nonsteroidal anti-inflammatory drug (NSAID) therapy
   B. Start prednisone 60 mg/day
   C. Give intra-articular injection of hyaluronate
   D. Limit walking
   E. Start methotrexate

4. Which of the following is a cause of secondary osteoarthritis?
   A. SLE
   B. Psoriasis
   C. Hemochromatosis
   D. Inflammatory bowel disease
   E. All of the above

● COMMENT

Osteoarthritis versus other arthritides • Osteoarthritis (OA) is the most common form of arthritis and prevalence increases with age, affecting about 50% of those over 65 years of age. Postmenopausal women have increased susceptibility to OA compared to men, and African Americans have a greater incidence of knee involvement than other ethnic groups. Osteoarthritis typically involves the weight-bearing joints including knees and hips as well as the hands. DIP bony enlargement (Heberden's nodes), proximal interphalangeal (PIP) bony enlargement (Bouchard's nodes), squaring of the first carpometacarpal (CMC) joint, and knee crepitus are common findings in OA. Morning stiffness usually lasts less than 30 minutes as opposed to rheumatoid arthritic stiffness, which usually lasts at least 1 hour. OA pain typically worsens with activity and improves with rest. Gout usually is an asymmetric arthritis with flares lasting days to weeks, commonly affecting the first metatarsophalangeal (MTP) joint. Polymyalgia rheumatica causes stiffness and pain to neck and proximal girdle joints and is accompanied by systemic complaints of fever, weight loss, and malaise. Psoriatic arthritis may cause similar joint distribution but would be unlikely at this age without preceding dermatologic lesions.

Diagnostic evaluation • The diagnosis of OA can be established with a good history and physical exam. However, x-rays can provide additional diagnostic support and confirm the extent of disease. Typical radiographic findings of early OA include osteophyte formation with the development of asymmetric joint space narrowing and subchondral bone sclerosis as the disease progresses. Later changes include subchondral cysts with bone remodeling at the joint ends. Bone demineralization is not a feature of OA and should raise the suspicion of an alternative diagnosis. Serum uric acid, CK, and rheumatoid factor level measurements are indicated if one suspects gout, myositis, or rheumatoid arthritis, respectively. The sedimentation rate is a nonspecific measure of inflammation and is usually normal in OA.

Treatment of OA • The treatment of OA in all patients should consist of patient education, reassurance, and physical therapy for strengthening of muscles, increased range of motion, and stability. If obesity is present, measures to address weight loss should be undertaken. Low-impact exercises such as walking or water aerobics are excellent methods of aerobic conditioning and maintaining function. If pain is mild to moderate, then acetaminophen, topical analgesics, and NSAIDs (cyclooxygenase-2 [COX-2] inhibitors for gastrointestinal [GI] side effects) are all good first-line agents. As disease progresses, intra-articular corticosteroid injections and opioids may offer benefit. Surgical therapy consisting of joint lavage, arthroscopic repair, and arthroplasty should be considered for severe, debilitating disease. Systemic steroids have no proven role in OA. Alternative therapy such as oral doxycycline and intra-articular hyaluronate injections are currently under investigation.

Primary versus secondary OA • The two forms of OA are primary OA and secondary OA. Primary OA typically affects the elderly, as described earlier whereas various other diseases may cause secondary OA, including hemochromatosis, Wilson's disease, pseudogout, gout, acromegaly, and ochronosis. These forms should be suspected in patients who have an atypical presentation: early age of onset, unusual joint involvement (shoulders, elbows, pelvis), joint effusions, atypical radiographic appearance, and evidence of systemic disease. Psoriasis and inflammatory bowel disease are associated with seronegative spondyloarthropathies. Systemic lupus erythematosus (SLE) causes a nondestructive, inflammatory polyarthritis.

Answers • 1-C 2-D 3-A 4-C

● CASE PRESENTATION

A 37-year-old female accountant has an 8-month history of swelling of her wrists. She notices that she wakes up feeling stiff and has difficulty opening cans or turning a doorknob, but toward the middle of the day, her symptoms improve. She states that in the last several weeks her fingers have become sore and slightly swollen. She also notes low-grade fever, malaise, and 5-pound weight loss over the past 2 months. She has taken ibuprofen for her joint pain with only mild relief. Her social history is negative for alcohol and illicit drug use, but she has a 20-pack-year smoking history. Her exam reveals low-grade fever of 100.4 F, blood pressure 115/84, pulse rate of 92/min, and normal cardiac, lung, and abdominal exam results. She has noticeable erythema, swelling, and tenderness of the first and second MCP and PIP joints of her hands with mild limitation upon extension of her wrists; the rest of her musculoskeletal exam results are normal.

1. What is the patient's most likely diagnosis?
   A. Carpal tunnel syndrome
   B. Gonococcal arthritis
   C. Rheumatoid arthritis
   D. OA
   E. Pseudogout

2. Which of the following tests should be ordered at this time?
   A. Needle aspiration of her joint
   B. Rheumatoid factor (RF)
   C. Uric acid level
   D. Anti–double-stranded deoxyribonucleic acid (DNA) antibody
   E. Antiribonuclear protein (RNP)

3. After making your diagnosis, you prescribe treatment for her symptoms. Which of the following is appropriate therapy at this time?
   A. Depocorticosteroid injection into the inflamed joints
   B. Methyl prednisolone (Medrol DosePak)
   C. Colchicine
   D. Weekly methotrexate
   E. Daily allopurinol

4. Your patient is at risk for which of the following complications?
   A. Ruptured Baker's cyst
   B. Erythema nodosum
   C. Pericardial effusion
   D. Cervical subluxation
   E. All of the above

● COMMENT

Differential diagnosis of rheumatoid arthritis • Rheumatoid arthritis (RA) is most common in women and often appears between the ages of 20 and 40 years. It is typically a symmetric arthritis and in 85% of cases involves the wrists and hands, most commonly the PIP and MCP joints. Often low-grade fever (<100.5 F), mild anemia, and weight loss can accompany arthritis. Although she may have carpal tunnel syndrome as a result of her RA, carpal tunnel syndrome alone would not account for her systemic complaints and abnormal physical findings. Gout and pseudogout are less likely since these typically occur as monoarticular arthritis involving the foot or knees and last only a few days before resolution. Gonococcal arthritis is unlikely given that she lacks a rash and the typical migratory arthritis. Primary OA typically occurs in patients over 50 years of age and spares the MCP and PIP joints in favor of the DIP joints of the hands.

Diagnostic work-up of RA • Lab results that should be obtained include sedimentation rate of C-reactive protein to monitor systemic inflammation. In addition, RF and antinuclear antibody (ANA) should be measured as initial screening tests. X-rays of her hands and wrists could be taken to evaluate for bony erosions typical of RA. Arthrocentesis and uric acid levels should be done if septic arthritis or crystal arthropathy such as gout or pseudogout is suspected. Both anti–double-stranded DNA antibody and anti-RNP antibody are more specific for lupus and mixed connective tissue diseases, respectively, and therefore should be reserved for a patient with a positive ANA finding.

Treatment • Recent evidence indicates that patients diagnosed with RA with active synovitis (as in our patient) benefit from earlier treatment with disease-modifying agents of rheumatic disease (DMARDs). These include methotrexate, hydroxychloroquine, azathioprine, sulfasalazine, cyclophosphamide, and leflunomide. In addition, the newer anti–tumor necrosis factor-alpha (TNF-alpha) agents etanercept and infliximab have shown promise in slowing the disease process in RA patients. These may be used in conjunction with NSAIDs, which help relieve pain and swelling but have less impact on disease progression. Depocorticosteroid injections are reserved for RA patients with only a few joints involved and should be done by someone experienced in arthrocentesis. Although low-dose systemic steroids have a role in RA, methylprednisolone lasts only a few days and would not be appropriate. Allopurinol and colchicine are used for treatment of crystal arthropathy.

Extra-articular manifestations of RA • RA may affect virtually every organ system but is more frequent and usually worse in patients who have high RF titers. Patients may have a ruptured Baker's cyst; subcutaneous rheumatoid nodules (erythema nodosum); various eye abnormalities, including keratoconjunctivitis sicca; rheumatoid nodules on the pericardium; or pleura causing pericardial and/or pleural effusions; and weakening of the tendons that support the neck, which may cause cervical subluxation and permanent spinal cord damage if not treated quickly. The pleural fluid from RA patients typically is an exudative effusion with low glucose (often less than 30 mg/dL) and low complement concentrations.

Answers • 1-C   2-B   3-D   4-E

● CASE PRESENTATION

A 24-year-old white man enters the emergency room complaining of pain and swelling of his left knee for several days prior to the visit. On further questioning he notes that he also has some swelling on the posterior aspect of his right heel and that he had a self-limited episode of eye irritation approximately 2 weeks ago. He is otherwise healthy, although he has noticed some stiffness in his lower back. On physical exam, his vital signs are normal. His left knee has a mild effusion with normal range of motion and there is swelling along his right Achilles tendon. There are no other joints involved. There is a painless, serpiginous ulceration on the glans penis. His laboratory data reveal an elevated sedimentation rate and white cells in his urine. You perform arthrocentesis of his left knee. The results show a leukocyte count of 10,000 cells/mm^3, mostly neutrophils, and a negative Gram stain result.

1. What is the most likely diagnosis?
   A. Disseminated *Neisseria gonorrhoea* infection
   B. Ankylosing spondylitis
   C. Reactive arthritis (Reiter's syndrome)
   D. Rheumatoid arthritis
   E. Psoriatic arthritis

2. Which of the following lab tests should be performed initially?
   A. Human leukocyte antigen B27 (HLA-B27) antigen
   B. Cultures of throat and urethra
   C. Rheumatoid factor
   D. Antinuclear antibody
   E. Double-stranded deoxyribonucleic acid (DNA)

3. In terms of the data, the best treatment for his knee pain is:
   A. Ibuprofen and rest
   B. Oral prednisone taper
   C. Intra-articular injection of corticosteroid
   D. Oral colchicine
   E. Oral methotrexate

4. You decide to perform x-rays of his lumbar spine, knees, and ankles. Which of the following is the most likely x-ray finding?
   A. Bilateral, symmetric sacroiliitis
   B. Normal bone x-ray findings
   C. Erosions along the metatarsals of his bilateral feet
   D. Medial compartment narrowing of his knees

● COMMENT

Seronegative spondyloarthropathies • Seronegative spondyloarthropathies are a group of diseases that share features of spine involvement, sacroiliitis, enthesopathy, and an association with HLA-B27. In addition, they involve to varying degrees peripheral arthritis, uveitis, dermatitis, bowel inflammation, and heart disease. This group includes the prototypic ankylosing spondylitis (AS), reactive arthritis, psoriatic arthritis, and arthritis related to inflammatory bowel disease. This patient likely has reactive arthritis.

Ankylosing spondylitis (AS) • Ankylosing spondylitis is a chronic systemic inflammatory disease with sacroiliitis as its hallmark. It typically begins in late adolescence or early adulthood and is more common in men. Patients have low back pain with prolonged morning stiffness. This stiffness improves with movement and exercise. The hips and shoulders are the most common locations for peripheral arthritis, which occurs in about 30% of patients. HLA-B27 is present in at least 90% of white patients with AS. Radiographs reveal a bilateral and symmetric sacroiliitis. Intervertebral bony bridges form, giving rise to the appearance of "bamboo" spine on x-ray.

Reactive arthritis • Reactive arthritis, often called Reiter's syndrome when it includes the classic triad of arthritis, conjunctivitis, and urethritis, is an infection-induced systemic illness characterized primarily by an inflammatory synovitis. It is primarily seen in young adults and follows an enteropathic or urogenital infection, which may be inapparent. Thus it is important to perform a gastrointestinal and genitourinary review of systems and to obtain swabs for culture during the physical exam. The arthritis is typically asymmetric, oligoarticular (fewer than five joints), and confined to the lower extremities. Enthesitis is inflammation of the tendon-bone junction (enthesis) and commonly causes heel pain and sausage digits. Generally, radiographic findings are normal in the acute disease. Sacroiliitis is classically asymmetric on radiographs in Reiter's syndrome. The characteristic cutaneous lesions are circinate balanitis and keratoderma blennorrhagicum (scaling on the soles of the feet). In most patients, reduction of inflammation and restoration of function can be achieved with nonsteroidal anti-inflammatory drugs (NSAIDs) alone and should be the first line of therapy.

Psoriatic arthritis • Psoriatic arthritis occurs in approximately 5% of patients with psoriasis. It is typically an asymmetric, oligoarticular peripheral arthritis, though axial involvement is not uncommon. The classic pattern is involvement of the distal interphalangeal digits. Along with psoriatic plaques, the findings of significant nail pits and sausage digits (dactylitis) are consistent with psoriatic arthritis. Radiographically, destructive lesions of predominantly DIP joints in a "pencil-in-cup" pattern are classic.

Arthritis associated with inflammatory bowel disease (IBD) • The arthritis associated with IBD is typically acute, migratory, asymmetric, and pauciarticular (fewer than five joints). Associated extraintestinal manifestations of IBD and inflammatory peripheral arthritis are pyoderma gangrenosum, anterior uveitis, erythema nodusum, and aphthous stomatitis. Peripheral arthritis tends to mirror bowel activity, whereas axial involvement is independent of bowel activity and extent of disease.

Answers • 1-C 2-B 3-A 4-B

● CASE PRESENTATION

A 64-year-old white woman has complaints of bilateral shoulder pain. She states she was well until 5 days ago when she began having pain and stiffness in her upper arms. She noted the stiffness was worse in the morning and that for the past 2 nights she has been awakened with pain. She has also found getting out of bed in the morning difficult because of stiffness. Though she is normally very active, this past week she has felt exceedingly fatigued. Her medications include ibuprofen and hydrochlorothiazide. On exam, her vital signs are unremarkable. She has some tenderness in her bilateral upper arms with motion. Her strength is normal, and the rest of her exam results are unremarkable.

1. What is the most likely cause of her complaints?
    A. Bilateral subacromial bursitis
    B. Rotator cuff tear
    C. Polymyalgia rheumatica
    D. Rheumatoid arthritis
    E. Hypothyroidism

2. You order laboratory testing. The most diagnostic information will be revealed by which test?
    A. Rheumatoid factor
    B. Elevated erythocyte sedimentation rate (ESR)
    C. Hematocrit
    D. Creatinine
    E. Antinuclear antibody (ANA)

3. You decide to initiate treatment with prednisone 15 mg/day. She calls you 2 days later to let you know that she is doing well and back to her usual activities with no further stiffness. Two weeks later, she calls to tell you she has had a temporal headache for 2 days and this morning she has blurry vision in her right eye. You tell her to:
    A. Increase her prednisone immediately to 60 mg and go to the office.
    B. Take acetaminophen (Tylenol) for her headache and drink plenty of fluids.
    C. Make an appointment with her ophthalmologist.
    D. Stop her prednisone and call if she does not feel better in several days.
    E. Add ibuprofen to her prednisone for additional anti-inflammatory effects.

4. The patient does as instructed. The next step will be:
    A. Computed tomography (CT) scan of head
    B. Cataract surgery on right eye
    C. Nuclear scan of thyroid
    D. Temporal artery biopsy
    E. Carotid Doppler ultrasonography

● COMMENT

Diagnosis and treatment of polymyalgia rheumatica (PMR) • PMR is an inflammatory syndrome of unknown cause characterized by pain and stiffness in the shoulder and/or pelvic girdles. This syndrome rarely affects individuals less than 50 years old and becomes more common with increasing age. Pain that limits mobility is common at night and is usually insidious in onset. The shoulder is often the first area to be affected. Constitutional symptoms and arthritis are common. Physical findings are less striking than the history might suggest. Movement may increase the pain that is generally felt in the proximal extremities. The characteristic lab finding is an elevated ESR, often greater than 100 mm/hr. The treatment of PMR is glucocorticoid therapy. Prednisone in an initial dose of 10–20 mg/day usually evokes a dramatic and rapid response. Most patients are better in 1 to 2 days.

Association of PMR and temporal arteritis • It is important to know that PMR and temporal (also known as giant cell) arteritis (TA/GCA) frequently occur simultaneously or sequentially in individual patients. PMR has been noted in 40% to 60% of patients with TA. Of PMR patients in North America 15% to 20% have coexistent TA. Signs suggestive of TA include headache, jaw claudication, visual disturbance, and scalp tenderness. TA may cause fever of unknown origin in the elderly. Palpation of arteries can elicit tenderness or may indicate enlargement, bruits, or loss of pulsation. Sudden blindness is the most dreaded complication of TA and occurs in 15% of patients.

Diagnosis and treatment of TA • TA is a large vessel vasculitis and may affect the aorta and its major branches, in addition to the cranial circulation. Again, the ESR is the most common laboratory abnormality, ranging from 60 to 80 mm/hr. Biopsy of the most abnormal segment of the temporal artery should be performed to confirm the diagnosis. The pathologic evaluation reveals a granulomatous inflammatory reaction centered on a disrupted internal elastic lamina. Since this disease is characterized by patchy arterial involvement, a negative biopsy result does not rule out the disease. The treatment of choice is the initiation of high-dose corticosteroid therapy (60 mg/day). Treatment should begin immediately when the clinical suspicion of the disease is high, with a biopsy obtained within 7 days.

Answers • 1-C   2-B   3-A   4-D

● CASE PRESENTATION

A 37-year-old black woman reports to her primary care physician pain and weakness in her arms, neck, and hips. She states she was doing well until approximately 1 month ago when she noted difficulty getting out of her armchair and climbing stairs at work. She also began having constant aches in her upper arms and thighs. The day before seeing her physician, she had choked while eating steak, and that prompted her visit. Her only significant past medical history was of heavy alcohol use, although she has been avoiding alcohol over the last year. She denied any illicit drug use and was taking no medications. On physical exam, her vital signs were unremarkable. She had significantly decreased strength in her bilateral deltoids and hip flexors, as well as marked weakness on cervical flexion. She had no rashes or joint effusions.

1. What is the most likely diagnosis for this patient?
   A. PMR
   B. Dermatomyositis
   C. Rheumatoid arthritis
   D. Fibromyalgia
   E. Polymyositis

2. Which of the following is *least* likely to aid in the diagnosis of this patient?
   A. Electrocardiogram
   B. Magnetic resonance imaging (MRI)
   C. Nerve conduction velocities with electromyography
   D. Muscle biopsy
   E. Creatinine kinase

3. You decide to start treatment of this patient with medication. The initial drug of choice would be:
   A. NSAID (Ibuprofen)
   B. Methotrexate
   C. Colchicine
   D. Corticosteroids
   E. Intravenous immunoglobulins

4. Which of the following diseases should be considered in the differential diagnosis of this patient?
   A. Hypothyroidism
   B. Rhabdomyolysis
   C. Hypercalcemia
   D. Myasthenia gravis
   E. All of the above

● COMMENT

Clinical findings • Polymyositis is an autoimmune inflammatory disease of striated muscle. There is a bimodal age distribution, with one peak at 10 to 15 years of age and the other at 45 to 50 years. Women and African Americans are more commonly affected. The dominant clinical feature is symmetric proximal muscle weakness. Patients usually have an insidious onset of disease, often noticing a gradual increase in difficulty in climbing steps, rising from a seated position, or raising the arms overhead. In addition, myalgia is a frequent feature. Arthralgias, Raynaud's phenomenon, dysphagia, and interstitial lung disease are seen less commonly. Patients who also have discoloration of their eyelids (heliotrope rash), scaling over their MCP and PIP joints (Gottron's papules), fissuring of the fingerpads (mechanic's hands), or an erythematous shoulder/upper arm rash (shawl sign) have dermatomyositis.

Diagnosis • The diagnosis of polymyositis is based on symmetric proximal muscle weakness along with elevated serum levels of muscle enzymes (creatinine kinase, aldolase, lactate dehydrogenase [LDH]), myopathic changes demonstrated by electromyography (EMG), and evidence of inflammation on muscle biopsy. These criteria along with skin disease are utilized to diagnose dermatomyositis. EMG reveals characteristic changes, but it is not diagnostic and the finding can be normal 10% of the time. Magnetic resonance imaging (MRI) is useful in demonstrating areas of muscle inflammation, edema, and necrosis. This test is useful in helping the physician select the site of muscle biopsy and allows for more definitive diagnosis. Myositis-specific autoantibodies, including anti-Jo1, can be useful in predicting clinical manifestations. The electrocardiogram (ECG) is rarely abnormal.

Treatment • Corticosteroids are the standard first line of therapy in polymyositis. Clinical improvement is usually noted within the first several weeks of therapy. Other immunosuppressive therapeutic agents such as methotrexate or azathioprine may be added in resistant cases. Physical therapy plays an important role in treatment as inflammation subsides.

Differential diagnosis • Polymyositis is the most common of the idiopathic inflammatory myopathies, which include dermatomyositis, juvenile dermatomyositis, myositis associated with other collagen vascular diseases, and myositis associated with neoplasia. An age appropriate malignancy work-up must therefore be included in the evaluation. Other causes of muscle weakness and elevated creatine kinase levels should be considered, including hypothyroidism, hypercalcemia, glycogen storage diseases, myasthenia gravis, rhabdomyolysis, and toxin- or medication-induced myopathies. Polymyalgia rheumatica is a condition characterized by axial muscle pain without weakness or elevated enzyme levels.

Answers • 1-E 2-A 3-D 4-E

● CASE PRESENTATION

A stuporous 68-year-old man is taken to the emergency room by his wife. She reports her husband became ill with fevers and weakness progressing over the last week. She noted excessive urination for the last several days with vomiting, increasing confusion, and lethargy over the last day. Past medical history is positive for mild chronic obstructive pulmonary disease and social history significant for smoking a pack of cigarettes daily for the past 50 years. Temperature is 38 C, blood pressure is 100/48, pulse is 110 beats/min, and respiration is 24 breaths/min. He is arousable only by sternal rub. Exam reveals dry mucous membranes, decreased breath sounds in the basilar left lung field, and no wheezing. Chest x-ray shows a left lower lobe infiltrate and hilar fullness. Serum chemical findings are remarkable for sodium of 158 mEq/L, calcium of 14.1 mEq/L, phosphorus of 5.2 mEq/L, albumin of 3.0 mEq/L, blood urea nitrogen (BUN) of 34 mEq/L, and creatinine of 2.4 mEq/L. Hematologic studies show a white blood cell count of 18,000/mm³, and a differential with 58% granulocytes and 20% bands. A complete blood cell count and serum chemistry panel including those indicated yielded normal findings 6 months ago.

1. Complications of severe hypercalcemia include which of the following?
   A. Mental confusion
   B. A short QT interval on electrocardiogram (ECG)
   C. Anorexia and nausea
   D. Cardiac arrest
   E. All of the above

2. The patient's hypercalcemia is most likely due to which of the following?
   A. Hyperparathyroidism exacerbated by hypercalcemia of critical illness
   B. Squamous lung cell carcinoma, causing humoral hypercalcemia of malignancy
   C. Pneumococcal sepsis
   D. Milk-alkali syndrome
   E. Hypervitaminosis D

3. Which of the following would be expected on further laboratory testing?
   A. Elevated intact parathyroid hormone level (iPTH) due to tumor secretion
   B. Suppressed iPTH level
   C. Elevated 1, 25-hydroxyvitamin D level
   D. Increased parathyroid hormone–related peptide (PTHrP) level
   E. B and D

4. Initial first-line therapy for this patient should include which of the following?
   A. Furosemide diuresis
   B. Vitamin D supplementation
   C. Intravenous normal saline solution
   D. Calcitonin, intravenous phosphate, and pamidronate disodium
   E. All of the above

● COMMENT

Complications • Symptoms are more common at calcium levels greater than 12 mg/dL and include increased urination, anorexia, nausea, vomiting, constipation, fatigue, and mental confusion. A short QT interval can be noted on the ECG and cardiac dysrhythmias can occur. Renal insufficiency, renal tubular defects, nephrolithiasis, and nephrocalcinosis can also occur. Severe hypercalcemia can manifest itself with coma and result in cardiac arrest.

Differential diagnosis of hypercalcemia • The causes of hypercalcemia are myriad, but most cases (>90%) are due to either hyperparathyroidism or cancer. This patient has hypercalcemia and findings consistent with postobstructive pneumonia. Hypercalcemia of malignancy is the most likely diagnosis. Overall, hyperparathyroidism is much more common than hypercalcemia of malignancy and is the expected diagnosis in the otherwise well patient with mild hypercalcemia. On the other hand, ill patients with severe hypercalcemia often harbor advanced malignancy, which is usually readily evident if not previously diagnosed. Milk-alkali syndrome is an unusual cause of hypercalcemia, which was more frequent before the advent of H₂ histamine blockers and proton pump inhibitors, when milk and sodium bicarbonate (alkali) were used to treat peptic ulcer disease. Elevated 1,25-hydroxyvitamin D level is also a less common cause of hypercalcemia. It can occur with excess dosages of 1,25-hydroxyvitamin D or with granulomatous and lymphoproliferative diseases, in which there is excessive and inappropriate conversion of 25-hydroxy to 1,25-hydroxyvitamin D. Critical illness, and especially sepsis, is associated with hypocalcemia, not hypercalcemia.

PTHrP and iPTH • Humoral hypercalcemia of malignancy is mediated by tumor secretion of PTHrP, a parathyroid hormone–like protein often associated with squamous cell carcinomas. Elevation of iPTH level is consistent with hyperparathyroidism and iPTH levels should be suppressed with other causes of hypercalcemia. Ectopic secretion of iPTH is exceedingly rare.

Therapy of severe hypercalcemia • Hypercalcemia causes severe dehydration due to nephrogenic diabetes insipidus, vomiting, and impairment of the thirst mechanism. First-line therapy is intravenous fluids, which restore glomerular filtration and allow calcium excretion through saline diuresis. Though furosemide is calciuric, its use is contraindicated during the initial resuscitation of dehydrated patients. Pamidronate disodium and calcitonin are helpful in the management of severe hypercalcemia, but intravenous phosphate is contraindicated, especially in patients with higher serum levels of phosphorus, as it can complex with calcium and cause nephrocalcinosis.

● CASE PRESENTATION

A 79-year-old white woman initially entered your office concerned that she might have osteoporosis. Her 82-year-old sister recently slipped on a tile floor and fractured her hip. The patient denies any known family history of osteoporosis though her mother had "slumped shoulders" in older age. She is neither a smoker nor a drinker. She reports she has lost about a half an inch in height since youth and there is no history of fracture or kidney stones. She walks four times a week and drinks two glasses of milk daily but ingests no other dairy products and does not take calcium. Physical exam findings are unremarkable except for mild tachycardia (104 beats/min). Dual x-ray absorptiometry (DEXA) is obtained: the spine (lumbar region L1 to L4) shows a T-score of −3.1 and a Z-score of −1.5; the total hip shows a T-score of −2.5 and a Z-score of −1.1. She now reports to your office for further counseling.

1. Which of the following is true of her sister's fracture?
   A. It is unlikely to be osteoporosis related; fractures are an expected consequence of such traumatic falls.
   B. Her fracture is likely to be osteoporosis related, but this history is not relevant to your patient.
   C. Her fracture is very likely osteoporosis related, as are most fractures caused by low-impact injuries.
   D. Osteoporosis is rare without identifiable risk factors such as hyperthyroidism or hyperparathyroidism.
   E. Given her sister's age, a pathologic fracture due to malignancy is the likely cause.

2. What recommendations should you make to the patient regarding her calcium intake?
   A. None: her current intake is adequate.
   B. As her peak bone age was achieved decades ago, she should decrease her calcium intake to reduce the risk of kidney stones.
   C. She should increase her milk intake to one glass at each meal.
   D. Her total daily intake of calcium should be 1200 mg.
   E. She should take 2000 mg of supplemental calcium with vitamin D.

3. Your patient is curious about her T- and Z-scores. You correctly can advise her of the following:
   A. An average Z-score coupled with an osteoporotic T-score is suggestive of secondary (not age-related) osteoporosis.
   B. Her T-score, which is used to classify her bone density as osteoporotic, is a statistical measure of deviation based on population levels of young healthy adults (i.e., those at their peak bone mass).
   C. Her Z-score is used to classify her bone density; the T-score is used to assess therapy.
   D. The T-score compares the patient's bone density to that of age-matched controls.
   E. All of the above

4. What additional studies are likely to be helpful in assessing this patient?
   A. Bone scan and biopsy, with calcium, albumin, and urinary N-telopeptide
   B. Bone biopsy, with calcium, albumin, and urinary N-telopeptide
   C. Thyroid stimulating hormone, calcium, and parathyroid hormone–related peptide
   D. Thyroid stimulating hormone, calcium, and albumin
   E. No additional studies are needed

● COMMENT

Osteoporosis risk • In this patient's sister the fracture is typical for osteoporosis. Approximately 95% of such low-impact fractures are related to osteoporosis. Osteoporosis is defined as a reduction in bone mass and is extremely common in postmenopausal women, though men can be affected as well. Estrogen deficiency, smoking, endocrine disorders (hyperparathyroidism, hyperthyroidism, Cushing's syndrome), vitamin D deficiency, low body weight, and fair skin are among the risk factors for osteoporosis. A history of osteoporotic fractures in a first-degree relative significantly increases this patient's risk for osteoporotic fractures.

Calcium intake/osteoporosis therapy • Current Institute of Medicine guidelines call for a calcium intake of 1000 mg/day in adults less than 50 years old and 1200 mg/day in adults over 50 years. Such intake of calcium with an appropriate dosage of vitamin D has been shown to decrease the risk of fracture in elderly adults. About 300 mg of calcium is obtained per dairy serving (for example, 8 ounces of milk, 16 ounces of cottage cheese, 1 ounce of hard cheese). This patient's current intake of calcium of about 600 mg is insufficient and should be increased. The risk of kidney stones becomes a major concern when daily calcium intake approaches 2000 mg. Dietary intake of calcium (i.e., nonsupplemental) has actually been associated with a decreased risk of kidney stones, presumably because calcium binds to oxalate in the gut, rendering it nonabsorbable. Other treatments for osteoporosis that can decrease the fracture rates include estrogen replacement therapy, bisphosphonates, and raloxifene. Nasal calcitonin has been shown to decrease the pain associated with vertebral compression fractures.

DEXA interpretation • DEXA bone scanning yields site-specific bone densities. These densities are used to calculate the Z- and T-scores from population bone density data. Both the T- and Z-scores are measures of standard deviation (SD). The T-score relates a patient's bone density to that of young adults, a population at their peak bone density (think T for 20s). Bone density is classified by the T-score as normal (within 1 SD of young adult mean values), osteopenic (T-score less than −1 but greater than −2.5), and osteoporotic (T-score less than −2.5). The Z-score is age- and sex-specific; if severely abnormal, it suggests the need to exclude causes of osteoporosis beyond that expected with normal aging. By way of example, an 85-year-old woman with an average Z-score would have a T-score in the osteoporotic range and would be unlikely to have a secondary, or non-age-related, cause of her osteoporosis.

Evaluation of osteoporosis • The extent of laboratory work needed to investigate osteoporosis is controversial, including whether routine measurement of bone markers such as N-telopeptide is warranted. Osteoporosis can be associated with hyperparathyroidism, hyperthyroidism, multiple myeloma, and long-term steroid use and a thorough history and physical exam are critical. All would agree that routine bone marrow biopsy, which theoretically might show myeloma, is excessive and that routine bone scanning is not needed. However, many providers routinely obtain serum protein electrophoresis to exclude myeloma. An albumin corrected calcium level is clearly indicated, as hyperparathyroidism is a fairly common treatable cause of osteoporosis. A thyrotropin (TSH) level is also justified to exclude hyperthyroidism, especially given this patient's tachycardia.

Answers • 1-C   2-D   3-B   4-D

● CASE PRESENTATION

A 48-year-old man seeks care in your clinic. He has no current complaints except a desire to lose "10 or 20 pounds" with diet and exercise. Past medical history is positive for type 2 diabetes for 15 years only known to be complicated by microalbuminuria. He also suffers from gout and hypertension. He suffers no glycemic symptoms and his hemoglobin A1C is 8.1%. His only medications are glyburide 5 mg and lisinopril 10 mg daily. He eats a high-fat "fast food" diet. On exam, blood pressure is 132/82. There is no retinopathy apparent on undilated exam. No bruits are heard and the remainder of the cardiovascular exam results are normal. Neurologic exam is notable only for moderately diminished vibratory sensation in the feet and absent ankle jerks. Electrocardiogram (ECG) finding is normal. Routine electrolytes, renal, and hepatic tests are normal. Fasting lipid panel shows a triglyceride level of 220 mg/dL, a high-density lipoprotein (HDL) level of 51 mg/dL, and a low-density lipoprotein (LDL) level of 128 mg/dL. The patient is to return in 2 months for a repeat fasting lipid panel after being prescribed an American Heart Association low-fat diet.

1. What should be done prior to prescribing an exercise program for this patient?

   A. Echocardiogram to exclude diastolic dysfunction
   B. Left heart catheterization
   C. Nothing: the normal ECG finding places the patient at low risk
   D. Stress test
   E. Initiation of statin drug to promote atheroma plaque stability

2. What effect on LDL could reasonably be hoped for with improved diet?

   A. None
   B. 10 to 20 mg/dL drop
   C. 30 to 40 mg/dL drop
   D. 50 mg/dL drop
   E. 100 mg/dL drop

3. Two months later the patient returns after a negative stress test result and no evidence of retinopathy on formal ophthalmologic exam. Triglycerides are now 120 mg/L, HDL is 55 mg/dL, LDL is 118 mg/dL, and hemoglobin A1C is 7.3%. What further measures should now be taken?

   A. Do nothing: LDL is less than 130 mg/dL.
   B. Start insulin to reduce hemoglobin A1C to below 7%.
   C. Start niacin.
   D. Start statin therapy.
   E. Start gemfibrizol to lower triglycerides.

4. In addition to periodically checking transaminase levels, the following is indicated when treating with a statin drug:

   A. Periodic urine studies for myoglobinuria
   B. Monitoring for symptoms of weakness and myalgia
   C. Complete blood cell count to rule out agranulocytosis
   D. Yearly nerve conduction studies to exclude neuropathy
   E. Periodic slit lamp exams for cataracts

● COMMENT

Cardiovascular risk • Although exercise has been associated with reduced risk of cardiovascular events in diabetes and can assist with weight loss, blood sugar control, and cholesterol reduction, care must be taken when prescribing an exercise program for patients with diabetes. Patients with diabetes are at much higher risk (two to four times) of cardiovascular disease than nondiabetics and neuropathy can mask typical anginal symptoms. This patient also has microalbuminuria, which is a definite marker for coronary artery disease. The American Diabetes Association currently recommends stress testing in all diabetic patients older than age 30 who are beginning an exercise program. High-grade retinopathy should also be excluded with a dilated ophthalmologic exam before strenuous exercise is begun.

Dietary effect on hyperlipidemia • Diet is the first step in all therapy for hypercholesterolemia; however, its effects are relatively modest. Adherence to a low-saturated-fat diet will rarely reduce LDL cholesterol by more than 10% to 20%. This information can be helpful when deciding whether to start medication as initial therapy of hypercholesterolemia.

Target LDL in diabetes • Patients with diabetes and no history of coronary artery disease have cardiovascular event rates similar to those of nondiabetics who have already suffered a myocardial infarction. Recognizing this markedly increased risk, the most recent National Cholesterol Education Program recommendations label diabetes as a "coronary artery disease risk equivalent" and set a goal LDL level at less than 100 mg/dL. Most physicians would begin statin therapy in this patient for further LDL reduction. Niacin is contraindicated by his gout and would also likely worsen glycemic control. Gemfibrizol does lower triglyceride levels effectively, but triglycerides are already at target level (less than 150 mg/dL). This patient's hemoglobin A1C is above the goal level of less than 7%, but his blood sugar is improving with diet and exercise and this should be continued before adding further therapy. Some practitioners would argue to substitute metformin for glyburide to help with weight loss and lessen the risk of hypoglycemia.

Side effects of statins • During therapy with statin drugs, liver function should be tested periodically. Many physicians also routinely measure creatine kinase levels, though this is controversial. At a minimum, the patient should be instructed of the possibility of myositis and instructed to stop medication and seek medical advice if they experience myalgia or weakness. Urine myoglobin is not monitored and agranulocytosis and neuropathy are not expected side effects of statins.

Answers • 1-D 2-B 3-D 4-B

● CASE PRESENTATION

L. W. is an 18-year-old white man who was taken to the emergency room by his college roommate. The patient is extremely lethargic, and much of the history is gathered from the roommate. The roommate states that the patient had been complaining about abdominal pain, thirst, and fatigue for the past couple of weeks. On exam the patient is tachypneic (rate 28/min), has a temperature of 100.8 F and blood pressure of 90/60 lying down with a pulse rate of 110/min, and has a standing blood pressure of 70/50 with a pulse rate of 130 beats/min. His skin is dry with decreased turgor and his breath has a fruity odor. The lab results reveal Na of 130 mEq/L, K of 5.5 mEq/L, HCO_3 of 13 mEq/L, Cl 100 mEq/L, blood urea nitrogen (BUN) of 37 mg/dL, and glucose of 353 mg/dL. His urinalysis result is positive for ketones with a specific gravity of 1.016 and glucose 4+.

1. There are numerous pathophysiologic conditions that occur with diabetic ketoacidosis (DKA). Which one of the following is correct?
   A. Decreased hepatic production of glucose
   B. Decreased protein catabolism in the peripheral tissues
   C. Decreased hepatic production of ketones
   D. Increased peripheral glucose usage
   E. Increased lipolysis

2. Which of the following are "classic" clinical features of DKA?
   A. Rapid, deep breathing
   B. Breath odor of acetone
   C. Dry skin and mucous membranes
   D. Clouding of consciousness
   E. All of the above

3. In this patient, you should first:
   A. Initiate therapy with IV fluids, insulin infusion, and replacement of electrolytes
   B. Order a computed tomography (CT) of the abdomen to evaluate abdominal pain
   C. Give sodium polystyrene sulfonate (Kayexalate) and calcium gluconate to treat hyperkalemia
   D. Wait until the patient awakens to get a better history
   E. Initiate therapy with oral sulfonureas

4. Key differences between DKA and nonketotic hyperosmolar state include which of the following?
   A. Unlike patients with DKA, patients with nonketotic hyperosmolar state have sufficient insulin levels to prevent lipolyis and ketosis and therefore rarely have acidosis.
   B. Patients with nonketotic hyperosmolar state have much higher mortality rates.
   C. Patients with nonketotic hyperosmolar state require greater fluid resuscitation before insulin therapy than patients with DKA.
   D. Hyperglycemia is generally more profound in nonketotic hyperosmolar coma.
   E. All of the above

● COMMENT

Pathophysiologic features of DKA • DKA is a complex metabolic phenomenon that occurs in type I diabetics when the circulating insulin is insufficient and leads to a series of events. First are a lack of glucose uptake by peripheral tissues and absence of glucagon inhibition. These lead to increased hepatic gluconeogenesis, glycogenolysis, and inhibition of glycolysis. There is also protein catabolism in peripheral tissues, increasing amino acids in the circulation, which act as hepatic substrates for gluconeogenesis. Insulin deficiency also results in increased lypolysis, which leads to mobilization of free fatty acids. The increased free fatty acids are utilized in ketogenesis under the stimulation of glucagon. DKA can be precipitated by any event that leads to increased insulin need or decreased insulin availability. Examples include omission of insulin dosages, infections, myocardial infarction, injuries, and emotional stress.

Clinical findings • The classic clinical features of DKA include rapid, deep breathing (Kussmaul's), acetone (fruity) breath odor, marked dehydration such as dry skin and mucous membranes, orthostatic hypotension, clouding of consciousness, weakness, abdominal pain, and myalgias. Laboratory analysis is an important clue to the severity and response to therapy. Hyperglycemia, increased anion gap metabolic acidosis, potassium derangement, and ketosis are all present and should be monitored every 1 to 2 hours during therapy. The degree of hyperglycemia does not have to be marked.

Treatment of DKA • Therapy should be rapidly initiated. There are a number of components that should be addressed. First, fluid replacement should be initiated with normal saline solution, as the glucose-induced osmotic diuresis results in profound dehydration. Insulin must also be replaced early to increase glucose use in the tissues, counter the effects of glucagon on the liver, and decrease lipolysis. IV insulin should be continued until the anion gap closes. Therapy must also address mineral and electrolyte replacement, paying particular attention to potassium and phosphate levels. Finally, one must search for and address the precipitating cause of the DKA.

DKA versus nonketotic hyperosmolar state (NKHS) • NKHS and DKA are both manifested by hyperglycemia, dehydration, and frequently the presence of a precipitating event (infection, infarction, noncompliance, etc.). However, there are also several key differences. First, profound hyperglycemia (>700 mg/dL) is more characteristic of NKHS, resulting in more severe dehydration and hyperosmolarity. Therefore, there is greater need for fluid replacement in NKHS. Insulin deficiency is not complete, and lipolysis and resultant ketoacidosis are usually prevented. As might be expected from their generally older age and infirmity, patients with NKHS coma have a higher mortality rate than those with DKA.

Answers • 1-E   2-E   3-A   4-E

● CASE PRESENTATION

A 33-year-old previously healthy white woman reports heat intolerance, palpitations, and diarrhea for the past 6 to 8 weeks. Family history is negative for any endocrinopathies. Review of systems (ROS) is positive for anxiety and a 10-pound weight loss over the past 2 months; the remainder of the ROS findings are negative. On physical exam, the patient is 167 cm (66 in.) and weighs 53.5 kg (117 lb.); her pulse rate is 99/min, and her blood pressure 148/60 mm Hg. In general she appears in no acute distress. Her eyes are proptotic with noted lid lag, and her thyroid gland is prominent, with size estimated to be three times normal. The thyroid is smooth and firm and a bruit is appreciated. Neurologic exam reveals fine tremor of her hands and 3+ deep tendon reflexes. Results of lab studies are as follows: Serum thyrotropin less than 0.1mFu/L (0.4-6.0) serum free thyroxine 4.1 mg/dL (4.5-12.0 mg/dL).

1. Signs and symptoms of hyperthyroidism include which of the following?
   A. Dry skin
   B. Narrow pulse pressure
   C. Dry, coarse hair
   D. Amenorrhea
   E. All of the above

2. What is the patient's most likely diagnosis?
   A. Toxic adenoma
   B. Toxic multinodular goiter
   C. Hyperthyroid phase of Hashimoto's thyroiditis
   D. Diffuse toxic goiter (Graves' disease)
   E. Thyrotropin-secreting pituitary tumor

3. Which is the best way to differentiate thyroiditis from Graves' disease?
   A. Radioactive iodine uptake
   B. Thyroid antibodies (antimicrosomal, anti-TPO)
   C. Elevated serum free thyroxine (FT_4)
   D. Suppressed thyrotropin (TSH)
   E. Presence of a goiter

4. What is the most common complication of radioactive iodine treatment?
   A. TSH secreting pituitary tumor
   B. Lymphoma
   C. Hypothyroidism
   D. Thyroid storm
   E. Subacute thyroiditis

● COMMENT

Signs and symptoms • Hyperthyroidism is a disease that affects around 2% of women and 0.2% of men. The work-up primarily consists of the history and physical exam plus the laboratory data. The history and physical exam often reveal complaints of metabolic changes (heat intolerance, sweating, and weight loss), cardiovascular effects (tachycardia, atrial fibrillation, widened pulse pressure), diarrhea, skin changes (warm, moist skin), fine, silky hair, and central nervous system (CNS) effects (restlessness, emotional lability, and fine tremor). Oligomenorrhea and amenorrhea may also occur. Certain clinical findings reveal the underlying cause of hyperthyroidism. The presence of a thyroidal bruit and exophthalmos signify Graves' disease.

Differential diagnosis • Graves' disease is the most common cause of hyperthyroidism. In the preceding case, the patient had the physical findings of exophthalmos and thyroid bruit that helped to diagnose the young woman's underlying Graves' disease. Other common causes of hyperthyroidism include thyroiditis (subacute, silent, and postpartum), toxic multinodular goiter, toxic thyroid adenoma, and factitious illness such as self-administration of thyroxine. The use of radioactive iodine often helps to differentiate among these illnesses. In Graves' disease, there is diffuse uptake of the ^{131}I tracer seen with the scan, whereas in thyroiditis there is low uptake, and in toxic adenoma (solitary or multinodular) there is uneven distribution. Other rare causes are pituitary oversecretion of TSH, exogenous iodide, or cancerous sources (either thyroidal or extrathyroidal).

Treatment of Graves' disease • Initially, symptoms are controlled with propanolol. Treatment then consists of three main modalities: antithyroid drugs, radioactive iodine, and subtotal thyroidectomy. The mainstay of antithyroid drug therapy consists of methimazole or propylthiouracil (PTU). Both inhibit oxidation of iodide and coupling of iodotyrosines, leading to decreased production of the thyroid hormones. PTU has the added benefit of decreasing peripheral conversion of T_4 to T_3. The antithyroidal drugs are preferred in the clinical situation of slight to moderate elevation of thyroid hormone levels because of their greater potential to produce lasting remission. PTU is especially used in pregnancy, as it is safer than methimazole and radioactive iodine is contraindicated in pregnancy. The disadvantages of these therapies include drug toxicities such as agranulocytosis, skin rash, and joint pain. Radioactive iodine, which leads to a decrease in thyroid function in 6 to 12 weeks after a single dose, is most commonly used in patients above age 30. The disadvantages of this therapy include hypothyroidism, which occurs in close to 70% of patients 10 to 15 years after treatment, and the potential that multiple treatments may be needed to treat the patient successfully. Subtotal thyroidectomy is another treatment for hyperthyroidism. It is the treatment of choice in patients with large goiters as well as those who are poor candidates or refuse to initiate medical or radioactive iodine therapy. One must successfully treat the hyperthyroidism with medications before surgery to prevent thyroid storm, a life-threatening condition of extreme hyperthyroidism. There are also risks of anesthesia and surgical morbidity such as laryngeal nerve palsy or hypoparathyroidism that must be considered before initiating this therapy.

Answers • 1-D 2-D 3-A 4-C

● CASE PRESENTATION

A 32-year-old white woman enters your office for evaluation of 8 weeks of fatigue, constipation, and weight gain of 4.6 kg (10 lb). On review of systems she states that she has had cold intolerance and that her skin is drier than usual. Her past medical history is unremarkable.

On physical exam, her blood pressure is noted to be 124/96 and her pulse rate is 51/min. Examination of the neck shows an enlarged, firm thyroid gland without masses or adenopathy. Her deep tendon reflexes reveal a slowed relaxation phase. Laboratory studies reveal serum thyrotropin of 84.5 μU/mL and serum total thyroxine of 1.0 μg/dL.

1. Which of the following is this patient most likely to experience?
   A. Diarrhea
   B. Deepening of the voice
   C. Fine, silky hair
   D. Hyperactive deep tendon reflexes
   E. Amenorrhea

2. What is the patient's most likely diagnosis?
   A. Graves' disease
   B. Secondary hypothyroidism
   C. Papillary thyroid cancer
   D. Chronic thyroiditis (Hashimoto's thyroiditis)
   E. Iodine excess

3. The patient has been started on thyroid replacement therapy without complications. She returns 6 months later and states that she is pregnant. What should you anticipate?
   A. She will no longer require thyroid replacement.
   B. Her thyroid replacement dosage will decrease.
   C. Her thyroid replacement dosage will increase.
   D. She will experience thyroid storm.
   E. She will not need to change her thyroid replacement dosage.

4. Hypothyroidism should be treated daily with what?
   A. Thyroxine (T_4)
   B. Triiodothyronine (T_3)
   C. Thyroglobulin
   D. Thyroid extract
   E. T_4 and T_3

● COMMENT

Signs and symptoms • This patient is in a hypothyroid state. The lab data reveal an elevated TSH level in the face of a low total thyroxine level, a classic finding for this disease entity. The history also provides helpful clues. Patients with hypothyroidism often have clinical manifestations such as weakness, lethargy, dry skin, cold intolerance, constipation, puffy eyelids and face, weight gain, deepening voice, and menorrhagia. Clinical findings may include prolongation of the relaxation phase of deep tendon reflexes, diastolic hypertension, bradycardia, low amplitude QRS on electrocardiogram (ECG), and findings consistent with carpal tunnel syndrome.

Differential diagnosis • One of the first steps in the work-up of hypothyroidism is narrowing the differential diagnosis. Often, clinicians must differentiate primary (arising from the thyroid) and secondary (pituitary or hypothalamic) causes. A secondary cause is eliminated in this case as the TSH level is elevated, implying normal hypothalamic-pituitary axis. In narrowing the differential diagnosis of primary hypothyroidism, it is often helpful to distinguish nongoitrous from goitrous causes. Nongoitrous causes of hypothyroidism include primary thyroid atrophy and postablative hypothyroidism after either surgery or radioactive iodine ablation. Goitrous causes include chronic thyroiditis (Hashimoto's thyroiditis), iodine deficiency, and drug-induced (amiodarone or lithium, for example) causes. In this patient, the most likely diagnosis is thyroiditis. Additional tests to help diagnose Hashimoto's thyroiditis include thyroid peroxidase (anti-TPO) and antimicrosomal autoantibodies.

Thyroid replacement in pregnancy • During pregnancy, various changes occur that can affect the thyroid axis. One change is the increase in thyroid binding globulin (TBG), which leads to increased T_4 binding, transiently increasing T_4 requirements. Additionally, there are increased destruction of T_4 by deidonases located in the placenta, as well as an increased volume of distribution. These three changes can lead to increased requirements for exogenous thyroxine therapy. It is extremely important to follow these patients closely as some recent studies suggest neuropsychological abnormalities in the children of hypothyroid mothers.

Treatment • Treatment is relatively simple. Thyroxine (T_4) is the preferred choice because it has a longer half-life than triiodothyronine (T_3) and it is converted to T_3 in the liver. This conversion better approximates the circulating T_4 and T_3 seen in euthyroid individuals. Thyroid extract and thyroglobulin both contain variable amounts of T_4 and T_3. This variability leads to great difficulty in interpretation of serum T_4 and T_3 levels, making dosage adjustment nearly impossible. T_3 is inappropriate because it has a short half-life, so it must be given several times a day.

● CASE PRESENTATION

An 84-year-old male nursing home patient is admitted to the intensive care unit (ICU) with fever, hypotension, and somnolence. History is not obtainable but nursing home notes document a slow deterioration of mental status and increasing anorexia over the last week, and a past medical history of prostatic hypertrophy, steroid-dependent chronic obstructive pulmonary disease, and left hip replacement for avascular necrosis of the femoral head. Temperature is 38.5 C, pulse 105 beats/min, blood pressure 84/48, respirations 24 breaths/min. Physical exam reveals an obtunded older man. Eyes show dense cataracts. The heart is distant and regular. The chest anterior-posterior diameter is increased, and there is mild diffuse wheezing with no rales. The prostate is diffusely enlarged. Skin turgor is poor. Urinalysis reveals specific gravity 1.025, 3+ leukocyte esterase activity, and marked bacteria. Complete blood count (CBC) reveals a white blood cell count of 17,000/mm³ with 58% polymorphonuclear leukocytes and 14% bands. Serum chemical results show sodium of 130 mEq/L, potassium of 4.3 mEq/L, blood urea nitrogen of 28 mg/dL, creatinine of 3 mg/dL, and urine sodium of less than 10 mEq/L. Blood cultures are pending and cardiac enzyme findings are negative. The electrocardiogram (ECG) result is only remarkable for sinus tachycardia. Despite treatment with broad-spectrum intravenous antibiotics, aggressive fluid resuscitation, and dopamine infusion, the patient remains hypotensive and serum cortisol drawn at 2 pm returns with a level of 7 μg/dL (normal range is reported at 5 to 20 μg/dL).

1. Which of the following is the most likely cause of this patient's refractory hypotension?
   A. Previously unrecognized Cushing's disease
   B. High-output cardiac failure secondary to hyperthyroidism
   C. Right ventricular infarction
   D. Adrenal insufficiency
   E. Hypovolemia

2. Regarding the serum cortisol, what further measures are most appropriate?
   A. None, the cortisol level is normal for the early afternoon.
   B. A baseline cortisol and corticotropin (ACTH) level should be drawn the next morning and followed by a 250-μg cosyntropin stimulation test before beginning glucocorticoids, which could worsen sepsis.
   C. The patient's hyponatremia, hypotension, and low cortisol level are indications for fludrocortisone acetate (Florinef Acetate).
   D. Stress dose hydrocortisone or dexamethasone should be initiated.
   E. Abdominal computed tomography (CT) imaging of the adrenal glands is required.

3. The likely cause of hypoadrenalism, if proved, is which of the following?
   A. Previous Cushing's disease with recent infarction of pituitary adenoma
   B. Metastatic adrenal disease
   C. Previous treatment with suppressive dosages of glucocorticoids
   D. Adrenal hemorrhage
   E. Autoimmune adrenalitis

4. In ambulatory patients, which of the following is a common clinical manifestation of adrenal insufficiency?
   A. Hypertension
   B. Abdominal pain
   C. Basophilia
   D. Increased appetite
   E. Hyperglycemia

● COMMENT

Cause of hypotension • Adrenal insufficiency should always be considered in hypotensive patients not responding to usual therapeutic measures. This patient is likely suffering from urosepsis; however, his refractory hypotension and past medical history of glucocorticoid treatment suggest adrenal insufficiency. Cortisol levels are expected to be lower in the afternoon in a well person, but levels should be elevated at any time of acute stress. The best cortisol level for diagnosing adrenal insufficiency during critical illness is intensely debated, but suggested threshold levels range from 18 to 25 μg/dL. Accordingly, this patient's cortisol level is low by any standard. Right ventricular infarction, an occasionally unsuspected cause of hypotension, is unlikely given the negative cardiac enzymes and unremarkable ECG findings. Hypovolemia and high-output failure are not likely in this patient.

Treatment of suspected adrenal insufficiency • In emergent situations patients with suspected adrenal insufficiency should be treated presumptively with glucocorticoid replacement while awaiting laboratory confirmation. Blood can be drawn for cortisol levels immediately prior to beginning stress dose hydrocortisone (100 mg every 8 hours). Alternatively, 4 mg of dexamethasone, which does not interfere with cortisol assays, can be given and followed by a cosyntropin stimulation test. Fludrocortisone acetate is a mineralocorticoid without glucocorticoid activity.

Causes of adrenal insufficiency • The cause of the patient's adrenal insufficiency is likely previous steroid therapy, which is the most common cause. Generally, dosages of glucocorticoids equivalent to 5 mg/day of prednisone or greater given for more than 3 weeks are considered sufficient to cause clinically relevant adrenal insufficiency by suppressing the hypothalamic pituitary axis. Recovery of adrenal function may take up to a year after steroid therapy. Autoimmune adrenalitis, granulomatous infections, and surgical resection are other common causes. Bilateral tumor metastasis and adrenal hemorrhages are less common causes. Though adrenal insufficiency can occur after rapid reversal of Cushing's disease (after surgery or with pituitary infarction), this is a very unlikely diagnosis in this patient.

Clinical manifestations • Marked fatigue, abdominal pain, anorexia, weakness, weight loss, hypotension, salt craving, and hyperpigmentation are common manifestations of adrenal insufficiency. Hyponatremia and hyperkalemia (due to mineralocorticoid deficiency) occur most commonly in primary adrenal insufficiency. Eosinophilia and hypoglycemia can also occur.

Answers • 1-D 2-D 3-C 4-B

● CASE PRESENTATION

A 59-year-old woman complains of fatigue and a 40-pound weight gain. She notes progressive weakness for the last year and now has difficulty rising from a chair and brushing her hair. She has no headache or visual changes. Past medical history indicates recently diagnosed hypercholesterolemia, but she is on no medications. She drinks two glasses of wine nightly and is a non-smoker. Family history is unremarkable. Physical exam reveals moon facies, moderate hirsutism, acne, a dorsocervical fat pad, and decreased proximal muscle strength. Her blood pressure is elevated at 155/92 mm Hg. There are no bruises or striae. The chest x-ray result is normal. Morning cortisol level is 14 μg/dL after a 1-mg dose of dexamethasone at 11 p.m. (normal is less than 1.8 μg/dL) and urinary free cortisol level is significantly elevated at 177 μg/24 hr.

1. Which of the following can be said about this patient's abnormal 1-mg dexamethasone suppression test result and elevated 24-hour urinary free cortisol level?
   A. She definitely has a corticotropin (ACTH)-secreting pituitary adenoma.
   B. She has adrenal cancer.
   C. Her Cushing's syndrome is definitely due to ectopic ACTH production.
   D. The test results are likely false-positive.
   E. She has Cushing's syndrome, its cause to be determined.

2. Common clinical findings in Cushing's syndrome include which of the following?
   A. Peripheral redistribution of fat
   B. Hypopigmentation
   C. Hirsutism and acne
   D. Hypotension
   E. All of the above

3. Which of the following is the most reasonable next diagnostic test to differentiate adrenal sources from Cushing's syndrome related to excess ACTH level?
   A. Inferior petrosal sinus sampling
   B. Computed tomography (CT) of the adrenal glands
   C. Pituitary magnetic resonance imaging (MRI)
   D. Plasma ACTH level
   E. Repetition of previous studies after weight loss

4. Given the patient's age and sex, what is the most common cause of her Cushing's syndrome?
   A. Adrenal cancer
   B. Ectopic ACTH production due to small cell lung cancer
   C. Adrenal adenoma
   D. Cushing's disease secondary to pituitary adenoma
   E. Cushing's syndrome secondary to islet cell pancreatic tumor

● COMMENT

Diagnosis of Cushing's syndrome • This patient's presentation and laboratory findings indicate *Cushing's syndrome,* the clinical symptom complex of hypercortisolism regardless of cause. *Cushing's disease* is pituitary-dependent glucocorticoid excess. We cannot determine the cause, given the available data. The 1-mg dexamethasone suppression test is the initial screen and if serum cortisol is suppressed with dexamethasone, Cushing's is excluded. A positive test result (lack of suppression) requires confirmation as false-positive results can occur with depression, certain drugs (phenytoin), obesity, and chronic alcohol use. Twenty-four-hour urinary excretion of cortisol is the other screening test and can be used for confirmation.

Clinical manifestations • Central redistribution of fat results in "moon facies," central obesity, and the cervicodorsal "buffalo hump." Proximal muscle weakness occurs in about two-thirds of patients with Cushing's syndrome as a result of hypercortisolemia. Purple abdominal striae are present in about 50% of cases, but they are less common in older patients. Susceptibility to bruising and poor wound healing are other hallmarks. Hyperpigmentation occurs with excess ACTH. Hirsutism, amenorrhea, and acne reflect increased secretion of adrenal androgens and can be found in Cushing's syndrome of any cause. Virilization (hirsutism plus male-pattern balding, deepened voice, and clitoromegaly) occurs more often in adrenal cancers, which produce a greater excess of adrenal androgens. Glucose intolerance and hypokalemic alkalosis are often evident. Severe osteoporosis can result from glucocorticoid inhibition of osteoblast activity. Most patients are hypertensive. Cushing's syndrome due to exogenous steroid use can be associated with avascular necrosis and cataracts as well.

Differentiation of ACTH-independent versus ACTH-related Cushing's syndrome • The next step in evaluation is determining the cause of hypercortisolism. Because of availability of reliable serum ACTH assays this test has largely supplanted high-dose dexamethasone suppression testing as the first-line test. A low ACTH level implies autonomous adrenal hypercortisolism, whereas elevated ACTH levels imply pituitary overproduction or ectopic ACTH syndrome. Anatomic localization procedures (inferior petrosal sampling and radiography) are done after the differential diagnosis has been narrowed (e.g., pituitary MRI if ACTH level is elevated, adrenal CT if ACTH level is low). High dose dexamethasone testing can be used to differentiate ectopic ACTH syndrome (which does not cause suppression) from Cushing's disease (which does cause suppression).

Cause • The most likely cause of Cushing's syndrome in adults is pituitary overproduction of ACTH. Ectopic ACTH production and adrenal overproduction due to adenomas or cancer are less common causes.

Answers • 1-E   2-C   3-D   4-D

● CASE PRESENTATION

A 32-year-old white man with a history of persistent intravenous drug use enters the emergency department with a 1-week history of subjective fever, sore throat, rash, myalgias, and headache. He does admit to sharing needles on occasion. Past medical history is remarkable for hepatitis B approximately 5 years ago. Physical examination is remarkable for a temperature of 102.1 F, pharyngeal erythema, cervical lymphadenopathy, and a maculopapular facial and truncal rash. The patient also has oral thrush noted. Laboratory studies reveal a normal white blood cell count with some atypical lymphocytes noted on peripheral smear. Levels of aspartate aminotransferase (AST) and alanine aminotransferase (ALT) are moderately elevated, but the hepatitis B surface antigen is negative. Initial human immunodeficiency virus (HIV) antibody testing yields a negative result.

1. You suspect acute HIV infection. True statements about this syndrome include which of the following?

   A. Unprotected sexual intercourse is a major risk factor.
   B. Opportunistic infections can be part of this presentation.
   C. Symptoms are typically self-limited.
   D. Fulminant clinical and immunologic deterioration can occur.
   E. All of the above

2. These symptoms appear approximately how long after exposure?

   A. 4 to 6 months
   B. 24 to 72 hours
   C. 5 to 7 days
   D. 3 to 6 weeks
   E. 10 years

3. Which lab abnormality is seen with this syndrome?

   A. Marked eosinophilia
   B. Hyperbilirubinemia
   C. Granulocytopenia
   D. Decreased CD4 lymphocyte count
   E. All of the above

4. True statements regarding diagnosis include which of the following?

   A. A negative HIV antibody test result rules out acute HIV infection.
   B. Repeat HIV antibody testing in 6 months will likely have a negative result.
   C. HIV ribonucleic acid (RNA) or p24 antigen testing would likely have a positive result.
   D. Characteristic elevation of CD4 lymphocytes is virtually diagnostic.
   E. All of the above

● COMMENT

Acute HIV infection • This patient is likely suffering from the acute HIV syndrome, which is experienced by at least half of the patients infected by HIV. This syndrome is a mononucleosis-type syndrome associated with marked viremia and is characterized by fever, pharyngitis, lymphadenopathy, headache, lethargy, and an erythematous maculopapular rash. Opportunistic infections can occur during this phase of HIV infection. Neurologic manifestations, including aseptic meningitis, can occur as well. Fulminant deterioration can rarely ensue. HIV is transmitted by exposure to blood or body fluids from infected individuals, including by sexual contact.

Time course • The acute HIV syndrome typically occurs 3 to 6 weeks after exposure to the virus. This syndrome lasts for at least 1 week then gradually subsides. Patients then generally have a prolonged asymptomatic stage of many years before they begin experiencing opportunistic infections. This usually occurs when the CD4 lymphocyte count falls to approximately 200/μL, though effective antiretroviral therapy alters this natural history and improves survival rate.

Laboratory abnormalities • Common abnormalities associated with the acute HIV syndrome include lymphopenia (particularly CD4 lymphocytes) and the presence of atypical lymphocytes on peripheral smear. Granulocyte counts are not affected and eosinophilia is not characteristic of acute HIV infection. Hepatic transaminase levels are nonspecifically elevated. There is significant viremia evident on specific testing.

Diagnosis • Diagnosis of the acute HIV syndrome requires an accurate history and an appropriate degree of suspicion. Standard enzyme-linked immunosorbent assay (ELISA) and Western blot antibody testing often have negative results early in the course of infection. Most patients have seroconversion at approximately 3 to 4 weeks, though this can take as long as 6 months. Therefore, polymerase chain reaction (PCR) determinations of HIV RNA or p24 antigen testing are often necessary to diagnose acute HIV infection.

Answers • 1-E 2-D 3-D 4-C

● CASE PRESENTATION

A 48-year-old white homosexual man arrives at your clinic for a new patient evaluation. He reveals that has not seen any health care professional for more than 10 years and has been healthy but recently found out a former sexual partner was diagnosed with acquired immunodeficiency syndrome (AIDS) and he wants to be tested. A human immunodeficiency virus (HIV) antibody shows a positive result (both by enzyme-linked immunosorbent assay [ELISA] and by Western blot), and subsequent blood work reveals a CD4 count of 146.

1. Which of the following is contraindicated for this patient?
   A. Hepatitis B vaccine
   B. Varicella zoster virus vaccine
   C. Pneumococcal vaccine
   D. Hepatitis A vaccine
   E. Tetanus vaccine

2. Which of the following is considered a contraindication to giving any vaccination?
   A. Low-grade temperature
   B. Living in a household with a pregnant woman
   C. Previous mild reaction to an immunization
   D. Family history of allergy to vaccinations
   E. None of the above

3. Which of the following statements is true regarding adult immunizations?
   A. It is not cost-effective to screen high-risk populations for previous hepatitis B infection before giving the immunization.
   B. Screening for prior influenza infection before influenza vaccination can prevent serious vaccine reactions.
   C. At least 70% of adults who deny childhood chickenpox infection are immune to the varicella zoster virus.
   D. Patients with chronic obstructive pulmonary disease (COPD) should be given the pneumonia vaccine annually.
   E. Patients with chronic liver disease should not receive the hepatitis A vaccine.

4. Which one of the following patients should receive the pneumococcal vaccine?
   A. 58-year-old white man with alcoholism
   B. 32-year-old black woman with diabetes
   C. 68-year-old white woman with no medical problems
   D. 37-year-old black woman with nephrotic syndrome from lupus nephritis
   E. All of the above

● COMMENT

Adult immunizations • The varicella zoster vaccine should be given to high-risk individuals at high risk for infection, but it is a live vaccine and should not be given to immunosuppressed or pregnant patients. Adult immunizations are generally given because 1) the patient has a life-style or occupation that places him at particular risk (e.g., vaccinating health care workers for hepatitis B), 2) the patient has a disease that predisposes him to certain preventable infections (e.g., splenectomized patients vaccinated for encapsulated bacteria), or 3) the patient is at risk for severe disease from a preventable infection (e.g., hepatitis A in cirrhotic patients). The patient in this case has all three characteristics. HIV infection places him at risk for certain infections (such as pneumococcal infections), and can increase severity of those infections. Homosexuality is an indication for the hepatitis B and hepatitis A vaccinations. The tetanus vaccine is recommended for all patients at 10-year intervals.

Current utilization of vaccines • In the adult population, vaccines are tremendously underutilized. Currently 30% of people who qualify for the pneumococcal vaccine receive it, 55% of people eligible for the influenza vaccine receive it, and only 10% of those who meet criteria for the hepatitis B vaccine receive it. Misconceptions regarding contraindications contribute to this underutilization. Previous mild to moderate reaction to a vaccine, living in a household with a pregnant woman, current mild febrile illness, and a family history of allergy to a vaccine are not contraindications to immunization.

Prevaccination screening for disease • Certain groups have such a high incidence of hepatitis B (prostitutes and intravenous drug abusers) that it is cost-effective to screen them for prior infection before vaccinating them. All patients who give a childhood history of chickenpox should be considered immune and not be vaccinated. In fact, 70% to 90% of those who deny prior infection are immune; therefore, it is reasonable to check varicella zoster antibody titers before vaccinating. Infections that do not confer lifelong immunity, such as influenza and pneumococcus infection, need not be screened for before vaccination.

Target populations • Pneumococcal vaccine and influenza vaccine share many of the same target populations: patients who are older than 65 or live in chronic care facilities, chronic lung disease patients, immunocompromised patients, alcoholics, and patients with congestive heart failure (CHF), nephrotic syndrome, diabetes, and cirrhosis. Influenza vaccination is recommended for all health care workers. The hepatitis B vaccine target population includes health care workers, household contacts of patients with chronic hepatitis B infection, intravenous (IV) drug abusers, sexually promiscuous individuals, hemodialysis patients, and homosexual patients.

Answers • 1-B 2-E 3-C 4-E

● CASE PRESENTATION

A 22-year-old woman enters your outpatient clinic complaining of sore throat, fever, and malaise for 5 days. She reports fevers at home to a maximum of 102 F two days previously. She has difficulty eating secondary to pain and describes intermittent headache and dull back pain over the past 2 days. On exam, her temperature is 100.8 F, heart rate is 95, blood pressure is 110/64, and respiratory rate is 18. HEENT exam is significant for tonsillar erythema and enlargement with a thick exudate. There is tender 1-cm posterior chain cervical lymphadenopathy present bilaterally. Cardiovascular and lung exam results are normal. Abdomen is diffusely full, without rebound or guarding, and with normal bowel sounds. The rapid *Streptococcus* sp. test finding is negative. A complete blood count reveals white blood cell count (WBC) of 14,000/mm^3 with 40% neutrophils, 30% lymphocytes, and 25% atypical lymphocytes.

1. Rapid diagnosis and treatment of group A streptococcal pharyngitis can prevent which of the following?
   A. Rheumatic fever
   B. Postinfectious glomerulonephritis
   C. Splenic rupture
   D. *Clostridium difficile* colitis
   E. Development of lymphoma

2. What is the most appropriate next step in the management of this patient?
   A. Echocardiography to evaluate for valvular vegetations
   B. Admission for intravenous (IV) antibiotics
   C. Oral penicillin for 10 days and close clinical follow-up to prevent rheumatic fever
   D. Serum heterophile antibody testing and caution against vigorous activity
   E. Quarantine of the patient and administration of antibiotic prophylaxis for close contacts

3. Which of the following is the most common serious complication of infectious mononucleosis?
   A. Postinfectious glomerulonephritis
   B. Rheumatic fever
   C. Splenic rupture
   D. Acute liver failure
   E. Aplastic anemia

4. The patient is given a prescription for amoxicillin and returns in 3 days with a pruritic maculopapular rash. Which of the following is the next appropriate step?
   A. Finish 10-day course of antibiotics.
   B. Discontinue amoxicillin and change to a macrolide.
   C. Counsel the patient never to take penicillin again.
   D. Stop antibiotics and give supportive care.
   E. Desensitize the patient to penicillin.

● COMMENT

Complications of group A streptococcus pharyngitis • Group A streptococcus pharyngitis can be associated with acute complications including scarlet fever, peritonsillar or retropharyngeal abscesses, meningitis, and bacteremia. The postinfectious complications include acute rheumatic fever and poststreptococcal glomerulonephritis. Appropriately diagnosing and treating streptococcus pharyngitis prevents acute rheumatic fever, but treatment does not impact the development of poststreptococcal glomerulonephritis.

Differential diagnosis of pharyngitis • The acute sore throat is one of the most common reasons for visits to primary care physicians in the United States. Acute pharyngitis in adults can be attributed to many causes, including bacteria, viruses, atypical pathogens, malignancy, and chemical or traumatic injury. The main dilemma faced by a practitioner is the differentiation of pharyngitis caused by group A streptococcus so that the dreaded complication of rheumatic fever can be prevented. The combination of tender anterior cervical adenopathy, fevers of greater than 101.5 F and exudative pharyngitis is suggestive of streptococcal pharyngitis. A rapid *Streptococcus* sp. throat swab, a standard culture, or a combination of both can confirm the diagnosis. Our young patient presents classic symptoms of Epstein-Barr viral infection (infectious mononucleosis). These patients are usually aged 15 to 24 and experience severe malaise, fever, lymphadenopathy, and exudative pharyngitis. Atypical lymphocytosis is characteristic and even diagnostic in this infection. Presence of serum heterophile antibodies, as indicated by slide test for mononucleosis (Monospot), confirms the diagnosis of infectious mononucleosis.

Complications of infectious mononucleosis (IM) • Malaise and weakness can last weeks to months after infection, but traumatic injury to a grossly enlarged spleen is the most dangerous complication of this generally self-limited infection. Other relatively rare complications of IM include airway obstruction caused by pharyngeal adenopathy, hepatitis, autoimmune hemolytic anemia, thrombocytopenia, granulocytopenia, carditis, and encephalitis.

Treatment of infectious mononucleosis • After challenge with penicillin, most IM patients will have a pruritic, maculopapular rash, which does not represent a true allergy. The treatment is generally supportive, though excessive physical activity should be avoided for 6 to 8 weeks to reduce the risk of splenic rupture. Airway obstruction, severe hemolytic anemia, and persistent thrombocytopenia are indications for glucocorticoid therapy. Epstein-Barr virus (EBV) infection can also be associated with Burkitt's lymphoma, nasopharyngeal carcinoma, and B cell lymphomas (particularly in immunocompromised patients). EBV also causes oral hairy leukoplakia in human immunodeficiency virus (HIV) patients.

Answers • 1-A   2-D   3-C   4-D

● CASE PRESENTATION

The patient is a 36-year-old man with a history of splenectomy due to trauma several years earlier who enters the emergency room complaining of not feeling well over the last 2 days. The patient reports subjective fever and chills along with a nonproductive cough. The patient is on no medications and his review of systems is otherwise negative. He is uncertain about his immunization status. Physical examination reveals an ill-appearing white man in mild distress. Temperature is 102.5 F, blood pressure is 86/60, and pulse is 115/min. The findings of the remainder of the physical examination are largely within normal limits. Results of a complete blood count (CBC), metabolic panel, and blood cultures are pending.

1. Which of the following best describes this patient's immune defect related to his splenectomy?

   A. Decreased humeral immunity related to T-cell dysfunction
   B. Impaired cell-mediated immunity
   C. Impaired neutrophil motility
   D. Inability to remove opsonized bacteria from the bloodstream
   E. Complement deficiency

2. Which of the following organisms would you be most worried about in this patient?

   A. Herpes simplex virus
   B. Streptococcus pneumoniae
   C. Staphylococcus aureus
   D. Pseudomonas cepacia
   E. Cryptococcus neoformans

3. In a patient with a normal spleen who has recurrent neisserial infections, which immune defect would be most likely?

   A. T-cell-mediated immunity
   B. Impaired chemotaxis
   C. Terminal complement deficiency
   D. Loss of mucocutaneous integrity
   E. Impaired natural killer cell function

4. Which of the following is classically associated with hypogammaglobulinemia?

   A. Hodgkin's disease
   B. Sickle-cell disease
   C. Systemic lupus erythematosus (SLE)
   D. Chronic lymphocytic leukemia
   E. Acquired immunodeficiency syndrome (AIDS)

● COMMENT

Immune defects associated with asplenia • Asplenic patients are at markedly increased risk for serious bacterial infections. This risk is highest during the first 3 years after splenectomy. The increased susceptibility to bacterial infections is related to the inability to remove opsonized bacteria from the bloodstream. There is also a defect in the production of antibodies to T-cell-independent antigens and bacterial capsules.

Infective organisms in splenectomized patients • This immune defect makes the patient particularly susceptible to infections with encapsulated bacteria, including *Streptococcus pneumoniae*, *Haemophilus influenzae*, *Neisseria* sp. and *Capnocytophagia* spp. (infection related to dog bites). This makes it imperative that one immunize these patients against *pneumococcus* sp., *meningococcus* sp., and *Haemophilus influenzae* (preferably before splenectomy). Additionally, parasitic diseases such as babesiosis (endemic in New England) and malaria occur with increased frequency in splenectomized patients.

Recurrent neisserial infection • Neisserial infections occur with increased frequency in patients with hypogammaglobulinemia, splenectomized patients, and those with B-cell dysfunction or deficiency. However, recurrent infections with neisserial species such as *Meningococcus* or *N. gonorrhoeae* should lead to suspicion that the patient has a deficiency of the terminal complement components (C6 through C9), the so-called membrane attack complex.

Hypogammaglobulinemia • Hypogammaglobulinemia has classically been associated with chronic lymphocytic leukemia and multiple myeloma and results in an increased frequency of infections with *Streptococcus pneumoniae, H. influenzae,* and *N. meningitidis*. Hodgkin's disease is classically associated with abnormal T-cell function and results in an increased susceptibility to intracellular pathogens (*Mycobacterium, Listeria, Salmonella,* and *Cryptococcus* spp.). Acquired immunodeficiency syndrome (AIDS) is also associated with deficiency and dysfunction of T lymphocytes, which result in impaired cell-mediated immunity. Systemic lupus erythematosus (SLE) patients suffer from complement deficiencies and impaired phagocytosis. Sickle-cell patients have a number of immune defects including functional asplenia and alternate pathway complement deficiencies.

Answers • 1-D 2-B 3-C 4-D

● CASE PRESENTATION

A 68-year-old white woman with a past medical history significant for chronic obstructive pulmonary disease (COPD) is admitted to the intensive care unit (ICU) with respiratory failure from bilateral lower lobe pneumonia. She is initially started on ceftriaxone and azithromycin with little clinical improvement. After 24 hours she remains febrile and her respiratory status declines, requiring endotracheal intubation. Subsequently admission blood culture results are positive for *pneumococcus* sp. resistant to penicillin and ceftriaxone; therefore, vancomycin is added to her antibiotic regimen. One week later she remains intubated in the ICU. Her fevers had defervesced with addition of the vancomycin, until hospital day 8 when her fever was 102.8 F. Blood cultures drawn had negative results. Urine studies revealed more than 50 white blood cells per high powered field and subsequently grew out to more than 100,000 colonies of pansensitive *Escherichia coli*. She was started on ticarcillin. As of hospital day 13 the patient has improved dramatically clinically. She has been extubated for 48 hours and is transferred to the floor. Her central venous line is pulled, but her Foley catheter remains because of significant weakness and difficulty ambulating to the bathroom. On hospital day 15 the patient is continuing her slow recovery but has a fever of 101.5 F. Blood culture results again are negative; her urine culture grows out to more than 100,000 colonies of vancomycin-resistant enterococcus (VRE).

1. Which of the following antibiotics have largely had no resistance problems?
   A. Gentamicin
   B. Erythromycin
   C. Ciprofloxacin
   D. Penicillin
   E. None of the above

2. What is the most common mechanism of pneumococcal resistance to penicillin?
   A. Bacterial production of a β-lactamase
   B. Alteration of the bacteria's penicillin-binding proteins
   C. Alterations in bacterial deoxyribonucleic acid (DNA) topoisomerase
   D. Increase in bacteria's efflux mechanisms
   E. Methylation of bacterial ribosomes

3. What is the incidence of penicillin-resistant strains of *Pneumococcus* sp. nationally?
   A. Greater than 90%
   B. 60%
   C. 25%
   D. 10%
   E. Less than 5%

4. Which of the following were risk factors for this patient's VRE infection?
   A. Use of ticarcillin
   B. Length of time spent in the intensive care unit
   C. Presence of indwelling Foley catheter
   D. Use of vancomycin
   E. All of the above

● COMMENT

Antibiotic resistance • No class of antibiotics has not had the problem of antibiotic resistance. Currently there is a disturbing trend toward emergence of resistance at a rate faster than the development of new antibiotics. Bacteria have many ways of acquiring resistance including spontaneous mutations and acquisition of foreign genetic material via plasmids or transposons. Also disturbingly, acquisition of resistance usually does not affect the viability or virulence of the bacteria. All of this makes it imperative that physicians prescribe antibiotics judiciously to minimize exposure to antibiotics and slow the rate of emerging resistance.

Penicillin-resistant pneumococci • Pneumococci began to develop resistance to penicillin in the 1960s and this has become one of the most widespread resistance problems. There are marked geographic variations in the rates of resistance, but the nationwide average is around 25%. The mechanism of resistance is alteration in the penicillin-binding proteins, thus decreasing the bacteria's ability to bind penicillin to its cell wall. Unfortunately, the emergence of penicillin resistance has not been accompanied by a decrease in virulence, and these strains of *Pneumococcus* spp. are usually also resistant to other antibiotics as well. Vancomycin and the newer quinolones (levofloxacin, gatifloxacin, and moxifloxacin hydrochloride) are the mainstays of treatment for penicillin-resistant *Pneumococcus* sp., but quinolone-resistant pneumococci are already emerging.

Vancomycin-resistant *Enterococcus* sp. • Increasing rates of methicillin-resistant *Staphylococcus aureus* (MRSA) and penicillin-resistant pneumococcal infections have forced the use of vancomycin, which in turn has led to the increasing prevalence of vancomycin-resistant enterococci. Virtually unheard of until the mid- to late 1980s, VRE is now the second most common cause of nosocomial urinary tract infections and the third most common cause of nosocomial bacteremia in the United States. The mechanism of resistance usually involves the bacteria's production of a peptidoglycan precursor in its cell wall that has a much lower affinity for vancomycin. Risk factors for development of VRE infections include long hospital stays, particularly in the ICU; use of broad-spectrum antibiotics and vancomycin; and certain disease states. VRE is exceedingly common in dialysis patients in whom vancomycin use has been widespread. Linezolid and quinupristin & dalfopristin are antibiotics that have recently been approved for use in VRE infections.

Answers • 1-E   2-B   3-C   4-E

● CASE PRESENTATION

The patient is an 18-year-old white man from North Carolina who has a fever, myalgias, and headache of 2 days' duration. He recently returned from a July hiking trip, but he does not remember any tick exposure. He has no significant past medical history and reports no recent sick contacts. Physical exam reveals a temperature of 101 F, pulse of 110/min, and blood pressure of 110/70. The patient has a diffuse erythematous macular rash on the torso and extremities, including the palms and soles.

1. Which organism is the most likely cause of this syndrome?
   A. HTLV I
   B. Dengue virus
   C. *Borrelia burgdorferi*
   D. *Rickettsia rickettsii*
   E. *Rickettsia typhi*

2. Which statement best describes appropriate diagnosis and treatment of this syndrome?
   A. Therapy should be deferred until diagnosis is confirmed by convalescent serologic testing.
   B. Empirical antibiotic therapy based on the clinical diagnosis should be started.
   C. Therapy should never be instituted without known tick exposure.
   D. Diagnosis and therapy are not very important since the disease is self-limited.
   E. The patient should be placed in strict respiratory isolation and started on a four-drug regimen.

3. What is the treatment of choice for Rocky Mountain spotted fever (RMSF)?
   A. Amoxicillin
   B. Trimethoprim & sulfamethoxazole (TMP-SMZ)
   C. Doxycycline
   D. Metronidazole
   E. Ceftriaxone

4. Which organism would you suspect if the patient had the same symptom complex with an annular skin rash with central clearing and an erythematous border?
   A. HTLV I
   B. Dengue virus
   C. *Borrelia burgdorferi*
   D. *Rickettsia rickettsii*
   E. *Erhlichia chaffeensis*

● COMMENT

Rocky Mountain spotted fever (RMSF) • RMSF is characterized by fever, headache, and a macular rash (often begins on wrists and ankles, involves the palms, and moves centrally). Other nonspecific symptoms include malaise, myalgia, nausea, vomiting, and anorexia. Severe manifestations include respiratory failure, encephalitis (mental status changes, seizures, or coma), and widespread microvascular damage, resulting in edema. Laboratory testing often reveals marked thrombocytopenia. RMSF is caused by *Rickettsia rickettsii* and is transmitted to humans by wood ticks or dog ticks. A similar syndrome can be associated with *Ehrlichia* species, though rash is less common with these organisms.

Diagnosis • Initial diagnosis of RMSF is based on the clinical presentation and the recognition of possible tick exposure. Serologic tests are useful for confirmation, but results are usually negative at presentation. Treatment should certainly not be delayed while serologic test results are pending. In fact, therapy is much more effective when given early in the course of disease. Patients often do not recall a tick exposure, and if the remainder of the history is suggestive of RMSF, antibiotic therapy should be initiated.

Treatment for RMSF • The first-line treatment for most rickettsial infections, including RMSF, is doxycycline. Antibiotic treatment should be initiated on the basis of clinical suspicion, as noted. Otherwise, treatment is supportive. For patients with severe manifestations, intensive care unit (ICU) support is necessary. Treatment has led to a marked decline in the overall mortality rate from RMSF and most deaths are due to delayed presentation, diagnosis, or treatment.

Lyme disease • The described rash is typical for erythema migrans and is suggestive of Lyme disease. Lyme disease is caused by a spirochete, *Borrelia burgdorferi*, which is transmitted by ixodid tick bites. Stage 1 of Lyme disease is heralded by the characteristic skin rash. A severe headache, progression of the skin rash, neck stiffness, fever, chills, myalgias, arthralgias, and malaise accompany stage 2 disease. Neurologic or cardiac symptoms can occur several weeks to months later. Stage 3 disease implies a persistent infection and is characterized by recurrent arthritis in large joints.

Answers • 1-D 2-B 3-C 4-C

● CASE PRESENTATION

A 65-year-old white woman with no past medical history enters the Emergency Department (ED) after more than 1 week of fever, chills, and progressive dyspnea. Physical examination reveals a temperature of 103 F, pulse of 120/min, respiratory rate of 24 breaths/min, and a blood pressure of 116/76. Lungs are clear to auscultation, but cardiac examination is remarkable for a grade 3/6 systolic murmur audible over the entire precordium. Electrocardiogram (ECG) is only remarkable for sinus tachycardia. Chest x-ray is clear.

1. Which of the following is a major diagnostic criterion for infective endocarditis (IE)?
   A. Roth spots
   B. Valvular vegetation on echocardiogram
   C. Fever of greater than 100.4 F
   D. Vascular phenomena suggesting arterial emboli
   E. Diffuse ST segment elevation on ECG

2. Which of the following is the most common cause of community-acquired native valve endocarditis?
   A. Viridans streptococci
   B. Gram-negative rods
   C. Fungi
   D. Enterococci
   E. *Haemophilus, Actinobacillus, Cardiobacterium, Eikenella,* and *Kingella* species (HACEK) group bacteria

3. Which of the following is the most common physical finding associated with IE?
   A. Subungual (splinter) hemorrhages
   B. Janeway lesions
   C. Roth's spots on the retina
   D. Digital clubbing
   E. Heart murmur

4. Which of the following is an indication for surgical therapy in IE?
   A. Loud murmur
   B. Penicillin allergy
   C. Refractory heart failure due to valve dysfunction
   D. Acute presentation with infective endocarditis
   E. Presence of oscillating intracardiac vegetation

● COMMENT

Duke criteria • The Duke criteria are very sensitive and specific for the clinical diagnosis of IE. Patients having two major criteria, one major and three minor criteria, or five minor criteria can be diagnosed with IE. Major criteria include 1) positive blood culture results (two separate culture results with a typical organism and no obvious focus *or* three of four positive results of cultures drawn at least 1 hour apart) and 2) evidence of endocardial involvement on echocardiogram (oscillating valvular or perivalvular mass, abscess, partial prosthetic valve dehiscence, or new valvular regurgitation). Minor criteria include fever (>100.4 F), vascular or immunologic phenomena, echo consistent with IE (not meeting major criterion), and serologic evidence of infection or positive blood culture results that do not meet the major criteria.

Organisms • Community-acquired native valve IE is most commonly caused by the viridans group of streptococci or *Staphylococcus aureus*. Less common causes include the HACEK organisms (*Haemophilus, Actinobacillus, Cardiobacterium, Eikenella,* and *Kingella* species), *Enterococcus* species, and other organisms. Endocarditis in injection drug users is most often caused by *Staphylococcus aureus*. The cause of prosthetic valve IE varies by the time of onset. IE at less than 2 weeks after valve surgery often involves coagulase-negative *Staphylococcus* spp., *Staphylococcus aureus*, or gram-negative bacilli. After 12 months the organisms causing prosthetic valve IE resemble the distribution in native valve IE. Between 2 and 12 months after surgery, coagulase-negative *Staphylococcus* spp., *S. aureus*, and enterococci are the usual pathogens.

Physical exam • Cardiac murmurs are detected in the vast majority of IE patients at some point in their illness. Fever is also fairly ubiquitous (up to 90% of cases). The peripheral manifestations of IE are infrequent today presumably because of earlier diagnosis and treatment. These include Osler's nodes (nodules on fingers/toes due to local vasculitis), Janeway lesions (red macules on the palms/soles), Roth's spots (red retinal patches with white centers), and splinter (subungual) hemorrhages. Digital clubbing does occur in IE, but it is less common than cardiac murmurs.

Treatment • Antibiotics should be chosen on the basis of culture results and continued for 4 to 6 weeks for native valve IE and 6 to 8 weeks for prosthetic valve IE. Moderate to severe congestive heart failure due to valvular dysfunction, persistent bacteremia on appropriate therapy, and lack of effective antibiotic therapy are indications for surgical intervention in native valve IE. In prosthetic valve IE, indications for surgery include an unstable valve, relapse after optimal therapy, *S. aureus* endocarditis with an intracardiac complication, or persistent unexplained fever with negative culture findings.

Answers • 1-B 2-A 3-E 4-C

● CASE PRESENTATION

A 62-year-old man with type 2 diabetes mellitus, congestive heart failure, and hypertension arrives at your office with a 1-day history of subjective fever and shaking chills. He also notes a cough productive of yellow-green sputum and sharp pain on his right side with deep breathing or coughing. His symptoms started suddenly last night. Past medical history (PMH) is as noted. He is a nonsmoker and does not drink alcohol.

On exam, he is an ill-appearing white man with a temperature of 102.4 F, pulse of 110/min, respiratory rate of 30 breaths/min, and a blood pressure of 122/62. The pulse oximeter reads 90% on room air. The patient is edentulous. Pulmonary exam reveals evidence of consolidation overlying the right lower lobe. Chest x-ray confirms right lower lobe infiltrate.

1. Which of the following is a physical exam sign of lung consolidation?
   A. Decreased tactile fremitus
   B. Vesicular breath sounds
   C. Hyperresonance to percussion
   D. Egophony
   E. All of the above

2. Which factors would impact your decision whether to admit this patient to the hospital?
   A. Age greater than 65
   B. Coexistent renal disease
   C. Respiratory rate of 30 breaths/min
   D. Glucose level of greater than 250 mg/dL
   E. All of the above

3. Which of the following is the most likely cause of this patient's pneumonia?
   A. Oral anaerobes
   B. *Pseudomonas aeruginosa*
   C. *Staphylococcus aureus*
   D. *Streptococcus pneumoniae*
   E. *Chlamydia psittaci*

4. Which of the following statements are true regarding therapy for community-acquired pneumonia (CAP)?
   A. Twice-daily drugs are preferable to once-daily drugs because of greater compliance.
   B. Single-agent macrolide therapy is recommended for first-line therapy in virtually all cases.
   C. Antibiotic therapy for CAP should be started on the basis of the results of sputum cultures.
   D. Penicillin resistance among *Streptococcus pneumoniae* isolates is currently minimal.
   E. A macrolide antibiotic plus a third-generation cephalosporin is a recommended first-line regimen for CAP in patients with comorbidities.

● COMMENT

Physical examination • Bronchial breath sounds, dullness to percussion, increased tactile fremitus, whispered pectoriloquy, rales, and egophony are all signs of consolidation on physical examination. Egophony occurs when a spoken *E* is heard as an *A*. This occurs in pulmonary consolidation or overcompressed lungs just below a pleural effusion. Decreased tactile fremitus would be evident over a pleural effusion. Hyperresonance to percussion is most common in emphysema. Vesicular breath sounds are the breath sounds normally heard over the entire lung surface.

Risk stratification • Patients with significant mortality risk should be admitted for inpatient therapy. Advanced age is perhaps the major single risk factor for a poor outcome in pneumonia. Underlying chronic diseases, such as cancer, hepatic disease, cardiac disease, cerebrovascular disease, and renal disease, also confer a higher mortality rate in CAP. Other significant risk factors for increased mortality rate in CAP include markedly abnormal vital signs (pulse $\geq$125/min, respiratory rate $\geq$30 breaths/min, hypotension), mental status changes, acidemia, hypoxemia, hyponatremia, and hyperglycemia.

Cause of CAP • This patient has a fairly typical presentation for *Streptococcus pneumoniae* infection. These findings include sudden onset of symptoms, high fever, pleuritic chest pain, and lobar consolidation on chest x-ray. In most patients with CAP, the exact causative organism is unknown. Oral anaerobes would be unlikely in this patient, since he is edentulous. Atypical presentations for CAP include an indolent onset, nonproductive cough, low-grade fever, and patchy consolidation on chest x-ray. This presentation is more commonly caused by organisms such as *Chlamydia pneumoniae*, *Mycoplasma pneumoniae*, and possibly *Legionella pneumophila*.

Treatment • *Streptococcus pneumoniae* is the most common pathogen in CAP, and the antibiotic regimen chosen must cover this organism. Penicillin resistance in *Streptococcus pneumoniae* isolates has increased exponentially over the last several years. Unfortunately, this can also be a marker for resistance to other classes of antibiotics. Single-agent macrolide antibiotic therapy is not recommended for patients who are 65 years or older or who have significant comorbidities. Current recommendations for these patients include a macrolide plus a β-*lactam* (such as a second- or third-generation cephalosporin) or an antipneumococcal fluoroquinolone. The use of sputum cultures to diagnose CAP is controversial, and antibiotic therapy should certainly not be withheld until sputum results are available. Once-daily dosage of outpatient antibiotics is associated with much better compliance than twice- or thrice-daily dosing.

Answers • 1-D 2-E 3-D 4-E

● CASE PRESENTATION

A 32-year-old white woman with a history of HIV infection has a 4-week history of fatigue, nonproductive cough, dyspnea, and intermittent fever. The patient has not had any ongoing care, and her most recent CD4 count from 2 years earlier was 180/μL. Her vital signs reveal a temperature of 100.5 F, a pulse of 130/min, and a respiratory rate of 30. Her lungs are clear to auscultation. PaO_2 is 65 mm Hg on room air blood gas.

1. *Pneumocystis carinii* pneumonia (PCP) is your tentative diagnosis. Which of the following supports the diagnosis of PCP?

   A. Insidious onset of symptoms over several weeks
   B. CD4 count of less than 200/μL
   C. Marked hypoxemia with a paucity of findings on pulmonary exam
   D. Elevated lactate dehydrogenase (LDH)
   E. All of the above

2. Which chest x-ray finding best supports this diagnosis?

   A. Bilateral diffuse infiltrates
   B. Lobar infiltrates
   C. Bilateral pleural effusions
   D. Curly B lines
   E. Air bronchograms

3. The host immune dysfunction with highest risk of PCP is:

   A. Complement deficiency
   B. Impaired neutrophil motility
   C. Impaired cellular immunity
   D. Postsplenectomy status
   E. Neutropenia

4. The patient is started on intravenous (IV) trimethoprim & sulfamethoxazole (TMP-SMZ) to treat PCP. Her hypoxemia should prompt the addition of which of the following?

   A. Aerosolized pentamidine
   B. Inhaled β-agonists
   C. Multivitamin with folic acid
   D. Oral glucocorticoids
   E. Fluconazole

● COMMENT

Clinical manifestations of PCP • PCP often has a several-week history of fever, nonproductive cough, and shortness of breath. This insidious presentation is particularly common in HIV patients with PCP, and clinicians must maintain an appropriate level of suspicion. Patients are usually tachypneic and tachycardic at presentation, but the pulmonary exam is often remarkably normal. Hypoxemia can be dramatic and patients may be cyanotic on presentation. There are no specific lab abnormalities, but the LDH level is frequently elevated in patients with PCP. Definitive diagnosis is established by detecting the organism (by staining or immunofluorescence) in induced sputum or bronchoalveolar lavage (BAL) sample.

Characteristic chest x-ray • Chest x-ray classically reveals bilateral diffuse, interstitial infiltrates in PCP. However, cavitary lesions, nodular densities, and pneumothorax have also been described. Bilateral upper lobe infiltrates are more common in patients who receive aerosolized pentamidine prophylaxis. Chest x-ray may be normal early in the illness. Pleural effusions and manifestations of lobar pneumonia are uncommon in PCP.

Predisposing immune dysfunction • Defects in cellular immunity predispose patients to *Pneumocystis carinii* infection. The incidence of PCP increases dramatically when the CD4 count falls below 200/μL in patients with HIV infection. Though the majority of PCP cases occur in acquired immunodeficiency syndrome (AIDS) patients, a number of other groups are at risk for infection, including children with primary immunodeficiencies, patients on chronic corticosteroid immunosuppression, and premature infants.

Treatment of PCP • Initial antibiotic therapy for PCP is TMP-SMX. Alternative therapies include IV pentamidine or trimetrexate for moderate to severe disease, and trimethoprim & dapsone, atovaquone, or clindamycin hydrochloride and primaquine phosphate for mild to moderate cases. Glucocorticoid therapy with prednisone has been shown to decrease the respiratory decompensation often seen with the onset of therapy for moderate to severe PCP. Glucocorticoids are indicated for PCP patients with PaO_2 values of less than or equal to 70 mm Hg or an alveolar-arterial oxygen gradient of 35 mm Hg or above and improve survival rate in this population. HIV patients with CD4 counts below 200/μL should receive prophylaxis against PCP.

Answers • 1-E 2-A 3-C 4-D

● CASE PRESENTATION

A 78-year-old woman with type 2 diabetes mellitus, hypertension, and coronary artery disease is admitted to the ICU for an acute myocardial infarction. She is intubated for respiratory failure and has successful angioplasty of an occluded left anterior descending artery. On hospital day 4 she has increasing oxygen requirements and increased production of green sputum. Physical examination reveals a temperature of 102.7 F with a pulse of 120/min. Blood pressure is 160/88 and lung exam reveals rales over the left lower lobe. A portable chest x-ray reveals a new left lower lobe infiltrate.

1. The differential diagnosis of pulmonary infiltrates in a hospitalized patient includes which of the following?
   A. Congestive heart failure
   B. Atelectasis
   C. Pneumonia
   D. Adult respiratory distress syndrome
   E. All of the above

2. Which of the following factors predispose to the development of hospital-acquired pneumonia?
   A. ICU admission
   B. Ulcer prophylaxis with sucralfate
   C. Intact mental status
   D. Hospital stays of 24 hours or less
   E. All of the above

3. Which organism is the most likely cause of hospital-acquired pneumonia?
   A. *Candida albicans*
   B. *Chlamydia pneumoniae*
   C. *Pseudomonas aeruginosa*
   D. *Streptococcus pneumoniae*
   E. All of the above

4. The choice of therapy for hospital-acquired pneumonia is partially based on which of the following?
   A. Knowledge of the prevalent institutional nosocomia pathogens
   B. Pattern of infiltrates on chest x-ray
   C. Degree of leukocytosis
   D. Severity of fever
   E. All of the above

● COMMENT

Differential diagnosis of pulmonary infiltrates in the hospitalized patient • Diagnosis of pneumonia in the hospitalized patient can sometimes be quite difficult. Pulmonary infiltrates result from pneumonia, congestive heart failure, postoperative atelectasis, or adult respiratory distress syndrome. Fever and leukocytosis can be variable. Likewise, other clinical signs and symptoms may be subtle, including a new cough, change in sputum character, or increasing oxygen requirements.

Risk factors for hospital-acquired pneumonia • Patients admitted to the ICU are at the highest risk for nosocomial pneumonia, particularly intubated patients. Most hospital-acquired pneumonia is related to aspiration, so any alteration in the level of consciousness, placement of a nasogastric tube, or a decreased gag reflex increases the risk. Postoperative patients, patients with chronic pulmonary disease, or patients treated with agents that lead to a rise in the gastric pH (e.g., H_2 blockers) all increase the risk of hospital-acquired pneumonia. Sucralfate does not increase the gastric pH and does not increase the risk of hospital-acquired pneumonia. The patient's oropharynx is typically colonized with many species within 48 hours of hospitalization, so longer hospitalizations are associated with an increased risk of nosocomial infection.

Common causes • Gram-negative aerobic bacteria are the most common cause of nosocomial pneumonia. *Pseudomonas aeruginosa* is the most common isolate, though *Staphylococcus aureus* is common as well. Because aspiration is the most common cause, oral anaerobes are another consideration. *Streptococcus pneumoniae* and *Chlamydia pneumoniae* most commonly cause community-acquired pneumonia.

Treatment • Clinicians should work toward minimizing risk factors for aspiration to help prevent hospital-acquired pneumonia. Antibiotic therapy for hospital-acquired pneumonia is usually empirical, with attention to the aforementioned organisms. Additionally, there is a great deal of institutional variability in pathogens and in antimicrobial resistance. Therefore, any treatment decision should be made with a good understanding of local patterns of infection and resistance.

Answers • 1-E 2-A 3-C 4-A

● CASE PRESENTATION

A 32-year-old woman from China is admitted to your service reporting a 4- to 6-week history of intermittent fevers, drenching night sweats, and a 15-pound weight loss. She has a cough productive of thick whitish sputum that has occasional bloody specks present. She relates that her grandfather in China died of a respiratory infection when she was a young child. Chest x-ray reveals a right upper lobe infiltrate. Physical exam shows an O_2 saturation of 91% on room air and egophony over the right upper lung field.

1. In addition to placing this patient on supplemental oxygen, appropriate therapy should include which of the following?
   A. Placing the patient in respiratory isolation in a negative-airflow room
   B. Administering a tuberculin skin test purified protein derivative (PPD)
   C. Collecting sputum samples for acid-fast bacilli (AFB) smears and cultures
   D. Initiating four-drug antibiotic therapy aimed at treating *Mycobacterium tuberculosis*
   E. All of the above

2. After 48 hours the patient is stable and her PPD is found to have an indurated area of 12 mm with an additional 3 mm of surrounding erythema. Which of the following statements is *false*?
   A. The PPD result is positive as the indurated area is greater than 10 mm and indicates prior exposure to tuberculosis (TB).
   B. The patient's history of living in China is a significant risk for TB exposure.
   C. The antibiotic coverage can be reduced to a two-drug regimen at this time.
   D. Family members and close contacts of the patient should be screened for TB.
   E. A PPD of greater than 5 mm is considered a positive result in patients with human immunodeficiency virus (HIV) or those immunosuppressed for organ transplantation.

3. Which of the following patients should receive antibiotic prophylaxis against tuberculosis?
   A. A healthy, asymptomatic 56-year-old man who lives alone whose PPD measures 14 mm
   B. A healthy immigrant from Mexico with a PPD of 5 mm
   C. The daughter of the patient described, who has a productive cough and a PPD of 9 mm
   D. A 29-year-old man who is asymptomatic but remembers his father's being hospitalized for tuberculosis in his childhood and has a PPD of 13 mm
   E. A 77-year-old nursing home resident with a PPD of 9 mm

4. Regarding antibiotic therapy for *M. tuberculosis*, which of the following statements is correct?
   A. A positive PPD result requires antibiotic treatment with standard four-drug therapy.
   B. Isoniazid, rifampin, pyrazinamide, and ethambutol should be continued for 6 months in all patients with a documented tuberculosis infection.
   C. There is little concern about development of resistance to the standard antibiotic regimen for TB.
   D. Directly observed therapy is no longer indicated for TB therapy.
   E. After 2 months of therapy consisting of at least three drugs, the TB patient should likely continue therapy with isoniazide (INH) and rifampin alone for 4 more months.

● COMMENT

Management of suspected TB • Any patient whose clinical presentation raises suspicions of tuberculosis should be considered as having an active infection. Appropriate measures include respiratory isolation, supplemental oxygen (if indicated), antimicrobial therapy if there is high suspicion (as in this case), and obtaining of three sputum samples for AFB culture and smear. A PPD finding may not be positive in the early stages of an acute infection, but in this patient with a possible distant exposure it should be positive.

PPD positivity • The area of induration, not erythema, determines PPD positivity. This delayed hypersensitivity reaction is indicative of past exposure to TB but does not indicate active infection. A PPD is positive at 5 mm in those with HIV, those who have had recent close contacts with TB patients, organ transplantation patients, patients on long-term high-dose prednisone, and those with a high probability of infection. A PPD of 10 mm is positive in patients from endemic areas (such as Asia and Latin America), residents and employees of nursing homes and hospitals, and those with chronic systemic diseases (diabetes, cancer, leukemia or lymphoma, intravenous [IV] drug users, or postgastrectomy status). Anyone not fitting into these categories (essentially young healthy people) is not considered to have a positive finding unless the induration is 15 mm or greater.

TB prophylaxis • A positive PPD result without evidence of an active infection should be treated with isoniazid for at least six months in individuals less than 35 years of age. For those over 35 a clinical decision must be based on the relative risk of development of an active infection in the future. All patients in the high- and intermediate-risk groups (5 mm and 10 mm positive) should receive prophylaxis regardless of age. HIV patients should receive 12 months of therapy. In this question, the patients in A, B, and E have negative PPD results, patient C should be treated for active TB as she would be considered at high risk and her PPD finding is positive at more than 5 mm. The patient described in choice D fulfills criteria for prophylaxis.

Treatment • Proper antibiotic treatment of TB is vital, as significant resistance patterns, likely due to incomplete antibiotic regimens, have been noted in numerous areas in America. This situation has improved with the institution of directly observed administration of antibiotics by health departments. The standard therapy for TB is starting with isoniazid, rifampin, pyrazinamide, and ethambutol or streptomycin. In areas where INH resistance is known to be less than 4%, ethambutol or streptomycin can be dropped when susceptibilities show efficacy of INH, rifampin, and pyrazinamide. After 2 months of this therapy, INH and rifampin alone can be continued for 4 more months (6 months total).

Answers • 1-E 2-C 3-D 4-E

● CASE PRESENTATION

A 78-year-old man with a history of stage IIIB non–small cell lung cancer reports a 3-hour history of acute shortness of breath and pleuritic chest pain on the right. On exam, the patient is afebrile, pulse rate is 120/min, respiratory rate is 30/min, blood pressure is 140/80, and O_2 saturation is 89% on room air. Chest exam reveals decrease in tactile fremitus, dullness to percussion, and absent breath sounds at right posterior lung base. Electrocardiogram (ECG) reveals sinus tachycardia. Ventilation/perfusion scan result is read as high-probability.

1. The most frequent inherited predisposition to hypercoagulability is which of the following?
    A. Protein C deficiency
    B. Antithrombin III deficiency
    C. Protein S deficiency
    D. Factor V Leiden mutation
    E. Antiphospholipid antibodies

2. Which of the following is a common consequence of pulmonary embolism (PE)?
    A. Increased alveolar-arterial (Aa) gradient (PAO_2-PaO_2)
    B. Ventilation of unperfused lung
    C. Pulmonary hypertension
    D. Bronchoconstriction
    E. All of the above

3. True statements regarding the diagnosis of PE include which of the following?
    A. Pretest probability is crucial in test ordering.
    B. VQ scanning is the "gold standard" for diagnosis
    C. A low-probability VQ scan finding essentially rules out PE
    D. The most common ECG finding in PE is an S wave in lead I and a Q wave in lead III
    E. All of the above

4. Thrombolytic therapy in the setting of a PE is indicated for which of the following?
    A. Pleuritic chest pain
    B. Heparin-induced thrombocytopenia
    C. Systemic hypotension
    D. Tachycardia
    E. None of the above

● COMMENT

Risk factors for pulmonary embolism • The patient has a pulmonary embolism (PE). His risk factor for PE is malignancy. Other risk factors for precipitating a thromboembolism include immobilization; surgery, especially orthopedic procedures involving the lower extremity; use of oral contraceptives; pregnancy; and indwelling central catheters. For younger patients without risk factors who have PE or deep vein thrombosis (DVT), one should consider an inherited hypercoagulable state. The most common inherited hypercoagulability is activated protein C resistance of factor V Leiden. Other inherited hypercoagulable states include deficiency in protein C, protein S, or antithrombin III; prothrombin mutations; and disorders of plasminogen.

Physiologic consequences in PE • Hypoxemia and a widened Aa gradient are classic findings in PE. Lung that is not perfused continues to ventilate, causing mismatches (discussed later). Pulmonary hypertension, right ventricular failure, and hypotension occur with massive PE. Bronchospasm can be appreciated as well.

Diagnostic testing • The typical chest x-ray finding in a patient with PE is normal. However, abnormalities such as focal oligemia (Westermark's sign) or a peripheral wedge-shaped infiltrate (Hampton's hump) can suggest the diagnosis of PE in a dyspneic patient. The most common ECG finding is sinus tachycardia, though one can see the S_1Q_3 suggestive of right axis deviation. V/Q scanning remains the principal imaging modality for diagnosing a PE. This test can reveal defects in lung perfusion coupled with preserved ventilation as one observes with PE. A normal lung scan result virtually excludes a PE, and a high-probability finding rules in a PE. It is important to note that a low- or intermediate-probability scan finding requires further diagnostic testing if the clinical suspicion is high enough. Pulmonary angiography currently is the definitive test to establish the diagnosis of PE. However, one may seek evidence of a DVT in the lower extremity by ultrasound before pulmonary angiography. Computed tomography (CT) pulmonary angiography is emerging as an effective alternative imaging technique as well, and studies are ongoing.

Treatment • The treatment of PE with DVT consists of anticoagulation. Heparin, low-molecular-weight heparins, and warfarin are all FDA approved for this role. The duration of therapy for PE is 1 year (indefinite with persistent risk factor, proximal DVT for 6 months, and calf-vein thrombosis for 3 months). Those patients who are at high risk for anticoagulation, have active bleeding, or have recurrent thromboembolism despite adequate anticoagulation are candidates for inferior vena caval filters. Finally, tissue-type plasminogen activator (tPA) has been FDA approved for a subset of patients with massive PE and either severe right ventricle (RV) hypokinesis or systemic hypotension.

Answers • 1-D 2-E 3-A 4-C

● CASE PRESENTATION

A 68-year-old white man with chronic obstructive pulmonary disease (COPD), hypertension (HTN), diabetes mellitus (DM), and 50-pack-year smoking history arrives at the emergency room reporting malaise, weight loss, low-grade fever, and a cough productive of yellow sputum for 4 days. On physical exam, he has decreased breath sounds at the right base and chest radiograph shows an infiltrate that obscures the hemidiaphragm and heart border on the right and layers out on a decubitus film. No mass is noted. A diagnostic thoracentesis is performed; it yields 60 mL of clear straw colored fluid with a pH of 7.45, lactate dehydrogenase (LDH) of 427 Iu/L (serum 250), total protein level of 4.6 g/dL (serum 6.2), glucose of 50 mg/dL, and 260 white blood cells (WBCs) with a negative Gram stain finding.

1. The pleural fluid analysis suggests that this effusion is a(n):
   A. Transudate
   B. Empyema
   C. Exudate
   D. Mixed transudate and exudate

2. Which of the following laboratory data are *least* helpful in determining transudative versus exudative pleural effusions?
   A. Pleural fluid-serum protein ratio greater than 0.5
   B. Pleural fluid-serum LDH ratio greater than 0.6
   C. Pleural fluid LDH greater than 45% of the normal serum LDH
   D. Pleural fluid pH

3. Which of the following is the *most* likely cause of the pleural fluid accumulation in this patient?
   A. Congestive heart failure
   B. Malignancy
   C. Tuberculosis
   D. Parapneumonia
   E. Empyema

4. Which of the following is the most appropriate management of this pleural effusion?
   A. Chest tube drainage
   B. Antibiotics to cover for community-acquired pneumonia
   C. Antibiotics and chest tube drainage
   D. Surgical thoracotomy to drain fluid
   E. Chest tube drainage followed by talc pleurodesis

● COMMENT

Transudative versus exudative effusion • This effusion is exudative in nature. The criteria for determining transudative versus exudative pleural effusions include a fluid-serum total protein ratio of more than 0.5 or fluid-serum LDH ratio of more than 0.6 (or fluid LDH > 45% of the accepted normal serum LDH). The pH is not helpful in this determination but can be helpful in deciding the cause of the pleural fluid accumulation. Leading causes of exudative effusions include bacterial pneumonia, malignancy, tuberculosis (TB), pulmonary embolus, and collagen vascular disease. Common causes of transudative effusions include congestive heart failure (CHF), cirrhosis, nephrotic syndrome, and pulmonary embolus.

Differential diagnosis • The pleural effusion in this case is most consistent with a simple parapneumonic effusion, which is the most common exudative effusion, occurring in approximately half of patients with a bacterial pneumonia. CHF generally results in a transudative effusion most commonly on the right. Tuberculosis could be the cause, but the patient does not have the symptoms associated with TB (fevers, night sweats) and the fluid glucose level and pH are usually lower. Malignancy is a possibility given the patient's age, smoking history, COPD, and weight loss, but parapneumonic effusions are more common and no mass is seen on chest x-ray. Empyema is characterized by more than 1500 white blood cells (WBCs), a positive Gram stain, and a low pH. Normal pleural fluid pH is greater than 7.6 and a value below 7.3 is seen only in empyema, esophageal rupture, chronic rheumatoid arthritis, malignancy, TB, systemic lupus erythematosus (SLE), and urinothorax. The fluid to serum glucose ratio is less than 0.5 in all of the conditions except urinothorax. The pleural fluid glucose is quite low in rheumatoid arthritis.

Treatment • Parapneumonic effusions can be treated with appropriate antibiotics alone if discovered early enough, before they enter the fibrinopurulent stage (3 to 10 days). Once bacterial invasion into the pleural space occurs, the space must be drained along with initiating appropriate antibiotic coverage. Surgical thoracotomy is generally reserved for empyemas that have organized and solidified beyond the point where usual drainage procedures can be successful. Talc pleurodesis is used in the case of symptomatic recurrent pleural effusions such as those secondary to malignancy (lung or breast). In this case, the absence of organisms in the pleural space and the early presentation of the patient indicate that antibiotics alone should be sufficient to treat the underlying pneumonia with eventual spontaneous resolution of the pleural effusion.

Answers • 1-C 2-D 3-D 4-B

● CASE PRESENTATION

A 57-year-old woman arrives at her internist's office reporting coughing up blood on three occasions over the past 24 hours. She is unable to quantify the amount of blood but answers that it is less than a "small cup." She denies any smoking history or tuberculosis exposure. On examination, her vital signs are stable and breath sounds are normal in all lung fields. Her physician admits her to the hospital for further monitoring.

1. Which of the following is the most common cause of hemoptysis worldwide?
   A. Bronchogenic carcinoma
   B. Tuberculosis
   C. Bronchiectasis
   D. Bronchitis
   E. Pulmonary infarction

2. The patient does well for 24 hours with only scant hemoptysis. Which of the following tests is *least* indicated in her evaluation?
   A. Complete blood count
   B. Sputum culture and smear
   C. Single-breath diffusion capacity
   D. Arteriography with embolization
   E. Fiber-optic bronchoscopy

3. No source of bleeding is found on initial testing. The patient is ready to be discharged from the hospital when she begins to cough violently, producing 500 mL of bright red blood. Her O_2 saturation falls to 78% and decreased breath sounds are heard at the left base. Which of the following measures is *least* indicated at this time?
   A. Placement of the patient with left side down
   B. Transfusion of 2 units of packed blood cells
   C. Placement of a balloon catheter into the site of bleeding
   D. Endobronchial intubation with a double-lumen tube
   E. Emergent arteriography with embolization

4. The patient undergoes successful embolization of the bleeding site and recovers without complication. Which of the following is the most likely source of bleeding in hemoptysis?
   A. Pulmonary arteries and branches
   B. Bronchial arteries and branches
   C. Pulmonary vein
   D. Superior vena cava
   E. Left main coronary artery

● COMMENT

Common causes • There are numerous causes of hemoptysis, making specific diagnosis very difficult. These include bronchitis, bronchiectasis, bronchogenic carcinoma, tuberculosis (TB), bacterial pneumonia or abscess, fungal infections (*Aspergillus*), pulmonary infarction, mitral stenosis, endobronchial foreign bodies, atrioventricular (AV) fistulas, Wegener's granulomatosis, Goodpasture's syndrome, and coagulopathies. The most common cause is bronchitis, likely because the disease itself is so common. This is particularly true of mild hemoptysis in the outpatient setting. TB, bronchiectasis, and lung cancer are more common causes of life-threatening hemoptysis. It is also important to realize that hemoptysis can be very difficult to differentiate from hematemesis and nasopharyngeal bleeding so a careful history and examination of these areas are vital.

Evaluation • Each of these tests may be indicated in the evaluation of hemoptysis, but the patient's condition is stable and the bleeding is minimal, so arteriography is not warranted. Studies such as complete blood count (CBC), prothrombin time (PT) and partial thromboplastin time (PTT), and sputum culture can be helpful. Single-breath diffusion capacity (DLCO) is elevated in a large proportion of patients with intrapulmonary bleeding and therefore can be helpful. Chest x-rays may identify an abnormal area but may be clear or may show an alveolar infiltrate that is caused by blood aspirated from elsewhere in the lungs. V/Q scan can be useful if there is suspicion that the bleeding is related to a pulmonary embolism. Fiber-optic bronchoscopy is valuable for its ability to identify endobronchial lesions and the site of bleeding and its potential to treat bleeding. The timing of bronchoscopy is somewhat controversial as coughing induced by the procedure may worsen the bleeding and widespread blood may interfere with visualization.

Treatment • Although each of these procedures may need to be performed on a patient who is actively bleeding, it is important to realize that the greatest danger to patients with hemoptysis is asphyxiation, *not* blood loss. Transfusion is not indicated in this case because the condition was formerly stable and the amount of blood loss, although indicating massive hemoptysis, is not likely to cause hemodynamic compromise in an acute condition. Placement of the patient with the affected side down allows airflow into the "good" lung. If the patient's airway is at risk or bleeding is ongoing, intubation or balloon tamponade may be warranted; emergent arteriography to find and stop the bleeding would be indicated at this time.

Source of bleeding • Although bleeding can originate in any of the blood vessels feeding the thorax, more than 90% of hemoptysis is from the bronchial artery and its branches or collaterals from systemic arteries such as the axillary, intercostal, or diaphragmatic arteries. Pulmonary arteries, capillaries, and veins are involved less than 10% of the time.

Answers • 1-D   2-D   3-B   4-B

● CASE PRESENTATION

A 20-year-old man enters the emergency room (ER) with worsening shortness of breath and audible wheezing for 6 hours. The patient has a history of asthma diagnosed at the age of 7. On physical exam, he is afebrile, with a pulse of 110/min, respiratory rate of 26/min, and blood pressure of 140/85. Lung exam reveals diffuse, bilateral expiratory wheezes and tachypnea. Tachycardia is noted on cardiac examination. An arterial blood gas evaluation is ordered; it shows a pH of 7.32, pCO_2 of 48, and pO_2 of 70 on room air. Chest x-ray demonstrates hyperinflation.

1. Which statement summarizes the definitive definition of asthma?
   A. Reversible airway obstruction
   B. Clinical history of shortness of breath and wheezing
   C. Presence of eosinophils in pulmonary secretions
   D. Positive skin test reaction to extracts of airborne allergens
   E. All of the above

2. Which of the following is the most important clinical information to indicate impending respiratory failure in a patient with an asthmatic attack?
   A. Decreased CO_2
   B. Respiratory acidosis
   C. Increased wheezing
   D. Decreasing pulsus paradoxus
   E. Forced expiratory volume in 1 second (FEV_1) of less than 50% of personal best

3. The most plausible explanation for hypoxemia in asthma is which of the following?
   A. Ventilation/perfusion (V/Q) mismatch
   B. Diffusion impairment
   C. Alveolar hypoventilation
   D. Impaired perfusion
   E. All of the above

4. Which of the following should *definitely* be included in this patient's maintenance therapy after his acute exacerbation?
   A. Inhaled ipratropium bromide
   B. Oral theophylline
   C. Inhaled or oral albuterol
   D. Anti-inflammatory therapy with inhaled corticosteroids
   E. All of the above

● COMMENT

Asthma • Asthma is an episodic disease characterized by both acute bronchospasms and chronic inflammation within the tracheobronchial tree. The diagnosis of asthma is established by demonstrating reversible airway obstruction. *Reversibility* is defined as a 15% or greater improvement in the FEV_1 (forced expiratory volume in 1 second) after the administration of a bronchodilator (e.g., albuterol). There are a number of physical findings in asthma. Acute bronchospasm can lead to diffuse wheezing and cyanosis can result from marked hypoxemia. Pulsus paradoxus is a drop in systolic blood pressure of more than 10 mm Hg with inspiration and is an exaggeration of a normal physiologic response. During inspiration, pressures in the thoracic cavity diminish and venous return increases. Filling of the right ventricle (RV) impedes left ventricle (LV) filling to a small degree, leading to a slight decrease in cardiac output and blood pressure with inspiration. Severe bronchospasm and cardiac tamponade exaggerate this response and are important causes of pulsus paradoxus.

Impending respiratory failure • An arterial blood gas (ABG) during an acute asthmatic attack reveals hypoxemia, hypocarbia, and respiratory alkalemia. The development of respiratory acidosis is a sign of impending respiratory catastrophe. Pulsus paradoxus is also a sign of severe bronchospasm.

V/Q mismatch • V/Q mismatch is one of the most important causes of hypoxemia. V/Q mismatch implies regional hypoventilation in which perfusion is still present. Hypoxemia from asthma is due to V/Q mismatch. An extreme form of V/Q mismatch is called *shunting* (i.e., no ventilation, but perfusion is still present). Supplemental oxygen corrects V/Q mismatch; however, it does not correct it in cases of shunting. Other causes of hypoxemia include diffusion abnormalities, high altitude, and hypoventilation.

Treatment of asthma • The treatment of an acute asthma exacerbation includes oxygen as needed, inhaled short-acting beta-agonists (albuterol), intravenous corticosteroids, and antibiotics if there is evidence of bacterial respiratory infection. Maintenance therapy for asthma should begin with anti-inflammatory therapy such as inhaled corticosteroids or possibly an oral leukotriene inhibitor. Additionally, long-acting beta-agonists, such as salmeterol, provide additional benefit. Short-acting beta-agonists should be used only as needed for acute symptoms.

Answers • 1-A 2-B 3-A 4-D

● CASE PRESENTATION

A 58-year-old man arrives at your office with a 1-year history of dyspnea on exertion. The patient is an active smoker of more than 80 pack-years. Review of systems is otherwise negative. On physical exam temperature is 98 F, respiratory rate is 18/min, blood pressure is 120/78, and O_2 saturation is 96% on room air. Lung exam reveals decreased breath sounds bilaterally with a prolonged expiratory phase. The rest of the examination findings are essentially normal. Chest x-ray shows hyperinflated lung fields. Pulmonary function test demonstrates a forced vital capacity (FVC) of 3.83 L (78% predicted), forced expiratory volume in 1 second (FEV_1) of 1.85 (54% predicted), and FEV_1/FVC of 48%.

1. Which of the flow volume loops and FEV_1's best describes obstructive dysfunction when interpreting pulmonary function test results?
   A. A
   B. B
   C. C
   D. All of the above

2. Which of the following best describes restriction when interpreting pulmonary function test results?
   A. Decreased FEV_1
   B. Decreased FEV_1/FVC ratio
   C. Decreased total lung capacity (TLC)
   D. Increased TLC
   E. Increased FEV_1

3. Which of the following diseases are associated with obstructive patterns on pulmonary function tests (PFTs) (up to four possible)?
   A. Emphysema
   B. Chronic bronchitis
   C. Pneumoconiosis
   D. Asthma
   E. Bronchiectasis

4. In chronic obstructive pulmonary disease (COPD), long-term treatment with which of the following is known to improve mortality?
   A. Corticosteroids
   B. Inhaled beta-agonists
   C. Supplemental O_2 if paO_2 is less than or equal to 55
   D. Inhaled ipratropium bromide
   E. All of the above

● COMMENT

Pulmonary function test (PFT) and flow volume loop (FVL) • One can quantify the amount of air in the lungs and determine the rate at which air can be expelled. The expiratory flow rates can be plotted against lung volumes to generate a flow-volume loop. There are four lung volumes: 1) inspiratory reserve volume (IRV), 2) tidal volume (TV), 3) expiratory reserve volume (ERV), and 4) residual volume (RV). The first three lung volumes are directly measured, but RV is an indirect measurement. A capacity is a measurement of two or more lung volumes. 1) total lung capacity (TLC) = IRV + TV + ERV + RV or VC + RV, 2) vital capacity (VC) = IRV + TV + ERV, 3) inspiratory capacity (IC) = IRV + TV, 4) functional residual capacity (FRC) = ERV + RV.

When evaluating PFTs and FVLs, diseases are characterized as obstructive or restrictive dysfunctions. As illustrated previously, the flow volume loop A is considered obstructive, on the basis of the scooping of the expiratory limb of the FVL. In addition, it is shifted to the left, suggesting hyperinflation. On a restrictive loop, the expiratory limb is narrow, peaked like a mast on a ship, and shifted to the right on the X-axis, suggesting low lung volumes. This is illustrated in Figure 8(C). Figure 8(B) represents a normal flow volume loop. The hallmark of obstruction is a decrease in expiratory flow rate, that is, decreased FEV_1. The FEV_1/FVC ratio is also decreased. TLC can be normal or elevated by hyperinflation and RV increased by air trapping. The hallmark of restriction is reduction in lung volumes (i.e., reduced TLC). The FEV_1 may also be reduced; however, there is a proportional reduction in FVC such that the FEV_1/FVC ratio is normal or elevated. A normal ratio is roughly 80 or higher but decreases with age similarly to FEV_1, which also has an age-related decline after the age of 35.

Obstructive patterns on PFTs • Respiratory diseases, which have an obstructive pattern, include asthma, COPD (emphysema or chronic bronchitis), cystic fibrosis, bronchiectasis, and bronchiolitis.

Restrictive patterns on PFTs • Examples of diseases that display a restrictive pattern include idiopathic pulmonary fibrosis (IPF), pneumoconioses, sarcoidosis, obesity, paralysis of the diaphragm, and chest wall deformities such as kyphoscoliosis.

Oxygen therapy • Oxygen therapy is the only modality proved to decrease the mortality rate of COPD patients. Supplemental O_2 is indicated if arterial O_2 levels are 55 or less or O_2 saturation is equal to or less than 88%. Medications such as bronchodilators, theophylline, and corticosteroids may improve symptoms but not mortality rate. The role of corticosteroids in COPD therapy is particularly controversial. They are clearly indicated in the treatment of acute exacerbations, but only a minority of patients respond to long-term treatment with corticosteroids.

A = FEV_1- 1.85L
B = FEV_1- 3.6L
C = FEV_1- 3.0L

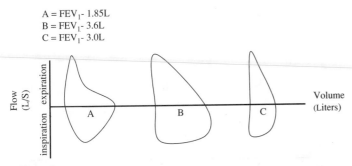

• *Figure 8*

Answers • 1-A 2-C 3-A, B, D, E 4-C

● CASE PRESENTATION

A 48-year-old severely obese man is referred for evaluation of daytime hypersomnolence. The patient reports falling asleep while driving a vehicle and has been involved in multiple car accidents over the past year. His wife reports that he has 15 to 20 seconds of apnea during sleep and is a heavy snorer. On physical exam, pulse is 90/min, and blood pressure is 175/90. He is 5 feet 10 inches, and weighs 290 pounds. Cardiac exam reveals a right ventricular heave with a right-sided S_4 sound. There is an accentuated P_2 component of the second heart sound and a systolic murmur that is loudest at the right lower sternal border. Extremities reveal bilateral edema.

1. Which of the following is the patient's most likely diagnosis?
   A. Obstructive sleep apnea
   B. Major depression
   C. Narcolepsy
   D. Sleeping sickness
   E. Chronic fatigue syndrome

2. True statements regarding therapy for the patient's condition include which of the following?
   A. Alcohol or sedatives may help the patient feel more rested.
   B. Weight loss may paradoxically worsen his symptoms.
   C. Nasal continuous positive airway pressure is indicated for severe disease.
   D. Surgery is the best first-line therapy.
   E. All of the above

3. You determine that the patient has cor pulmonale, which is due to pulmonary hypertension. Physical exam findings consistent with cor pulmonale include which of the following?
   A. Increased jugular venous pressure
   B. Ascites
   C. Pulsatile hepatomegaly
   D. Lower extremity edema
   E. All of the above

4. Which of the following maneuvers increases tricuspid regurgitant murmurs?
   A. Inspiration
   B. Expiration
   C. Standing
   D. Valsalva's maneuver
   E. B, C, and D

● COMMENT

Obstructive sleep apnea (OSA) • This patient has obstructive sleep apnea (OSA), complicated by cor pulmonale. OSA results from occlusion of the upper airway during sleep, leading to transient cessation (apnea) or diminution (hypopnea) of airflow. Obesity and alcohol or sedatives exacerbate this condition. Symptoms include excessive snoring, daytime somnolence, and morning headaches. The resultant nocturnal hypoxemia may lead to dysrhythmias, pulmonary hypertension, and cor pulmonale. OSA can also be associated with nephrotic syndrome due to focal segmental glomerulosclerosis (FSGS). Diagnosis generally requires an overnight sleep study with polysomnography.

Treatment of OSA • A mainstay of treatment for severe OSA is continuous positive airway pressure (nasal CPAP), which can be titrated during the overnight sleep study. Other treatments include weight loss and avoidance of alcohol. Surgery (uvulopalatopharyngoplasty) is indicated for refractory cases, but the failure rate is substantial.

Clinical manifestations of cor pulmonale • Cor pulmonale is enlargement of the right ventricle (RV) with right ventricular failure. The diseases that can cause RV failure can be divided into pulmonary vascular diseases (examples include primary pulmonary hypertension, OSA, and pulmonary emboli) and respiratory diseases (most common is chronic obstructive pulmonary disease [COPD], but any disease process affecting the lungs can lead to the development of cor pulmonale). Patients may have peripheral edema, ascites, pulsatile liver, distended neck veins with prominent V waves of tricuspid regurgitation, cyanosis due to hypoxemia, and low cardiac output. A prominent second heart sound (P_2) is suggestive of pulmonary hypertension.

Tricuspid regurgitation (TR) • Like mitral regurgitation (MR), TR is a systolic murmur. Regurgitant murmurs, like stenotic murmurs, increase in intensity if flow is increased across the valve. Applying this principle, if venous return is increased to the right side of the heart, the murmur of TR should increase. Inspiration causes a decrease in intrathoracic pressures and therefore increases venous return. Standing, Valsalva's maneuver, or expiration decreases venous return, which results in decreased filling of the right ventricle. Therefore, the sound of TR decreases in intensity.

Answers • 1-A 2-C 3-E 4-A

● CASE PRESENTATION

A 23-year-old black woman arrives at your office with a chronic cough and new skin lesions on her legs. She reports a chronic, nonproductive cough for 3 months with intermittent, low-grade fevers. She also reports arthritis involving both knees and the left wrist. On physical exam, the patient is afebrile, pulse is 78/min, respiratory rate is 12/min, and blood pressure is 120/78. Physical exam is notable only for painful, raised, nonblanching erythematous lesions overlying both shins. There are five lesions, each measuring 2 by 3 cm. Lab results are remarkable for an elevated serum calcium of 12.9 mg/dL. You refer the patient for bronchoscopy and transbronchial biopsy, which reveals noncaseating granulomas.

1. Which of the following can be associated with this condition?
   A. Diabetes insipidus
   B. Cardiac arrhythmias
   C. Anterior uveitis
   D. Cranial nerve palsies
   E. All of the above

2. The patient's skin lesions most likely represent which of the following?
   A. Rheumatoid nodules
   B. Erythema multiforme
   C. Pyoderma gangrenosum
   D. Erythema nodosum
   E. Ecthyma gangrenosum

3. The most common cause of death in patients who have this illness is:
   A. Infections
   B. Respiratory failure
   C. Renal failure
   D. Cardiomyopathy
   E. Progressive central nervous system (CNS) disease

4. What is the likely mechanism of hypercalcemia in this patient?
   A. Hyperparathyroidism
   B. Production of parathyroid hormone (PTH) related peptide
   C. Increased 1-alpha hydroxylation of vitamin D
   D. Decreased calcium excretion
   E. All of the above

● COMMENT

Sarcoidosis • Sarcoidosis is a chronic, multisystem disease of unknown cause. It is characterized by the formation of noncaseating granulomas in numerous organ systems. Noncaseating granulomas are not pathognomonic for sarcoidosis. Other disorders characterized by noncaseating granulomas include berylliosis, eosinophilic granuloma, and granulomatous vasculitides such as Wegener's granulomatosis.

Sarcoidosis can involve any organ system in the body. Ninety percent of patients diagnosed with sarcoidosis have an abnormal chest x-ray finding at some point. Intrathoracic lymphadenopathy and reticulonodular infiltrates can be seen on radiographs. Anterior uveitis can occur in 25% of patients. Mild cholestasis from liver involvement can be seen. Hypercalcemia can lead to nephrocalcinosis and nephrolithiasis. Cardiac arrhythmias or overt heart failure occur in 5%. Neurologic manifestations can include seizures, cranial or peripheral neuropathy, pituitary involvement, and chronic meningitis.

Cutaneous manifestations • Approximately 25% of patients with sarcoid have skin involvement. The skin lesions can consist of erythema nodosum, lupus pernio, plaques, or subcutaneous nodules. The patient's tender, indurated lesions over the anterior shin are most consistent with erythema nodosum. Rheumatoid nodules are seen in rheumatoid arthritis. Erythema multiforme is associated with drugs or certain infections (herpes simplex virus, mycoplasma). Pyoderma gangrenosum is seen in Crohn's disease and ecthyma gangrenosum occurs in pseudomonal sepsis.

Outcome • Respiratory failure is the most common cause of death of patients with sarcoidosis. Approximately 20% of patients have progressive symptoms, implying that, for most patients, sarcoidosis has a relatively benign course. Significant involvement of the eye, heart, or central nervous system (CNS), or progressive lung disease should trigger treatment with corticosteroids.

Hypercalcemia • Hypercalcemia from sarcoidosis is due to enhanced gut absorption via 1,25-dihydrovitamin D. This form of vitamin D is produced by activated macrophages within these granulomas. These activated macrophages are able to convert inactive vitamin D to its active form by 1-alpha hydroxylation of 25-dihydrovitamin D.

● CASE PRESENTATION

A 58-year-old man reports progressive onset of breathlessness with exercise and a dry, nonproductive cough for the past 3 months. Otherwise, review of systems yields negative findings. The patient does have a 50-pack-year smoking history. On physical exam, auscultation of lungs reveals late inspiratory Velcro-like crackles at both lung bases. Cardiac exam reveals right-sided heave and an accentuated P_2 component of the second heart sound is appreciated. Examination of the extremities reveals digital clubbing. Pulmonary function tests denote a restrictive defect. The chest x-ray finding is the presence of coarse reticular-nodular infiltrates at both lung bases.

1. What is the most likely diagnosis for your patient?
   A. Chronic obstructive pulmonary disease (COPD)
   B. Non–small cell lung cancer
   C. Idiopathic pulmonary fibrosis
   D. Sarcoidosis
   E. Congestive heart failure (CHF) with pulmonary edema

2. Which inorganic dust is associated with pleura-based plaques and interstitial changes at the lung base?
   A. Asbestos
   B. Coal dust
   C. Silica
   D. Beryllium
   E. Byssinosis

3. Which of the following can be associated with drug-induced interstitial lung disease?
   A. Amlodopine
   B. Amiodarone
   C. Digoxin
   D. Captopril
   E. All of the above

4. Which of the following findings are consistent with idiopathic pulmonary fibrosis?
   A. Pleural effusion
   B. Left ventricular dysfunction
   C. Radiographic findings of honeycombing
   D. Arthritis
   E. All of the above

● COMMENT

Idiopathic pulmonary fibrosis (IPF) • IPF is a specific form of interstitial lung disease (ILD) that represents a chronic fibrosis of the lung. Men are affected more often than women. Patients typically seek medical attention after age 60 and most patients are between the ages of 40 and 70. Typically, patients have symptoms for 6 months before seeking medical attention, signifying the insidious nature of this disease. Smoking is considered a risk factor for IPF. Extrapulmonary manifestations of IPF are limited. Digital clubbing can be noted in approximately 50% of cases. Cor pulmonale and cyanosis may also be present and, when seen, signify moderate to severe disease. The definitive diagnosis of IPF rests on pathologic confirmation via lung biopsy. IPF is a progressive disorder, which has a median survival expectancy of 28 months. Corticosteroids and other immunosuppressant medications are the mainstay of therapy; however, clinical response is only achieved in 10% to 20% of patients. Lung transplantation is also accepted therapy in those with advanced disease who do not respond to medical therapy.

Asbestosis • The combination of pleura-based calcified plaques and basilar interstitial changes is consistent with asbestosis. Prior asbestos exposure (shipyard workers, pipe fitters) places a patient at increased risk for bronchogenic carcinoma and mesothelioma.

Other causes of ILD • There are over 150 causes of ILD, for which IPF represents only one clinical entity. The classification scheme of ILD based on cause includes drugs (i.e., nitrofurantoin, methotrexate, amiodarone, radiation); connective tissue disease (i.e., systemic lupus erythematosus [SLE], rheumatoid arthritis, scleroderma, dermatomyositis); occupational exposures (i.e., silica, asbestos, beryllium, organic dust); pulmonary vasculitis (i.e., Churg-Strauss syndrome, Wegener's granulomatosis); and other systemic disorders (i.e., sarcoidosis, Goodpasture's syndrome, pulmonary histiocytosis X). As is evident, a very detailed medical history and physical exam are needed to make an accurate diagnosis. The combination of pleura-based plaques and ILD suggests asbestosis.

Honeycombing • Honeycombing is a descriptive radiographic term, describing lung fibrosis. These are thick, linear densities that form the shape of a honeycomb. In IPF, the fibrosis tends to occur in a peripheral location. You may be given chest radiographs to interpret and match with the disease process that produces the abnormalities seen. For example, asbestosis has linear densities with or without honeycombing with calcified pleural plaques at the lung bases. Silicosis has small nodules to large conglomerate masses in the upper lobes. Eggshell calcifications of hilar nodes can also be present with silicosis.

Answers • 1-C 2-A 3-B 4-C

● CASE PRESENTATION

A 28-year-old woman with a history of asthma enters the emergency room (ER) for acute shortness of breath and worsening wheezing over the past 6 hours. Physical exam reveals a temperature of 98.2 F, pulse of 120/min, respiration rate of 40/min, and blood pressure of 140/80. Lung exam reveals faint wheezes and diminished breath sounds bilaterally. Over the next 30 minutes, the patient experiences increasing respiratory distress and decreasing alertness. Arterial blood gas immediately reveals a pH of 7.16, pCO_2 of 80, and pO_2 of 55 on 4-liter nasal cannulae. Emergent intubation is performed. The patient is placed on assist-control mode of ventilation; respiratory rate is 20/min, tidal volume is 800 mL, and FiO_2 is 100%. Five minutes later, the patient becomes profoundly hypotensive with a systolic blood pressure of 70 mm Hg.

1. Which of the following could explain this patient's hypotension?
   A. Tension pneumothorax
   B. Oxygen toxicity
   C. Intrinsic positive end expiratory pressure (auto–PEEP)
   D. Nosocomial gram negative sepsis
   E. A and C

2. Which of the following is a physiologic effect of auto-PEEP on the cardiovascular system?
   A. Decreased preload
   B. Increased cardiac output
   C. Increased afterload
   D. Increased preload
   E. C and D

3. Changing which parameter on a mechanical ventilator affects paO_2?
   A. PEEP
   B. Expiratory flow rate
   C. Respiratory rate
   D. Tidal volume
   E. All of the above

4. In an intubated and paralyzed patient on pressure support of 15 cm H_2O pressure, what is the expected minute ventilation?
   A. 10 liters
   B. 5 liters
   C. 15 liters
   D. 0 liters
   E. None of the above

● COMMENT

Cause of hypotension • In this patient hypotension developed secondary to intrinsic or auto-PEEP. Auto-PEEP is present when the pressure at the alveolar spaces exceeds airway opening pressure. Auto-PEEP occurs when there is insufficient time for the lungs to empty completely before inspiratory flow is initiated again. Over time, there is a cumulative increase in positive intrathoracic pressure. Patients who are prone to development of auto-PEEP are those who have asthma, chronic bronchitis, emphysema, or high inspiratory rates secondary to respiratory failure. Tension pneumothorax should be excluded for any patient on a mechanical ventilator when hypotension develops.

Effects of auto-PEEP • Auto-PEEP has several important effects on both the cardiovascular and respiratory systems. The application of positive intrathoracic pressure causes a decrease in preload, leading to a decrease in cardiac output. It also decreases afterload. In terms of the respiratory system, auto-PEEP increases the work of breathing and predisposes the patient to increased risk of pneumothoraces.

How to correct hypoxemia • Hypoxemia can be corrected through several steps. One can increase FiO_2, increase extrinsic PEEP, or increase inspiratory time. Sustained levels of O_2 greater than 60% cause acute lung injury. Therefore, it is imperative to lower FiO_2 to less than 60%. The application of extrinsic PEEP or increased inspiratory time can lead to better alveolar recruitment and can improve oxygenation when toxic levels of oxygen are being administered.

Modes of ventilation • Ventilators are either volume-cycle or pressure-cycle. Assist-control (AC) and synchronized intermittent mandatory ventilation (SIMV) modes are volume-cycled. In these modes, the physician must set a rate, tidal volume, and inspiratory flow rate. In AC mode, a fixed tidal volume is given at a predetermined rate. If the patient takes a breath spontaneously, the ventilator assists the inspiratory effort fully by delivering a full tidal volume. Unlike AC mode, the SIMV mode does not assist spontaneous breaths beyond the predetermined tidal volume and rate. The two pressure cycle modes are pressure support (PS) and pressure control (PC). In PS, the ventilator responds to an inspiratory effort by raising pressure to a selected level and maintaining that pressure level until inspiratory effort has ceased. Respiratory rate is determined entirely by the patient; therefore, he or she must have an intact respiratory drive to ensure adequate ventilation. In a paralyzed patient on PS, minute ventilation is zero! PC ventilation is similar to PS in that the physician sets the airway pressure, but a backup respiratory rate can also be set in this mode. The tidal volume and alveolar ventilation in PC mode are inversely related to the compliance of the respiratory system. If a patient has stiff lungs as a result of acute respiratory distress syndrome (ARDS) (i.e., poor lung compliance), higher airway pressures are required to increase tidal volume or minute ventilation.

Answers • 1-E 2-A 3-A 4-D

● CASE PRESENTATION

A 54-year-old white man with a history of obesity, type 2 diabetes mellitus, and hyperlipidemia seeks a routine follow-up today. He reports that he has been doing well overall and denies polyuria, polyphagia, or polydipsia. He is compliant with the dosage of metformin and atorvastatin calcium. Physical exam is remarkable for a blood pressure of 145/95 in both arms, which is consistent with his last two readings. His hemoglobin A1C is 6.8% and low-density lipoprotein (LDL) cholesterol is 92 mg/dL. Urine microalbumin finding is negative.

1. What is this patient's target blood pressure?
   A. It is less than or equal to 160/95.
   B. It is less than 130/85.
   C. His excellent lipid and diabetic control make tight blood pressure control less important.
   D. It is less than 140/90.
   E. None of the above

2. Which of the following factors should prompt the initiation of pharmacologic therapy in a hypertensive patient?
   A. Left ventricular hypertrophy on electrocardiogram (ECG)
   B. Coronary artery disease
   C. Diabetes mellitus
   D. Proteinuria
   E. All of the above

3. What is the best class of antihypertensive agent for this patient?
   A. Beta-blocker
   B. Calcium channel blocker
   C. Angiotensin converting enzyme inhibitor
   D. Alpha-blocker
   E. Loop diuretic

4. Adequate blood pressure control is associated with which of the following?
   A. A decline in overall mortality rate
   B. Decreased risk of congestive heart failure (CHF)
   C. Decreased risk of stroke
   D. Decreased incidence of renal failure
   E. All of the above

● COMMENT

Blood pressure goals • Optimal blood pressure is less than 120/80, and normal blood pressure is less than 130/85. The goal of hypertension therapy varies, depending on the individual patient. All patients should be treated to a target of less than 140/90, but some populations merit more aggressive control. For example, diabetic patients and patients with heart failure should be treated to a blood pressure of less than 130/85. Patients with renal insufficiency and proteinuria (>1g/24 hr) have a target blood pressure of less than 125/75. Unfortunately, relatively few hypertensive patients have achieved blood pressure goals.

Indications for pharmacologic therapy • Hypertension treatment is based on the severity of blood pressure elevation and the overall risk stratification of the patient. All patients with hypertension or high normal blood pressure (130 to 139/85 to 89) should have life-style modification, including a low-sodium diet, weight loss, limiting of alcohol intake, and increase in aerobic exercise. Patients with a blood pressure greater than or equal to 160/100 should also receive simultaneous drug therapy. Additionally, patients with clinical cardiovascular disease, target organ damage (such as left ventricular hypertrophy, proteinuria, or hypertensive retinopathy), or diabetes should be treated initially with drug therapy and life-style modification regardless of the degree of blood pressure elevation. This includes patients with high normal blood pressure. Patients with cardiovascular risk factors and relatively mild hypertension can have a trial of life-style modification before the initiation of drug therapy.

Choice of agents • Beta-blockers and diuretics have the most supporting evidence of efficacy and should be the initial choice for uncomplicated conditions. There are a number of compelling indications for particular classes of antihypertensives including the use of angiotensin converting enzyme inhibitors (ACEIs) in diabetic patients. ACEIs are also the initial antihypertensive choice for CHF patients, though beta-blockers, diuretics, and angiotensin receptor blockers are other reasonable choices. Patients with a recent myocardial infarction (MI) should be treated with a beta-blocker and possibly with an ACEI as well. Isolated systolic hypertension should be treated with diuretic therapy, though there is some evidence for calcium channel blocker or ACEI therapy in these patients.

Risks associated with hypertension • Hypertension is a major contributor to coronary artery disease, cerebrovascular disease, CHF and end-stage renal disease. Adequate treatment has been proved to decrease morbidity and mortality rates related to these conditions.

Answers • 1-B   2-E   3-C   4-E

● CASE PRESENTATION

The patient is a 72-year-old black man with a history of well-controlled hypertension, hyperlipidemia, tobacco abuse, and peripheral vascular disease who arrives at your office for routine follow up. He continues to smoke two packs per day. He is compliant with his hydrochlorothiazide dosage. Blood pressure measurements have been consistently in the 120/80 range for several years. However, physical exam findings today are remarkable for a blood pressure of 165/105. Funduscopic exam yields a benign result. He does have an abdominal bruit in the hypogastric region. Renal function and electrolyte levels are within normal limits.

1. Which of the following should prompt a work-up for secondary causes of hypertension?
   A. Family history of hypertension
   B. Acute worsening of well-controlled blood pressure
   C. Hypertension that requires two agents to achieve control
   D. Mild to moderate hypertension at diagnosis
   E. Onset of hypertension after age 25

2. The patient's presentation suggests which secondary cause of hypertension?
   A. Pheochromocytoma
   B. Coarctation of the aorta
   C. Renal artery stenosis
   D. Cushing's syndrome
   E. Hyperthyroidism

3. Significant hypokalemia would be most consistent with which of the following causes of hypertension?
   A. Hyperaldosteronism
   B. Hyperthyroidism
   C. Coarctation of the aorta
   D. Pheochromocytoma
   E. Polycystic kidney disease

4. In addition to hypertension and headaches, patients with pheochromocytoma are most likely to report which of the following?
   A. Hypoglycemia
   B. Bradycardia
   C. Profuse diaphoresis
   D. Weight gain
   E. Flushing

● COMMENT

Work-up for secondary causes of hypertension • All patients with hypertension should have a careful history and physical examination searching for any clues to an identifiable cause of hypertension. Further, newly diagnosed hypertensive patients should undergo testing including serum creatinine, urinalysis, serum potassium, and electrocardiogram (ECG).

The onset of hypertension in particularly young patients (<25 years) or those older than 55 years should prompt further investigation. Significant worsening of previously well-controlled blood pressure can also herald secondary hypertension. Further, patients whose blood pressure is refractory to therapy with adequate doses of three antihypertensives merit addition work-up.

Renal artery stenosis • The patient's prior history of vascular disease, tobacco abuse, and abdominal bruit makes renal artery stenosis (RAS) the most likely diagnosis. Atherosclerotic RAS is more common in men and occurs later in life. The lesion is at the ostium of the renal artery and is not typically amenable to balloon angioplasty. Fibromuscular dysplasia is the type of RAS that occurs more commonly in young women. The lesion is midvessel and is readily treatable with angioplasty. Renal arteriography is the gold standard for diagnosing RAS; captopril renogram (triple renal scan) and renal artery duplex ultrasound are noninvasive alternatives.

Hyperaldosteronism • Primary hyperaldosteronism or Conn's syndrome is suggested by significant hypokalemia in a hypertensive patient who is not on diuretic therapy. Serum aldosterone levels are elevated and plasma renin activity is depressed in primary hyperaldosteronism. Volume expansion with normal saline solution fails to suppress aldosterone levels. RAS can also be associated with hypokalemia that is due to stimulation of aldosterone production in the adrenal by elevated renin levels.

Pheochromocytoma • Pheochromocytoma is a catecholamine-secreting tumor associated with hypertension (paroxysmal or sustained) and classic symptoms including sudden headache, marked diaphoresis, and palpitations. Patients often have weight loss. Glucose intolerance and orthostatic hypotension can be noted as well. Flushing is uncommon with pheochromocytoma. The diagnosis is suggested by elevated levels of metanephrines, catecholamines, and vanillylmandelic acid (VMA) in a 24-hour urine collection. The tumor may then be localized with computed tomography (CT) scanning or a methyliodobenzyl guanidine (MIBG) scan.

Answers • 1-B 2-C 3-A 4-C

● CASE PRESENTATION

A 59-year-old white woman was admitted to the psychiatric hospital for depression with suicidal ideation. She has a history of hypertension (HTN) and gastroesophageal reflux disease (GERD) and a long history of recurrent depression. On admission she was placed on a selective serotonin reuptake inhibitor (SSRI) antidepressant and continued on her hydrochlorothiazide and omeprazole. After a week of hospitalization, she was being considered for electroconvulsive therapy and preprocedure lab results revealed serum sodium concentration of 123 mmol/L (normal: 135-144 mmol/L). Other electrolytes and renal function were normal. The renal consultation team was called, and on exam, her mucous membranes were dry and she was mildly orthostatic. The nursing staff reports a history of normal oral intake and no compulsive water drinking. Serum osmolarity was low at 260.

1. For the patient described which of the following is the most likely cause of the hyponatremia?

   A. Depression
   B. Small cell lung cancer
   C. SSRI antidepressants
   D. Hydrochlorothiazide
   E. Congestive heart failure

2. Which of the following is a common serious symptom of severe hyponatremia?

   A. Cardiac arrest
   B. Seizures
   C. Respiratory failure
   D. Renal failure
   E. Diarrhea

3. Syndrome of inappropriate antidiuretic hormone (SIADH) secretion is a common cause of hyponatremia. Causes of SIADH include which of the following?

   A. Intracranial masses
   B. Small cell lung cancer
   C. Mechanical ventilation
   D. Medications
   E. All of the above

4. Treatment of hyponatremia consists of treating the underlying cause, restricting free water, and providing volume support. The complication of central pontine myelinolysis can occur when:

   A. The sodium concentration is not corrected.
   B. Seizures develop.
   C. The sodium concentration is overcorrected or corrected too quickly.
   D. Hyponatremia recurs after successful treatment.
   E. Hyponatremia is due to SIADH from an intracranial process.

● COMMENT

Differential diagnosis of hyponatremia • Hyponatremia is the leading electrolyte abnormality in hospitalized patients. The first step is to determine the serum osmolarity. Most often it is low, but hyperlipidemia and hyperproteinemia can cause a pseudohyponatremia with a normal serum osmolarity. Hypertonic hyponatremia is generally caused by markedly elevated serum glucose. Once hypotonic hyponatremia is documented, the differential diagnosis is based on the volume status of the patient (Table 2).

TABLE 2

Hypovolemic	Euvolemic	Hypervolemic
• Diuretics	• Syndrome of inappropriate antidiuretic hormone (SIADH)	• Congestive heart failure (CHF)
• Volume loss	• Psychogenic polydipsia	• Cirrhosis
• Adrenal insufficiency	• Hypothyroidism	• Nephrotic syndrome
• Salt wasting renal disease		

This patient appears dehydrated and is clinically hypovolemic; thus her diuretic is the likely culprit.

Symptoms • Hyponatremia most commonly causes neuromuscular irritability, resulting in fatigue, lethargy, muscle spasm, hiccups, and seizures. Symptoms can develop at higher levels if the sodium level falls acutely, but most symptoms are manifested at a level of 120 mmol/L or less.

SIADH • SIADH secretion can occur with many disease processes. A long list of drugs can cause the syndrome. Classically it is a paraneoplastic manifestation of small cell lung cancer, but other neoplasms are also associated. Essentially any abnormality in the head or chest, including use of a ventilator, can cause the syndrome. A similar clinical presentation can be caused by hypothyroidism, but the mechanism of disease is different. For a diagnosis of SIADH, the patient must be euvolemic and have normal adrenal and thyroid function. Simultaneous serum and urine osmolarities reveal a urine osmolarity inappropriately concentrated.

Treatment of hyponatremia • The first step in the treatment of a hypovolemic, hyponatremic patient is hydration with normal saline solution. In mild cases when the patient is not dehydrated, free water restriction to 1 to 1.5 liters/day is effective and allows the sodium to rise slowly. Three percent saline solution, "hotsalt," can be given emergently if rapid correction is needed because of seizures. This should be done cautiously and only to raise the sodium level above 120 mmol/L. The speed at which the condition developed can dictate the speed at which it should be corrected. A general rule of thumb is that sodium level should be increased by no more than 0.5 to 1.0 mmol/liter/hr. Correcting slowly prevents the neurologic damage of central pontine myelinolysis.

Answers • 1-D 2-B 3-E 4-C

● CASE PRESENTATION

A 45-year-old man was rescued by the emergency medical service (EMS) after being involved in a severe automobile accident, suffering crush injuries to his lower extremities. On arrival in the ER, the patient is conscious and alert. There are multiple fractures of the upper and lower extremities. After initial stabilization, the patient gives a history of no medical problems. Exam reveals tachycardia and the presence of compound fractures of the lower extremities. Before surgery, lab specimens are drawn. The serum potassium level is 7.4 mg/dL (3.5-5.0 mg/dL), and the serum creatinine level is elevated at 2.1 mg/dL. Urinalysis reveals glucosuria and pigmented casts. A serum creatine kinase (CK) is elevated at 35,000 mg/dL. An electrocardiogram (ECG) reveals sinus tachycardia with prominent peaked T waves. Rhabdomyolysis is diagnosed and aggressive hydration is initiated.

1. A repeat ECG reveals some widening of the QRS complex. Which treatment would you give initially?
   A. Calcium gluconate
   B. Insulin
   C. Sodium bicarbonate
   D. Sodium polystyrene sulfonate (Kayexalate)
   E. Furosemide

2. Which of the following lowers the serum potassium concentration most rapidly?
   A. Calcium gluconate
   B. Insulin
   C. Sodium bicarbonate
   D. Sodium polystyrene sulfonate
   E. Ibuprofen

3. Which of the following drugs can be associated with hyperkalemia?
   A. Nonsteroidal anti-inflammatory drugs (NSAIDs)
   B. Angiotensin converting enzyme (ACE) inhibitors
   C. Angiotensin receptor blockers
   D. Spironolactone
   E. All of the above

4. Which of the following is *least* likely to lead to hyperkalemia?
   A. Metabolic acidosis
   B. Renal failure
   C. Tumor lysis syndrome
   D. Cushing's syndrome
   E. Adrenal insufficiency

● COMMENT

Clinical manifestations of hyperkalemia • Hyperkalemia can be a life-threatening state. Neuromuscular weakness can occur, and the cardiac manifestations are potentially lethal. The ECG findings progressively include T-wave prominence (peaked T waves), prolongation of the QRS, sine wave degeneration of the QRS complex, and asystole.

Treatment • Intravenous calcium should be given first to patients with significant ECG changes. This stabilizes the myocardial membrane but does not affect the potassium concentration. Insulin is the quickest way to shift K^+ into the cells, and dextrose should also be administered to prevent hypoglycemia. Sodium bicarbonate and beta-agonists also can shift K^+ into cells, but this effect takes longer. Definitive treatment includes removing K^+ from the body, by means of sodium polystyrene sulfonate (Kayexalate), a binding resin, or dialysis. In this case, aggressive hydration and alkalization of the urine are indicated to treat the underlying rhabdomyolysis.

Drug-induced hyperkalemia • Any drug that disrupts the renin-angiotensin-aldosterone axis has the potential to cause hyperkalemia, including ACE inhibitors, angiotensin receptor blockers, and beta-blockers. NSAIDs inhibit renin, as well as causing glomerular hemodynamic changes. Spironolactone competitively inhibits aldosterone.

Other causes • Hyperkalemia results from 1) abnormal release from cells, as in rhabdomyolysis and tumor lysis syndrome; 2) abnormal renal excretion of K^+ from renal failure, mineralocorticoid deficiency, or drug effects; or 3) abnormal shifting of potassium. Acidosis causes K^+ in the cytosol to be exchanged with hydrogen ions in the serum, leading to hyperkalemia.

Answers • 1-A 2-B 3-E 4-D

● CASE PRESENTATION

The patient is a 46-year-old male with a history of marked alcohol abuse, who entered the emergency department reporting a 3- to 4-day history of midepigastric pain, nausea, and vomiting. The patient denies hematemesis. He has eaten very little in the last 3 days. Past medical history is unremarkable. Social history is remarkable for the consumption of 12 beers per day, though he has not had anything to drink over the last 3 days. Physical exam reveals an ill-appearing white man with dry mucous membranes. Vital signs are remarkable for a pulse of 110/min with normal blood pressure. Otherwise, the patient does have some midepigastric tenderness on deep palpation. Physical exam is otherwise normal. Laboratory data reveal serum sodium concentration of 136 mEq/L, potassium of 3.6 mEq/L, chloride of 100 mEq/L, and serum bicarbonate of 12 mEq/L (normal: 22-32 mEq/L). Renal function, blood glucose, amylase, and lipase are within normal limits. Arterial blood gas reveals a pH of 7.20, pCO_2 of 26, and pO_2 of 90. Urinalysis is remarkable for ++ ketones.

1. Which of the following best characterizes this patient's acid-base abnormality?
   A. Increased anion gap metabolic acidosis with respiratory compensation
   B. Non–anion gap metabolic acidosis
   C. Combined respiratory and anion gap metabolic acidosis
   D. Respiratory alkalosis with metabolic compensation
   E. None of the above

2. What is the most likely cause of this patient's acid-base abnormality?
   A. Diabetic ketoacidosis
   B. Renal tubular acidosis
   C. Uremia
   D. Alcoholic ketoacidosis
   E. Salicylate toxicity

3. Which of the following is characteristic of severe metabolic acidosis?
   A. Kussmaul respiration
   B. Lethargy (possibly progressing to coma)
   C. Peripheral arterial vasodilatation with hypotension
   D. Predisposition to pulmonary edema
   E. All of the above

4. Which of the following is the most appropriate therapy for this patient?
   A. Aggressive hydration with D5 normal saline solution
   B. Intravenous insulin drip until the anion gap closes
   C. Hemodialysis
   D. Intravenous sodium bicarbonate
   E. Outpatient treatment for alcoholic gastritis with a proton pump inhibitor

● COMMENT

Identification of a high anion gap acidosis • This patient has metabolic acidosis, which is better defined as low serum bicarbonate level. There is also evidence of respiratory compensation. Metabolic acidosis can be further characterized by determining the anion gap [$Na - (Cl + HCO_3)$]. The anion gap represents unmeasured anions in the plasma and is 24 mmol/liter in this patient (normal 10 to 12 mmol/liter). When acid anions accumulate in the serum, this leads to a high anion gap acidosis. One can predict the appropriateness of respiratory compensation for respiratory acidosis by the following formula: $pCO_2 = (1.5 \times HCO_3) + 8$. Using this formula, the predicted pCO_2 in this case should be 26.

Differential diagnosis of high anion gap metabolic acidosis • Alcoholic ketoacidosis is characterized by extensive alcohol abuse followed by little or no oral intake. The patient likely does have an element of alcoholic gastritis that precipitated his nausea, vomiting, and inability to eat. The four principal causes of high anion gap acidosis are lactic acidosis, ketoacidosis, ingested toxins (ethylene glycol, methanol, salicylates, paraldehyde), and renal failure. Some find it helpful to use a mnemonic device such as MUDPILES (methanol, uremia, diabetic or alcoholic ketoacidosis, paraldehyde, ironiazide [INH], lactic acidosis, ethylene glycol, salicylates) to remember the differential diagnosis.

Sequelae of severe metabolic acidosis • Severe metabolic acidosis (pH less than 7.2) is associated with deep respiration, particularly increased vital capacity (Kussmaul respiration). Cardiac contractility may be depressed and peripheral arteries may be vasodilated, with the potential to lead to cardiovascular collapse and shock. Additionally there is venous contraction and a predisposition to pulmonary edema. Patients are often lethargic and can progress to coma.

Treatment • In this case, primary treatment should be directed at correcting the patient's volume status and providing some carbohydrate substrate for metabolism with D5 normal saline solution. Hypophosphatemia, hypokalemia, and hypomagnesemia are often present and should be corrected. Other causes of high anion gap metabolic acidosis can be corrected by addressing the underlying abnormality. Diabetic ketoacidosis should be treated with intravenous insulin infusion and hydration. Uremia may require hemodialysis and oral bicarbonate replacement. Methanol or ethylene glycol ingestion can be treated with hemodialysis in severe cases. Intravenous infusion of ethanol or the new alcohol dehydrogenase inhibitor fomepizole can lessen toxicity due to these ingestions. The use of intravenous sodium bicarbonate therapy in high anion gap metabolic acidoses is controversial, but it is often done in severe acidosis to increase the pH to 7.25.

Answers • 1-A   2-D   3-E   4-A

● CASE PRESENTATION

A 52-year-old black man with a long history of type 2 diabetes, hypertension, and hyperlipidemia arrives at your office to establish care. He reports that he has been doing reasonably well overall and denies any polyuria, polyphagia, or polydipsia. Vital signs are normal, including a blood pressure of 124/68. Physical examination is otherwise remarkable for decreased light touch and position sense in a stocking and glove distribution. Current medications include metformin 1 g twice a day, hydrochlorothiazide 12.5 mg/day, and atorvastatin 10 mg orally per day. Laboratory testing reveals a normal sodium level of 138 mEq/L, potassium of 5.9 mEq/L (normal: 3.5-5.0 mEq/L), chloride of 112 mEq/L, HCO_3^- of 18 mEq/L (normal: 22-32 mEq/L), blood urea nitrogen (BUN) of 28, creatinine of 1.4 mg/dL (normal: 0.6-1.4 mg/dL), and blood glucose of 148 mg/dL. Liver function test results are within normal limits.

1. What is the likely cause of the patient's metabolic acidosis?
   A. Diabetic ketoacidosis
   B. Type I renal tubular acidosis
   C. Lactic acidosis related to metformin
   D. Type IV renal tubular acidosis
   E. Uremic acidosis

2. Which of the following best characterizes the pathophysiologic characteristics of type IV renal tubular acidosis (RTA)?
   A. Proximal tubular wasting of bicarbonate
   B. Hyporeninemic hypoaldosteronism
   C. Defect in distal tubular hydrogen ion secretion
   D. Reaction to increased gastrointestinal loss of bicarbonate
   E. Mineralocorticoid excess

3. Which of the following is a true statement regarding normal anion gap metabolic acidoses?
   A. The sole cause of normal anion gap acidoses is RTA.
   B. A common cause in diabetics is ketoacidosis.
   C. Type I (distal) RTA occurs with hypokalemia and hyperchloremia.
   D. Type IV RTA is often accompanied by hypokalemia.
   E. All of the above are true

4. Which of the following statements is true regarding therapy of RTAs?
   A. Primary therapy for type IV RTA is usually directed at controlling hyperkalemia.
   B. Type I RTA requires significantly higher doses of $NaHCO_3$ therapy than type II (proximal) RTA.
   C. Type II RTA can be treated with the carbonic anhydride inhibitor acetazolamide.
   D. Type I and type II RTAs frequently require therapy for hyperkalemia.
   E. All of the above are true.

● COMMENT

Type IV RTA   •   This patient has a classic picture of a type IV RTA. He is diabetic with relatively mild renal insufficiency and has a mild hyperchloremic metabolic acidosis and hyperkalemia. This is the most common type of RTA. As noted, the acidosis is generally mild and hyperkalemia is often the most striking feature. It can also be seen in patients treated with angiotensin converting enzyme inhibitors, potassium-sparing diuretics, or nonsteroidal anti-inflammatory drugs.

Pathophysiologic features of type IV RTA   •   The most common underlying abnormality in type IV RTA is hyporeninemic hypoaldosteronism associated with diabetic renal disease. However, resistance to the effects of aldosterone can occur as well. Regardless, the lack of mineralocorticoid activity results in significant hyperkalemia. Hyperkalemia inhibits ammonium production by the renal tubules and thus decreases the buffer capacity for hydrogen ions in the urine. The result is metabolic acidosis.

Normal anion gap metabolic acidosis   •   Normal anion gap (hyperchloremic) metabolic acidosis generally occurs as a result of HCO_3^- loss from the gastrointestinal tract or from a defect in renal acidification. Gastrointestinal (GI) bicarbonate losses can result from diarrhea, ureteroileostomy, or external pancreatic or small bowel drainage. Types I (distal), II (proximal), and IV are the three major types of RTA. Types I and II RTA both result in hyperchloremic metabolic acidosis and hypokalemia. Type I RTA is rare and is due to a defect in distal tubular hydrogen ion secretion. Causes include autoimmune disorders, drugs (amphotericin B, toluene), hypercalciuria, and obstructive uropathy. Patients often have nephrocalcinosis and/or nephrolithiasis. The primary defect in type II RTA is reduced proximal tubular reabsorption of HCO_3^- and may occur in isolation or as part of a more generalized defect in proximal tubular function (Fanconi's syndrome). Types I and II RTA may be differentiated by the fact that type II RTA requires much higher dosages of sodium bicarbonate ($NaHCO_3$) for treatment. Further, type I RTA patients have more severe acidosis and never have the capacity for acidification of urine pH below 5.4.

Therapy for RTA   •   Therapy for type IV RTA involves correction of the underlying hyperkalemia with diuretics such as furosemide or with a binding resin like sodium polystyrene sulfonate (Kayexalate). $NaHCO_3$ can correct the acidosis. Mineralocorticoids can lead to volume overload and hypertension. Effective treatment for types I and II RTA involves oral bicarbonate replacement, though huge doses of replacement therapy are necessary in type II RTA because of the underlying defect. K^+ replacement may be necessary for both types, though the requirements are much higher for type II RTA.

Answers   •   1-D   2-B   3-C   4-A

● CASE PRESENTATION

A 63-year-old man with a history of hypertension (HTN), benign prostatic hypertrophy (BPH), gastroesophageal reflux disease (GERD), and alcohol abuse entered the emergency department after 3 days of abdominal pain, nausea, and vomiting. On the day of admission, he reports that the over-the-counter analgesics he has been taking for pain are no longer effective. Physical exam reveals hypotension with a blood pressure of 80/56 and marked epigastric tenderness. Acute pancreatitis was diagnosed and amylase, lipase, and liver function tests were elevated. His creatinine level was 2.6 mg/dL (normal: 0.6-1.4 mg/dL) with a blood urea nitrogen (BUN) level of 60 mg/dL (normal: 8-20 mg/dL). On review, the previous creatinine level was 1.1 mg/dL 2 years ago. A work-up of pancreatitis and acute renal failure was initiated.

1. True statements regarding serum creatinine include which of the following?
   A. Creatinine is a sensitive indicator of renal function.
   B. Creatinine is freely filtered and minimally secreted.
   C. Serum creatinine is largely unaffected by medications.
   D. Serum creatinine is impacted by urinary pH.
   E. All of the above

2. Prerenal azotemia is associated with which of the following?
   A. Fractional excretion of Na^+ less than 1%
   B. Prompt resolution with treatment
   C. Inactive urinary sediment
   D. BUN/creatinine ratio greater than 20:1
   E. All of the above

3. The best renal imaging study in the initial evaluation of acute renal failure (ARF) is:
   A. Intravenous pyelolgram
   B. Magnetic resonance imaging (MRI) of abdomen
   C. Ultrasound
   D. Plain abdominal radiograph
   E. Computed tomography (CT) intravenous pyelogram.

4. The most common intrarenal cause of acute renal failure in a hospitalized patient is:
   A. Acute tubular necrosis
   B. Acute glomerulonephritis
   C. Acute interstitial nephritis
   D. Acute diabetic nephropathy
   E. Prerenal azotemia

● COMMENT

Creatinine and ARF • Creatinine is not a sensitive indicator of renal function. A small rise in serum creatinine may in fact indicate a significant, over 50%, loss of renal function. Creatinine can rise acutely and not be above the upper limit of the laboratory standard yet still indicate renal failure. Creatinine is a marker of glomerular filtration rate (GFR) because it is freely filtered in the glomerulus and only mildly secreted. Certain drugs, such as cimetidine and trimethoprim, can block this secretion. Muscle mass is a primary determinate of serum creatinine because it is a muscle by-product and continually released at a constant rate. Urine pH does not affect creatinine.

Prerenal renal failure • The diagnosis of ARF is divided into three segments: prerenal, renal, and postrenal causes. Prerenal renal failure is characterized by a decrease in the effective circulating blood volume and a subsequent decrease in renal perfusion. The kidney is able to autoregulate its blood flow and pressure, but when these mechanisms are overcome, creatinine level rises, indicating a decrease in GFR. Potential causes include hemorrhage, volume depletion, and heart failure. The combination of nonsteroidal anti-inflammatory drugs (NSAIDs) and angiotensin converting enzyme (ACE) inhibitors can also decrease intraglomerular perfusion pressure. The BUN/creatinine ratio is typically high because the kidney retains BUN at a higher rate than creatinine. The fractional excretion of sodium (FeNa = [urine Na × plasma creatinine/plasma Na × urine creatinine] × 100) is a measure of the amount of the filtered sodium excreted. When volume depletion is present, the kidney avidly retains Na^+ and thus causes a FeNa of less than 1%. There should not be any cells, casts, or protein in the urine. Restoration of circulating volume causes the renal function to return to normal.

Imaging in ARF • Renal ultrasound is the best imaging technique in ARF because it helps rule out postrenal obstruction, a readily reversible cause of ARF. It readily documents the presence of two kidneys and hydronephrosis, if present. Documenting bilateral kidneys is not trivial, because bilateral obstruction is needed to cause renal failure. Renal size can also be determined to help determine the chronicity of renal insufficiency.

Acute tubular necrosis • Renal causes of ARF can be divided into three groups, glomerular, tubular, and interstitial. The most common renal cause of ARF in hospitalized patients is acute tubular necrosis (ATN). ATN is characterized by muddy brown granular casts in the urine and a FeNa greater than 1%. Common causes include aminoglycosides (or other drugs), radiocontrast dye, sepsis, and hypotension.

Answers • 1-B 2-E 3-C 4-A

● CASE PRESENTATION

A 25-year-old black man without significant past medical history reports a 2-day history of dark-colored urine, nausea, and vomiting, and a 1-day history of disorientation. A chart review reveals that the patient was treated with antibiotics for impetigo about 2 weeks ago. Physical examination reveals blood pressure of 190/120, pulse of 105/min, respiratory rate of 18/min, temperature of 99.6 F, and O_2 saturation of 90% on room air. Other physical exam findings are pertinent for mild nuchal resistance and trace pedal edema. Funduscopic exam reveals papilledema. The patient does not have any rash or arthritis. Laboratory studies show a negative urine drug screen, blood urea nitrogen (BUN) of 42 mg/dL (normal: 8-20 mg/dL), creatinine of 2.6 mg/dL (normal: 0.6-1.4 mg/dL), and total creatine kinase (CPK) of 1500 Iu/L (normal: 55-170). The urine myoglobin is negative and uric acid level is within normal limits. LFTs are within normal limits. Urinalysis (UA) shows trace protein, with numerous erythrocytes and red blood cell casts. Results of renal ultrasonography are unremarkable, and the findings of computed tomography (CT) of the head are normal. Lumbar puncture shows normal cerebrospinal fluid (CSF).

1. What is the most likely cause of this patient's renal insufficiency?

   A. Minimal change disease (MCD)
   B. Immunoglobulin A (IgA) nephropathy
   C. Poststreptococcal glomerulonephritis (PSGN)
   D. Rhabdomyolysis
   E. Membranous nephropathy (MN)

2. Which of the following studies would be most specific in helping establish the diagnosis of this patient's renal insufficiency?

   A. Serum IgA
   B. Kidney biopsy
   C. Antideoxyribonuclease
   D. Antinuclear antibody (ANA)
   E. Serum complement

3. What is the most likely cause of this patient's disorientation?

   A. Uremic encephalopathy
   B. Meningitis
   C. Early cerebrovascular accident
   D. Hypertensive encephalopathy
   E. Dehydration

4. Treatment of this patient should employ which of the following?

   A. Antihypertensives
   B. Decrease in salt and protein intake
   C. Antibiotics
   D. Diuretics
   E. All of the above

● COMMENT

Cause of acute renal insufficiency • The active urinary sediment, relative lack of proteinuria, and negative urine myoglobin finding narrow the differential diagnosis in this case. IgA nephropathy is rare in blacks and usually presents with asymptomatic hematuria. Therefore, this patient likely has acute glumerulonephritis (AGN), specifically poststreptococcal glomerulonephritis (PSGN) due to previous impetigo. Upper respiratory or skin infection by nephritogenic strains of group A beta-hemolytic *Streptococcus* sp. (GABHS) predisposes to the development of PSGN 1 to 3 weeks after the acute infection. PSGN is common in children and young adults. Features of PSGN are an abnormal urinalysis result ranging from asymptomatic microscopic hematuria to gross hematuria ("Coca-Cola"–colored urine), edema, mild to moderate proteinuria, oliguria, hypertension, and renal insufficiency. Creatinine level is usually less than 3.0 mg/dL.

Confirming a diagnosis of PSGN • There is no definitive study that confirms PSGN. The diagnosis is very likely if in the appropriate clinical setting there is exposure to GABHS documented by culture or serologic findings. However, serologic confirmation is usually the only way to confirm prior streptococcal infection. Antistreptolysin O (ASO) and antideoxyribonuclease are the appropriate studies; ASO is better for pharyngitis and antideoxyribonuclease is better for skin infection. It may be possible to document a significant rise in titer. Complement levels are usually low, but that finding is not specific for PSGN. The differential for low complement glumerulonephritis (GN) includes systemic lupus erythematosus (SLE), PSGN, subacute bacterial endocarditis (SBE), cryoglobulinemia, and membranoproliferative GN. Renal biopsy is usually not necessary unless there is no improvement in renal function and the cause is unclear. If biopsy is performed, it reveals a diffuse proliferative GN with some crescent formation due to epithelial cell hyperplasia.

Cause of disorientation • The sudden onset of excessively high blood pressure in a previously normotensive patient can precipitate hypertensive encephalopathy. This is not an uncommon complication in patients with AGN. Features of hypertensive encephalopathy include headache, disorientation, signs of meningism, and papilledema. HTN in this setting should be treated aggressively with intravenous (IV) antihypertensives.

Management of PSGN • Management is mainly supportive. Steroids may actually worsen the condition and immunosuppressants are not helpful. Antibiotics are given to eradicate GABHS infection. Hypertension is aggressively treated to prevent complications such as encephalopathy, worsening renal failure, and congestive heart failure. Diuretics may help with volume overload and oliguria. Most patients regain normal renal function, though microscopic hematuria and proteinuria may persist for years. In about 10% of patients rapidly progressive GN develops and may progress to end-stage renal disease.

Answers • 1-C   2-C   3-D   4-E

● CASE PRESENTATION

The patient is a 47-year-old man who is admitted to the hospital for evaluation and treatment of left lower extremity redness and swelling of 2 days' duration. The patient also reports some pain in his left inguinal region and subjective fevers. Past medical history is remarkable for chronic venous stasis in his left lower extremity due to injuries sustained in a motorcycle accident several years earlier. He has no known drug allergies. Physical examination reveals a temperature of 102.6 F, pulse of 110/min, and blood pressure of 130/70. His distal left lower extremity is erythematous, swollen, and hot to the level of the knee. There are no palpable cords, but he does have markedly tender left inguinal adenopathy. Admission lab results are remarkable for a white blood cell (WBC) count of 9.8/uL with 56% neutrophils, 30% bands, and 14% lymphocytes. Blood urea nitrogen (BUN) and creatinine are 18 and 0.9 respectively. Serum electrolytes are normal. Left lower extremity Doppler ultrasonography reveals no evidence of deep vein thrombosis. The patient is started on intravenous nafcillin and quickly defervesces. His left lower extremity cellulitis is improving nicely by the second day of antibiotics. Blood cultures drawn on admission have negative results. On the third day of antibiotics, the patient begins having low-grade fevers of up to 100.4 F. His lab results indicate BUN level of 49 mg/dL (normal: 8-22 mg/dL) and creatinine level of 2.4 mg/dL (normal: 0.6-1.4 mg/dL).

1. Which of the following statements regarding allergic interstitial nephritis (AIN) is true?

   A. Renal injury is usually evident with the first dose of the offending medication.
   B. Massive proteinuria is characteristic of AIN due to antibiotics.
   C. An erythematous skin rash sometimes accompanies AIN.
   D. Severe abdominal pain often accompanies AIN.
   E. All of the above

2. Which of the following medications have been reported to cause AIN?

   A. Penicillins and cephalosporins
   B. Nonsteroidal anti-inflammatory drugs (NSAIDs)
   C. Cimetidine
   D. Fluoroquinolones
   E. All of the above

3. Which of the following statements best summarizes the diagnosis of AIN?

   A. The absence of urine eosinophils essentially rules out AIN.
   B. The diagnosis of AIN is confirmed by characteristic glomerular lesions found on biopsy.
   C. Renal insufficiency coupled with an erythematous rash and eosinophilia is highly suggestive of AIN.
   D. Elevated creatinine level with a normal BUN level is characteristic of AIN.
   E. All of the above

4. Appropriate treatment for AIN includes which of the following?

   A. Plasmapheresis
   B. Discontinuation of the presumed offending agent only after renal biopsy confirmation of AIN
   C. Immunosuppressive therapy with methotrexate
   D. Discontinuation of the offending agent and consideration of corticosteroid therapy
   E. A, B, and C

● COMMENT

Clinical findings in AIN • AIN results in renal insufficiency due to interstitial infiltration of inflammatory cells in the kidneys. This tends to occur after several days to several months of exposure to an offending agent. In addition to the rise in creatinine, there is generally significant azotemia. Hyperkalemia and acidosis can result from tubular dysfunction. Peripheral eosinophilia is a relatively common finding in AIN. Associated clinical features sometimes include low-grade fever, a generalized erythematous skin rash, and arthralgias.

Causes of AIN • Medications, particularly antibiotics, are the most common causes of AIN. Penicillin (particularly antistaphylococcal penicillins), cephalosporins, sulfonamides, and fluoroquinolones are all well-described causes. Other drugs that have been linked to AIN include NSAIDs, H_2 blockers (cimetidine, ranitidine), rifampin, and allopurinol. As noted, AIN usually occurs after relatively long-term exposure to these medications, though it has been described after just a few doses.

Diagnosis • The only definitive way to diagnose AIN is to find characteristic tubulointerstitial changes on renal biopsy. However, the combination of skin rash, eosinophilia, and new-onset renal insufficiency is very sensitive for the clinical diagnosis of AIN. Unfortunately, it is uncommon to see all of these manifestations. Renal ultrasound generally reveals some nonspecific enlargement of the kidneys consistent with medical renal disease. Urinalysis typically reveals some hematuria and pyuria. Additionally, urine eosinophils are frequently shown by special staining. Substantial proteinuria is uncommon, though nephrotic range proteinuria can be a feature of NSAID-associated AIN.

Treatment • The cornerstone of treatment for AIN is the immediate cessation of the offending drug. Renal function gradually returns to normal, though some patients do not completely return to their previous level of renal function. Glucocorticoids have shown some benefit in uncontrolled trials, but this finding has yet to be confirmed. At this point, no overall benefit has been described for treatment with other immunosuppressants or plasmapheresis.

Answers • 1-C   2-E   3-C   4-D

● CASE PRESENTATION

A 68-year-old man with diabetes, benign prostatic hypertrophy (BPH), and hypertension (HTN) entered the Emergency Department with fever, chills, and foul-smelling urine. Physical exam revealed a disoriented, diaphoretic man. His temperature was 101.6 F, pulse was 110/min, respiration rate was 22/min, and blood pressure of 100/60. There was tenderness in the lower abdomen. Urinalysis shows numerous white blood cells (WBCs) and bacteria. Cultures of urine and blood both grow *Escherichia coli*. The patient was admitted to the intensive care unit with urosepsis. After admission, he experienced cardiac arrest. Cardiopulmonary resuscitation and ACLS protocols resulted in a pulse and blood pressure after 20 minutes. His hospital course continued to be stormy; after cardiac arrest his blood urea nitrogen (BUN) and creatinine levels rose significantly and he became hypoxemic. The chest x-ray result showed pulmonary edema. Electrocardiogram (ECG) did not reveal peaked T waves or QRS widening.

1. In the patient which of the following would be an indication for acute hemodialysis?

   A. Potassium level of 5.8 mg/dL
   B. pO_2 of 55 mmHg on room air
   C. Phosphorus level of 6.0 mg/dL
   D. BUN of 70 mg/dL
   E. Creatinine level of 4.8 mg/dL

2. Which of the following are symptoms of the uremic syndrome?

   A. Polycythemia
   B. Endocarditis
   C. Dysfunctional platelets
   D. Diarrhea
   E. All of the above

3. Which of the following drug intoxications can be effectively treated with hemodialysis?

   A. Digoxin
   B. Warfarin
   C. Lithium
   D. Phenytoin
   E. All of the above

4. Which of the following are efficiently cleared by hemodialysis?

   A. Potassium
   B. Phosphorus
   C. Albumin
   D. Magnesium
   E. All of the above

● COMMENT

Indication for acute dialysis • There are five indications for emergent dialysis. Remember them by the following pneumonic: A, acidosis; E, electrolytes (potassium); I, intoxication with dialyzable drugs; O, volume overload; U, uremia. All indications carry the disclaimer of "not responsive to medical therapy." This patient has pulmonary edema and hypoxemia caused by renal insufficiency and dialysis can effectively remove volume by means of ultrafiltration. Though he is hyperkalemic, this condition is not severe and his ECG does not reveal acute changes.

Uremic syndrome • There is no specific BUN at which a patient becomes uremic. Uremia is a clinical syndrome, characterized by encephalopathy, fatigue, nausea, vomiting, pericarditis, dysfunctional platelets, and anemia. These symptoms coupled with a rising BUN/creatinine ratio establish the diagnosis of uremia.

Intoxication • Hemodialysis is an effective treatment for drug intoxication, provided the drug has low molecular weight and is not protein-bound. Lithium and the alcohols (methanol, isopropyl alcohol, and ethylene glycol) fit these characteristics. Digoxin, warfarin, and phenytoin are all extensively protein-bound and are therefore not dialyzed effectively.

Molecular size • As mentioned, small molecules are effectively cleared because of a favorable diffusion coefficient. Therefore, potassium, urea, and water are easily removed with hemodialysis. As a molecule increases in size, its diffusibility decreases substantially. Magnesium, phosphorus, and proteins are poorly cleared by hemodialysis.

Answers • 1-B 2-C 3-C 4-A

● CASE PRESENTATION

A 55-year-old white man with no significant past medical history reports a 1-week history of facial and bilateral lower extremity swelling and abdominal discomfort. He also reports mild shortness of breath and pleuritic chest pain of 2 days' duration. These symptoms are improving. He denies tobacco or ethanol use.

On physical exam his blood pressure is 150/90, pulse is 100/min, respiratory rate is 24/min, and O_2 saturation on room air RA is 86% and 91% on 2 liter of O_2 by nasal cannula. Apart from slightly decreased air entry in the left lung base, cardiopulmonary exam is normal. Mild to moderate ascites is noted with minimal abdominal tenderness, and no other signs of chronic liver disease are noted. Bilateral pedal edema is present.

Laboratory data

Creatinine 1.4 mg/dL   Blood urea nitrogen (BUN) 20 mg/dL
Serum albumin 1.8 g/dL   Serum cholesterol 500 mg/dL
Other electrolytes and complete blood count (CBC) within normal limits
Cardiac enzymes normal
Arterial blood gas (ABG): pH 7.44, pCO_2 33 mm Hg, pO_2 60 mm Hg, O_2 saturation 88% on room air
Urinalysis 3+ protein
Prothrombin time (PT) and partial thromboplastin time (PTT) normal
Serologic result: negative antinuclear antibody (ANA) with normal complements
Hepatatitis profiles are negative
Chest x-ray result: blunting of left costophrenic angle and mild basal atelectasis; cardiac shadow is normal
Electrocardiogram (ECG): sinus tachycardia with right atrial enlargement

1. Which of the following characterizes nephrotic syndrome?
   A. Proteinuria
   B. Hyperlipidemia
   C. Hypoalbuminemia
   D. Peripheral edema
   E. All of the above

2. What is the most likely cause of this patient's nephrotic syndrome?
   A. Diabetic nephropathy
   B. Focal segmental glomerular sclerosis
   C. Membranous nephropathy (MN)
   D. Minimal change disease
   E. Lupus nephritis

3. Which of the following conditions can be a secondary cause of nephrotic syndrome?
   A. Diabetes mellitus
   B. Solid tumors
   C. Human immunodeficiency virus (HIV) infection
   D. Morbid obesity
   E. All of the above

4. What is the likely cause of shortness of breath in the patient?
   A. Congestive heart failure
   B. Pleura effusion
   C. Pneumothorax
   D. Pulmonary embolism (PE)
   E. Pericardial effusion

● COMMENT

Definition of nephrotic syndrome · Nephrotic syndrome (NS) is characterized by albuminuria (>3.5 g/day), hypoalbuminemia (<3.0 g/dL), and accompanying hyperlipidemia and edema. NS can be idiopathic or secondary to other systemic illnesses, drugs, or infections. Most cases are idiopathic glomerular diseases and require a kidney biopsy to make a definitive histologic diagnosis. Biopsy findings in idiopathic NS include minimal change disease (MCD), focal segmental glomerulosclerosis (FSGS), membranous nephropathy (MN), and membranoproliferative glomerulonephritis (MPGN).

Cause of idiopathic NS · Membranous nephropathy is the most common cause of idiopathic NS in adults and is the most likely cause in the patient described. MN is also the glomerulopathy most likely to be associated with thrombotic events and PE. FSGS disproportionately affects blacks; MCD is the most common cause of NS in children.

Secondary causes of NS · Infections, drugs, autoimmune diseases, and malignancies can all precipitate NS. Diabetes mellitus is the most common secondary cause of NS in the United States. Secondary causes of NS generally lead to one of the previously described histologic patterns except diabetes mellitus and amyloidosis. Drugs (particularly gold, penicillamine, and captopril), syphilis, hepatitis B, systemic lupus erythematosus (SLE), and solid tumors can lead to MN. Heroin abuse, HIV infection, morbid obesity, and sickle cell disease can precipitate FSGS. Hodgkin's disease and nonsteroidal anti-inflammatory drugs (NSAIDs) can lead to MCD. Some cases of membranoproliferative GN have been linked to hepatitis C infection.

Complications of NS · Complications of NS include anasarca, ascites, renal insufficiency, protein malnutrition, vitamin D deficiency, increased risk of atherosclerotic heart disease, and a hypercoagulable state with increased risk of thrombosis (especially renal vein thrombosis). This patient has most likely experienced a thrombotic event with subsequent PE. PE can result from venous thrombosis, including renal vein thrombosis, and should be suspected in cases of nephrotic syndrome with pulmonary signs or symptoms.

Answers · 1-E   2-C   3-E   4-D

● CASE PRESENTATION

A 49-year-old man enters your office describing moderate epigastric pain that has been getting progressively worse over several weeks. He has had similar pains in the past but never so severe. He describes the pain as a burning or gnawing pain without radiation. Pain is lessened by meals and over-the-counter antacids but "returns with a vengeance" 2 to 3 hours after meals. He is awakened by this pain at night at times and reports occasional nausea, bloating symptoms, and more frequent belching. He denies any weight loss. On exam he is tender in his epigastrium, and occult blood test (Hemoccult) yields a positive finding on digital rectal exam (DRE).

1. Risk factors for this patient's likely diagnosis do not include which of the following?
   A. Brother with ulcer disease
   B. Smoking history of 1 pack per day
   C. History of arthritis that requires high-dose ibuprofen
   D. History of three to four alcohol drinks per day
   E. Blood type O

2. Which of the following is the preferred diagnostic test in this patient?
   A. Serum blood test for *Helicobacter pylori*
   B. Esophagoduodenoscopy (EGD)
   C. Upper gastrointestinal (GI) series
   D. Abdominal computed tomography (CT) scan
   E. Trial of acid suppression medications

3. The most common cause of this condition is which of the following?
   A. Nonsteroidal anti-inflammatory drug (NSAID) therapy
   B. Zollinger-Ellison syndrome
   C. Tobacco abuse
   D. *Helicobacter pylori* infection
   E. None of the above (idiopathic)

4. Which of the following supports the diagnosis of Zollinger-Ellison syndrome (ZE)?
   A. Multiple ulcers in unusual locations
   B. Peptic ulcer disease (PUD) associated with steatorrhea or diarrhea
   C. Paradoxical increase in gastrin after intravenous (IV) secretin
   D. Ulcer disease refractory to medical therapy
   E. All of the above

● COMMENT

Risk factors for PUD • This patient has the classic symptoms of a duodenal ulcer. Classically gastric ulcers worsen with ingestion of food and less often have nocturnal symptoms. PUD usually results from one of four underlying causes: *Helicobacter pylori*, NSAIDs, high acid output states, or Crohn's disease of the stomach or duodenum. A family history of first-degree relatives and blood type O (bound preferentially by *H. pylori*) are risk factors, but spicy diet, personality type, occupation, and alcohol are not. Tobacco use increases the morbidity rate, decreases healing, and increases the recurrence rate.

Diagnosis • The diagnostic procedure of choice in nonperforated ulcer is EGD. An upper gastrointestinal (UGI) series is equally specific but less sensitive and does not allow biopsy or CLO testing for *H. pylori*. Complications of PUD include bleeding (5% require surgery; most are treated with EGD), obstruction (25% require surgery), perforation, and penetration that causes pancreatitis (requires surgery). Nonhealing, large, or irregular gastric ulcers should be biopsied and endoscopy should be repeated in 8 weeks after therapy.

Helicobacter pylori • *H. pylori* is a microaerophilic gram-negative organism thought to be the most common cause of PUD. It is believed to cause 80% to 85% of duodenal ulcers in the United States. The lifetime risk of PUD when infected with *H. pylori* is 15%. If it is successfully treated, *H. pylori* and ulcers rarely recur. It is found in the mucous layer above the gastric antral epithelium. Histologic exam or culture of biopsy is the gold standard for diagnosis but has low sensitivity. Serologic testing only indicates exposure. Urease tests allow detection of active disease by using a radiolabeled breath test or a CLO test with urea medium with a pH marker (requires biopsy of gastric mucosa). Treatment should consist of at least two appropriate antibiotics and acid suppression with a protein pump inhibitor (PPI preferred).

Zollinger-Ellison syndrome • ZE is a rare triad that refers to a non-beta-cell-islet cell tumor that produces gastrin, causing increased gastric acid secretion that results in severe ulcer disease. This syndrome should be suspected in refractory PUD, with multiple ulcers, if ulcers are in unusual locations, or if ulcer disease is associated with diarrhea or steatorrhea (due to malabsorption from increased acidification of duodenal contents). ZE is the cause of less than 1% of PUD and is associated with multiple endocrine neoplasia type 1 (20% of cases). ZE is diagnosed by elevated fasting gastrin levels, elevated acid output or paradoxical increase in gastrin after administration of secretin, or absence of an increase in gastrin after a standard meal. ZE should be treated aggressively with surgery if the tumor is localized or with high-dose PPI and/or octreotide for symptoms.

Answers • 1-D 2-B 3-D 4-E

● CASE PRESENTATION

A 36-year-old man enters your office with a cough and mild wheezing, which have been present for about 2 months but increasing in severity and frequency. He tells you that these symptoms are worse at night and occasionally wake him from sleep. He denies any history of asthma but does have frequent heartburn. He has not seen a physician for more than 10 years and has no family history of respiratory illnesses. Exam reveals normal vital signs and unremarkable findings. Chest x-ray findings are unremarkable.

1. What diagnostic maneuver should be performed initially in assessing this patient's symptoms?
   A. Pulmonary function testing
   B. Chest computed tomography (CT)
   C. Endoscopy
   D. Bernstein test
   E. Therapeutic trial of H_2 receptor antagonist or protein pump inhibitor (PPI)

2. Common manifestations of gastroesophageal reflux disease (GERD) can include which of the following?
   A. Retrosternal chest pain
   B. Heartburn
   C. Regurgitation
   D. Dysphagia
   E. All of the above

3. Initial treatment of GERD is:
   A. H_2 receptor antagonist for most patients
   B. Life-style modifications alone
   C. Proton pump inhibitors for most patients
   D. Over-the-counter antacids
   E. Dependent on severity and frequency of symptoms

4. Chronic GERD requires monitoring for which premalignant syndrome?
   A. Barrett's esophagus
   B. Squamous dysplasia of the esophagus
   C. *Helicobacter pylori*–associated gastritis
   D. Schatzki's ring
   E. Peptic stricture

● COMMENT

Diagnosis • It is neither necessary nor practical to initiate a diagnostic evaluation of every patient with heartburn. Mild to moderate GERD is usually treated empirically with life-style modifications and acid-reducing agents. Endoscopy is warranted when heartburn is refractory to medical management or accompanied by dysphagia or odynophagia or there is evidence of gastrointestinal (GI) bleeding. The absence of endoscopic findings does not exclude GERD. Ambulatory pH monitoring can be useful in the evaluation of patients with atypical reflux symptoms or those who do not respond to a trial of antireflux therapy. A pH probe is placed in the lower esophagus, to monitor acid reflux events and to correlate acid exposure to clinical symptoms.

GERD symptoms • The most common symptoms associated with GERD are heartburn (often retrosternal), regurgitation, and dysphagia, often temporally related to meals or bedtime. Respiratory symptoms mimicking asthma are often unrecognized as GERD-related. It is thought that esophageal irritation leads to bronchoconstriction, which is manifested as chronic cough and wheezing. Treatment with acid-reducing drugs and life-style modifications often eliminate the respiratory symptoms. GERD can also cause chest pressure and pain that can be confused with cardiac ischemia.

Treatment • Avoiding meals several hours before bedtime and foods that reduce lower esophageal sphincter tone (chocolate, alcohol, fatty foods, etc.) is an important adjunct to medical management. Raising the head of one's bed with bricks or blocks also can aid in symptom relief. Antacids give immediate relief but are usually inadequate except in the mildest cases. Histamine (H_2) antagonists and proton pump inhibitors are now the mainstay in medical management of GERD with the goal of increasing gastric pH to greater than 4. Patients with severe, chronic GERD not controlled medically are candidates for antireflux surgery.

Barrett's esophagus • Chronic or refractory GERD also warrants screening for evidence of Barrett's esophagus, a premalignant metaplasia of the gastroesophageal junction caused by chronic acid exposure. Barrett's esophagus is determined by pathologic examination; it indicates increased risk of adenocarcinoma of the esophagus. It is increasing in frequency for unclear reasons.

● CASE PRESENTATION

A 35-year-old white man arrives at his primary care physician with progressive difficulties in swallowing solids and liquids over a 1-year period. The patient notes a 10-pound weight loss, heartburn, chest pain, and frequent regurgitation of undigested food. On further questioning, the patient reports dyspepsia associated with difficulty belching. He states that he must eat more slowly in order to have adequate oral intake. Physical examination findings are normal. Chest x-ray reveals a widened mediastinum and absence of the gastric air bubble.

1. Which of the following is a true statement regarding dysphagia?
   A. Mechanical obstruction of esophagus is initially accompanied by dysphagia for liquids.
   B. Motility disorders present with dysphagia for liquids and solids.
   C. Oropharyngeal dysphagia is seldom associated with nasopharyngeal regurgitation.
   D. History is not typically helpful in diagnosing dysphagia.
   E. Esophageal cancer patients usually report less weight loss than patients with other types of obstruction.

2. Which of the following is a cause of esophageal dysphagia?
   A. Scleroderma
   B. Peptic stricture
   C. Lower esophageal rings
   D. Achalasia
   E. All of the above

3. Which of the following is the best initial test for the patient described?
   A. Barium swallow
   B. 24-hour pH probe
   C. Manometry
   D. Endoscopy
   E. Computed tomography (CT) chest scan

4. The patient has a barium swallow, which reveals abnormal esophageal motility and a "bird beak" narrowing. Manometry reveals aperistalsis and decreased relaxation of the lower esophageal sphincter. What is the most likely diagnosis?
   A. Lower esophageal ring
   B. Achalasia
   C. Scleroderma
   D. Squamous cell esophageal cancer
   E. Peptic stricture

● COMMENT

Clinical history • History can suggest the cause of dysphagia in the majority of cases. Dysphagia is loosely divided into mechanical obstructions and motility disorders. Mechanical dysphagia is due to intrinsic obstruction or external compression of the esophagus and is initially heralded by dysphagia for solids. Motility disorders commonly include dysphagia for liquids and solids. Oropharyngeal dysphagia involves difficulty in initiating swallowing, and nasopharyngeal regurgitation is common. Weight loss out of proportion to the difficulty in swallowing is classically associated with malignancy.

Esophageal dysphagia • Mechanical causes of esophageal dysphagia include lower esophageal rings, peptic strictures, injuries from toxins (lye or radiation), and esophageal carcinoma. Motor or motility disorders leading to esophageal dysphagia include achalasia, diffuse esophageal spasm, and scleroderma.

Evaluation of dysphagia • Patients who have a clinical history suggestive of achalasia require radiographic, manometric, and endoscopic evaluation to confirm the diagnosis. Barium swallow is typically used as the primary screening test and reveals a dilated esophagus that terminates in a typical "bird beak" narrowing. Manometry is required for confirmation and endoscopy is recommended to exclude malignancies at the gastroesophageal junction that may mimic achalasia (pseudoachalasia).

Achalasia • Achalasia is a disease of unknown cause that results from the degeneration of ganglion cells in the myenteric plexus in the esophageal wall. Therefore, there is loss of peristalsis in the distal esophagus and failure of relaxation of the lower esophageal sphincter. The symptom most characteristic of achalasia is dysphagia to liquids. Other symptoms include dysphagia to solids, difficulty in belching, weight loss, regurgitation, chest pain, heartburn, and hiccups. These symptoms are due primarily to failure of lower esophageal sphincter relaxation, which leads to a functional obstruction that persists until the pressure generated by the sphincter muscle is exceeded by the pressure of the retained material. The three characteristic manometric features are elevated resting lower esophageal sphincter pressure, incomplete lower esophageal sphincter relaxation, and aperistalsis. Those with achalasia have a substantially increased risk for the development of squamous cell esophageal cancer. The management of this disorder is aimed at its treatment, as there is no therapy that can reverse or impede its process. It appears that laparoscopic myotomy is generally superior for both the short- and long-term relief of dysphagia. Pneumatic balloon dilation also provides good short-term results. Botulinum toxin injections are less likely to produce a durable response.

Answers • 1-B 2-E 3-A 4-B

● CASE PRESENTATION

A 32-year-old white woman arrives at your office reporting abdominal pain for the past 4 months that is relieved with defecation. At defecation, the patient has straining and incomplete evacuation. She notes watery stools with mucus. She denies a history of weight loss, fever, or rectal bleeding. On exam, the patient is afebrile with stable vital signs. Mucous membranes are moist. Conjunctivae are pink. Heart sounds are regular. Abdominal exam reveals a soft abdomen with normoactive bowel sounds. Voluntary guarding is diffuse. No rebound or rigidity is noted.

1. Work-up for this patient should include which of the following?
   A. Complete blood count (CBC)
   B. Erythrocyte sedimentation rate (ESR)
   C. Stool studies
   D. Flexible sigmoidoscopy
   E. All of the above

2. Which of the following makes a diagnosis of irritable bowel syndrome more likely?
   A. Nocturnal symptoms
   B. Mucus in stool
   C. Fever
   D. Bright red blood per rectum
   E. All of the above

3. This condition may improve with avoidance of which of the following?
   A. Chewing gum
   B. Caffeine
   C. Lactose
   D. Carbonated beverages
   E. All of the above

4. Which of the following therapies may improve this condition?
   A. Dietary modification
   B. Psychosocial therapies
   C. Serotonin receptor antagonists
   D. Anticholinergic agents
   E. All of the above

● COMMENT

Irritable bowel syndrome (IBS) diagnosis • IBS is characterized by altered bowel habits with or without abdominal pain in the absence of organic disease (diagnosis of exclusion). The Rome criteria provide the best definition: 1) at least 3 months of continuous or recurrent abdominal pain or discomfort relieved by defecation or associated with a change in the consistency or frequency of stool and 2) two of the following that occur at least 25% of the time: altered stool frequency, altered stool form, altered stool passage, passage of mucus, and bloating or distention. In the United States, 9% to 22% of the population reports symptoms that would be diagnostic of IBS. A reasonable diagnostic approach involves a careful history and physical, ruling out occult blood loss; checking of nonspecific markers for inflammation (ESR); stool studies to rule out chronic infection (such as *Giardia* sp. infection); and consideration of colonic imaging.

Clinical features of IBS • The intensity, location, and timing of the abdominal pain are highly variable in patients with IBS. Abdominal pain in IBS may be exacerbated by meal ingestion or by stress and relieved by defecation or flatus. Significant weight loss and malnutrition are rare, as are nocturnal symptoms. Patients display alterations in bowel function that include constipation, diarrhea, or constipation alternating with diarrhea. Patients with constipation-predominant IBS report stools that are hard or pelletlike. Stools are loose and frequent but of normal daily volume in those with diarrhea-predominant IBS. The passage of blood, nocturnal diarrhea, malabsorption, or weight loss warrants an aggressive approach for organic disease. High incidences of dysfunction of the genitourinary organs, fibromyalgia, low back pain, fatigue, headaches, and insomnia have been reported with IBS.

Management and course of IBS • The physician should impart awareness that IBS is a functional disorder without long-term health risks. Patients should try to avoid gum, breath mints, and carbonated beverages and possibly limit dairy products as these may worsen symptoms. This sole approach is sufficient in 25% of the cases. The other 75% receive various trials and combinations of medications as no medication has proven therapeutic value. Constipation-predominant IBS should be managed by increasing stool water and bulk with bran, psyllium, methylcellulose, or osmotic laxatives. Diarrhea-predominant IBS treatment focuses on improving stool consistency by reducing stool frequency and urgency with opiate agents, antispasmodic agents, serotonin antagonists, and tricyclic antidepressants. The area of focused pharmacologic research involves agents that reduce visceral hypersensitivity. Psychotherapy, biofeedback, and hypnosis have been reserved for patients with clear dysfunctional behavior.

Answers • 1-E 2-B 3-E 4-E

● CASE PRESENTATION

A 17-year-old woman is taken to your office by her mother for evaluation of diarrhea. You notice that the patient seems withdrawn and her mother answers most of your questions. The mother reports that the patient has had increased frequency of defecation for the past several months with estimates of six to eight bowel movements today. When directed questions are asked of the patient, she states that she thinks her mother is overreacting and she does not feel that she has a problem. On physical exam, you find a thin body habitus, parotid enlargement, and evidence of enamel erosion on inspection of her oral cavity. Remainder of her exam yields essentially normal findings.

1. Chronic diarrhea is:
   A. A relatively rare disorder with a limited differential diagnosis
   B. Defined as the production of loose stools with or without increased stool frequency for more than 4 weeks
   C. Not associated with infectious causes
   D. Improved with abstinence from food
   E. All of the above

2. Your approach to this patient should begin with which of the following?
   A. 72-hour quantitative stool collection and analysis
   B. Colonoscopy
   C. Therapeutic trial of metronidazole
   D. Computed tomography of abdomen
   E. Careful history that includes exploration of the patient's body image and possible laxative use

3. Which of the following stool tests best classifies a diarrhea as secretory or osmotic in nature?
   A. Quantitative fecal fat determination
   B. Fecal leukocytes
   C. Determination of fecal osmotic gap
   D. Laxative screening
   E. None of the above

4. Which of the following could indicate fat malabsorption?
   A. Prolonged prothrombin time
   B. Steatorrhea
   C. Low beta-carotene level
   D. Low vitamin D level
   E. All of the above

● COMMENT

Definition of chronic diarrhea • There is a wide range of normal bowel movement patterns, from three per day to three per week. Diarrhea is an increase in frequency, amount, volume, or fluidity of stool. Normal is less than 200 g/day of stool. The American Gastroenterologic Association (AGA) defines chronic diarrhea as the production of loose stool with or without increased stool frequency for more than 4 weeks. It is a common malady and has a broad differential diagnosis.

Initial approach • The initial approach to all chronic diarrheas should consist of a thorough history and physical examination. The characteristics of onset, pattern, and duration should be identified. The presence of abdominal pain, significant weight loss, as well as aggravating and mitigating factors should be elicited. A history of malingering or suspicion of an eating disorder warrants laxative screening. A review of prescription and nonprescription drug use may yield a causative agent. The most important conclusion to draw from the physical exam is the extent of fluid and nutritional depletion. This patient has definitive evidence of an eating disorder and it is imperative to explore her body image.

Diagnostic evaluation • If a specific diagnosis is not obvious, quantitative stool collection or spot stool collection can yield important objective information about the type of diarrhea and its severity. In addition to stool weight, the following six groups of studies should be done to classify the diarrhea as watery (either secretory or osmotic), inflammatory, or fatty and narrow the differential.

— Stool sodium and potassium concentrations are measured and fecal osmotic gap calculated. Osmotic diarrheas are characterized by gaps greater than 125 mOsm/kg, whereas secretory diarrheas typically have gaps less than 50 mOsm/kg. Stool osmotic gap = $290 - 2([Na^+] + [K^+])$.

— Stool pH less than 5.6 is consistent with carbohydrate malabsorption.

— Positive fecal occult blood test results suggest presence of inflammatory bowel syndrome, neoplastic disease, or celiac sprue or other spruelike syndromes.

— Presence of fecal white blood cells can suggest inflammatory diarrhea.

— Excess stool fat (>14 g/24 hr) suggests malabsorption or maldigestion. Stool fat concentrations greater than 8% strongly suggest pancreatic exocrine insufficiency.

— Laxative screening should be performed.

Fat malabsorption • Fat malabsorption leads to floating, malodorous stools known as *steatorrhea*. It also leads to decreased absorption of vitamins A, D, E, and K. Beta-carotene is a metabolite of vitamin A, and the prothrombin time can be prolonged in vitamin K deficiency.

Answers • 1-B   2-E   3-C   4-E

● CASE PRESENTATION

A 21-year-old woman arrives at your office with colicky abdominal pain, intermittent nonbloody diarrhea, anorexia, and 21-pound weight loss over the past year. She has had increasing fatigue and bloating. Her diarrhea has been characterized by excretion of loose stools with mucus up to 10 times per day. Her estranged father had "some kind of bowel disease." On exam, she is a thin young woman with a pulse of 104/min that increases to 118/min on standing and is febrile, with a temperature of 101.2 F. She has dry mucous membranes and a palpable right lower quadrant (RLQ) mass on abdominal exam. A complete blood count (CBC) shows white blood cell (WBC) count of 9.4 K/cumm (normal: 4.8-10.8 K/cumm) with hypersegmented polymorphonuclear leukocytes; hematocrit (HCT) of 31%; mean corpuscular volume (MCV) of 99 fL; platelets of 556 K/cumm (normal: 140-440 K/cumm); normal electrolytes and liver enzymes except a decreased albumin level of 2.1g/dL; iron studies are consistent with iron deficiency; prothrombin time (PT) is 14 seconds.

1. What should be done first for the patient?

    A. Barium enema to rule out malignant lesion
    B. Azathioprine to control inflammatory response
    C. 0.9% NaCl solution for volume resuscitation
    D. Intravenous injections of iron and B_{12} to correct anemia
    E. Nasogastric tube for emergent enteral nutrition

2. Which of the following features characterizes Crohn's disease (CD)?

    A. Alternating areas of normal mucosa and linear ulcerations and cobblestoning
    B. Focal granulomas
    C. Inflammation limited to the mucosa with microabscesses of crypts of Lieberkühn
    D. Stricture formation with resultant obstruction
    E. All of the above

3. Which feature of ulcerative colitis increases the risk of development of colon carcinoma?

    A. Diagnosis more than 10 years ago
    B. History of toxic megacolon
    C. Pseudopolyps indicated by previous colonoscopy
    D. High steroid requirements for control of disease
    E. Finding of elevated alkaline phosphatase and liver biopsy result consistent with primary sclerosing cholangitis (PSC)

4. Which extraintestinal complications of inflammatory bowel disease (IBD) are least likely associated with ulcerative colitis?

    A. Rheumatoid factor–negative arthritis
    B. Pyoderma gangrenosum
    C. Primary sclerosing cholangitis
    D. Uveitis
    E. Calcium oxalate nephrolithiasis

● COMMENT

Crohn's disease (Table 3) • CD or regional enteritis is a chronic inflammatory disease of the gastrointestinal (GI) mucosa that occurs in any area from the mouth to the anus, but usually involves the terminal ileum and colon. It is lumped in the category of IBD with ulcerative colitis (UC) because they share some clinical features but differ in many respects as well. Both have a familial association and both are associated with an increased risk of colon cancer, although much less for Crohn's disease than for UC. In CD patients 40% have involvement of the small bowel, 30% of the colon alone, and 30% of both areas. There is a bimodal distribution of initial age of presentation: most occur between 12 to 30 years, and a second smaller peak occurs later in life. Incidence has been increasing. CD is a more indolent disease than UC and therefore less responsive to therapy. Because CD may affect the ileum and UC only involves the colon, complications associated with poor absorption in the ileum such as calcium oxalate kidney stones, cholesterol gallstones, B_{12} deficiency, hypocalcemia (vitamin D malabsorption), and bile acid–associated diarrhea are seen only in CD. Smoking affects both UC and CD but in different ways. In CD smokers are more likely to experience disease, whereas in UC, stopping may precipitate symptoms. Patients tend to have flares and remissions with colicky pain, systemic symptoms of fever, weight loss, anorexia, diarrhea (often without blood), anorectal fissures, fistulas, and abscesses. Diagnosis is by endoscopy with biopsies. Barium studies are contraindicated in acute flares because of the serious risk of toxic megacolon. Infectious causes should be ruled out as they may mimic IBS clinically and endoscopically. Acute flares should be treated with steroids or mesalamine preparations. Immune modulators such as azathioprine and 6-mercaptopurine require several months to affect disease but may be used to spare the patient from long-term steroids. Metronidazole and fluoroquinolones may be effective in perianal and fistulous disease. Recently the anti–tumor necrosis factor drug infliximab has shown great efficacy in patients with moderate to severe disease. Surgery is generally not curative and should be reserved for only severe complications.

Ulcerative colitis (Table 3) • UC is limited to the colon. It has a stronger bimodal distribution of initial presentation with the first peak between 15 to 30 years of age and the second at around 60 years. UC has a much higher risk of colon cancer than CD. This risk increases with duration of disease and extent of disease from rectum but not with severity of disease. All patients require scheduled colonoscopies after 10 years of disease activity to monitor for dysplasia. Of UC patients 30% have disease limited to proctitis, 50% have involvement of only the left colon, and 20% have pancolitis. UC more often occurs with bloody diarrhea and tenesmus than CD but has similar constitutional symptoms and extraintestinal symptoms, such as peripheral arthritis, sacroiliitis, erythema nodosum, pyoderma gangrenosum, uveitis, pericholangitis, and PSC. Uveitis and PSC are independent of disease activity, but other symptoms usually correlate. Alkaline phosphatase should be checked periodically to monitor for development of PSC. Treatment is similar to that of CD with steroids and salicylate preparations for acute flares and immunomodulators for prolonged therapy. Sulfasalazine and olsalazine require colonic bacteria to cleave bonds to be effective, and so they only work in the colon. Steroids may be given systemically or locally when disease is limited to the descending colon. Surgery is considered curative in UC and should be considered for patients with dysplasia on biopsy.

Answers • 1-C 2-E 3-A 4-E

TABLE 3

	Crohn's Disease	Ulcerative Colitis
Symptoms	More abdominal pain, less bloody diarrhea	More diarrhea with blood-mucus discharge, cramping
Location of involvement	Mouth to anus	Colon
Pattern of involvement	Skip lesions, normal mucosa between abnormal areas	Uniform continuous involvement from rectum with sharp margin
Histology characteristics	Transmural, granulomas, focal ulceration, cobblestone mucosa	Mucosal inflammation, crypt microabscesses, crypt distortion, diffuse inflammation
Radiographic findings	Terminal ileum involvement, deep ulcerations (Crohn's craters), normal haustra between lesions, strictures, fistulas, perianal disease with rectal sparing, inflammatory masses and abscesses, obstructions, string sign on small bowel follow through	Rectal involvement, shortened colon lead-pipe sign (no haustra), pseudopolyps, shallow ulcerations
Usual course of disease	More indolent	More acute
Tobacco effect	Exacerbates	? Protective

● CASE PRESENTATION

A 44-year-old African-American man with a history of heavy alcohol abuse enters the emergency room with nausea and vomiting, anorexia, and severe midepigastric abdominal pain. The patient states that he has had these symptoms for the past day. During this time, he has had no oral intake. He does note that he has had similar problems on two other occasions. On exam, the patient is uncomfortable and cannot lie still. His blood pressure is 110/60 with a pulse of 101/min. He is afebrile. The patient is orthostatic and has dry mucous membranes. His abdomen has hypoactive bowel sounds and is soft with voluntary guarding and midepigastric tenderness. Serum amylase and lipase levels are elevated suggesting pancreatitis.

1. Causes of this condition include which of the following?
   A. Ethanol
   B. Thiazide diuretics
   C. Trauma
   D. Hypercalcemia
   E. All of the above

2. True statements about the clinical presentation of this condition include which of the following?
   A. Midepigastric pain almost always heralds its onset.
   B. Patients generally prefer to remain perfectly still.
   C. Patients are generally more comfortable when recumbent.
   D. Diminished bowel sounds usually herald a surgical emergency.
   E. All of the above

3. Which of the following is not a complication of this condition?
   A. Necrosis
   B. Abscesses
   C. Acute respiratory distress syndrome (ARDS)
   D. Splenic vein thrombosis
   E. Hypercalcemia

4. Critical immediate therapy for this patient includes which of the following?
   A. Aggressive volume repletion
   B. Clear liquid diet
   C. Antibiotics
   D. Emergency endoscopic retrograde cholangiopancreatography (ERCP)
   E. All of the above

● COMMENT

Risk factors for acute pancreatitis • Gallstones and biliary sludge induce pancreatitis through transient obstruction of the main pancreatic duct. Ethanol induces pancreatitis by the following mechanisms: ductule obstruction by secreted protein concretions, altered fluidity of the pancreatic cell membrane, induced hypertriglyceridemia, and duct obstruction by an abnormally functioning sphincter of Oddi. Most patients with ethanol-induced pancreatitis have underlying chronic pancreatitis. This is consistent with the occurrence of an initial pancreatitis attack after years of significant alcohol intake. Chronic pancreatitis develops in only 5% of heavy drinkers. Blunt abdominal trauma can cause acute pancreatitis, as can manipulation of the pancreatic duct during ERCP. Other causes of acute pancreatitis include medications such as thiazides and hypercalcemia.

Clinical features • A boring visceral midepigastric abdominal pain is almost always the initial symptom of acute pancreatitis. It often radiates to the middle to lower back. Frequently, patients are restless and cannot remain still. Many patients sit leaning forward in an effort to minimize abdominal discomfort. Nausea and vomiting are almost always present. High fevers and rigors suggest coexistent infection. Bowel sounds can be diminished as a result of a superimposed ileus. Hypovolemia and hypotension result from the extravasation of fluids or from hemorrhage into the retroperitoneum. Rare patients with hemorrhagic necrosis experience periumbilical (Cullen's sign) or flank (Grey Turner's sign) ecchymoses. Jaundice, hepatomegaly, ascites, and encephalopathy may also be discovered.

Complications • Severe pancreatitis may cause peripancreatic fluid collections or pancreatic necrosis in the first 1 to 2 weeks. Either of these complications may become infected. Pseudocysts develop in 10% of patients. Pseudocysts may cause pain by compressing adjacent organs or by causing erosion into the mediastinum. Persistent (>6 weeks), large (>5 to 6 cm) pseudocysts or rapidly enlarging pseudocysts should be drained surgically, endoscopically, or percutaneously. Mild hypoxia is present in most patients with acute pancreatitis. Left-sided pleural effusions are often seen on chest x-ray. Other systemic complications include stress gastritis, ARDS, renal failure, splenic vein thrombosis, fat necrosis, and hypocalcemia.

Treatment • Initial treatment of acute pancreatitis involves aggressive fluid resuscitation. Patients are generally not allowed to eat or drink until symptoms improve, and persistent nausea and vomiting can be treated with nasogastric suctioning. Narcotics are often required for pain control. Complications are managed as noted.

Answers • 1-E 2-A 3-E 4-A

● CASE PRESENTATION

A 62-year old man enters the emergency room with a several-month history of progressive dyspnea, bilateral leg edema, increasing abdominal girth, and fatigue. He reports that he is now having a difficult time walking to the other end of his trailer without stopping to catch his breath. He denies chest pain, tobacco use, melena, and hematochezia but does report a 10-year history of hypertension, mild diabetes and drinking two to three beers per day. He reports a family history of diabetes, alcohol use, and liver disease. Physical exam reveals a tachypneic man in mild respiratory distress, crackles in bilateral lung fields, S_4 at apex, spider angiomas over the upper chest, hepatomegaly, shifting dullness on abdominal exam, testicular atrophy, and 3+ edema of bilateral legs. Lab results are hematocrit (HCT) of 43% (normal: 42-52%), platelets of 119K/cumm (normal: 140-440), aspartate aminotransferase (AST) of 56 Iμ/L (normal: 12-38), alanine aminotransferase (ALT) of 42 Iμ/L (normal: 10-45), glucose of 174 mg/dL, iron of 245 mg/dL (normal: 50 to 150), ferritin of 1193 ng/mL (normal: 20 to 400), and transferrin saturation of 84%.

1. The proposed mechanism of iron accumulation in this disorder is:
   A. Decreased elimination of iron to sweat glands due to lack of transporter
   B. Increased iron release from hemolysed blood and secondary deposition
   C. Increased intake of iron in Western diets
   D. Increased intake of iron due to drinking beer that is brewed in iron pots
   E. Increased iron absorption by mucosal cells in the small bowel

2. Which of these bacteria is associated with an increased infection rate in this iron overload state?
   A. *Vibrio vulnificus*
   B. *Listeria monocytogenes*
   C. *Yersinia enterocolitica*
   D. *Pasteurella pseudotuberculosis*
   E. All of the above

3. Most patients now diagnosed with hereditary hemochromatosis (HHC) are screened because:
   A. They display the features of cirrhosis.
   B. They are screened and found to have a hemachromatos (HFE) gene mutation after a relative was diagnosed with hereditary hemachromatosis (HHC).
   C. They are screened for the HFE gene after being diagnosed with diabetes.
   D. They are found to have an elevated iron level or ferritin level on routine lab tests.
   E. They are found to have an elevated hematocrit on routine complete blood count (CBC).

4. Which of the following statements regarding HHC is incorrect?
   A. There is increased risk of hepatocellular carcinoma.
   B. Younger onset and more severe disease occurs in men.
   C. Treatment of choice is chelation with deferoxamine.
   D. Calcium pyrophosphate crystal arthropathy is common.
   E. In the United States 1 in 10 whites is a carrier of an abnormal HFE gene.

● COMMENT

Cause of iron overload • HHC, also called *genetic hemochromatosis*, is the genetic cause of increased iron deposition into end organs. HHC is an autosomal recessive disorder of the HFE gene that causes an increased intestinal absorption of dietary iron. Iron absorption is two to three times that of normal persons, leading to an accumulation of 1 to 2 g/yr.

Clinical manifestations • Iron accumulates and is deposited in the liver, heart, pancreas, pituitary, synovium, skin, thyroid, and adrenal glands, causing eventual fibrosis and organ failure, which may result in cirrhosis, bronze or gray skin hyperpigmentation, secondary diabetes, arthropathy, dilated cardiomyopathy, cardiac arrhythmia, or secondary hypogonadism/testicular atrophy. Symptoms include weakness, fatigue, loss of libido, and congestive heart failure (CHF) symptoms. Hepatomegaly occurs in 95% of patients. Patients are at higher risk for infection with *Vibrio* spp. and the other "iron-loving" gram-negative organisms noted in question 2. HHC was previously thought to be a rare disorder, but more recent screening has shown that the gene defect is very common in whites. Symptoms usually are not manifested until 20 g of iron has accumulated, so patients generally seek medical attention after age 40. Women tend to be affected later in life because of iron losses associated with menses. Cirrhotic HHC patients are at very high risk for hepatocellular carcinoma.

Diagnosis of HHC • Classically the triad of hyperpigmentation, diabetes, and liver disease led to the diagnosis. Now the diagnosis is most often made after abnormal results of iron studies on routine lab work. The elevation of serum iron and ferritin levels and percent saturation of transferrin suggest the diagnosis, but evaluating a liver biopsy finding and quantifying the amount of iron seen make the definitive diagnosis. In HHC iron is seen in both the Kupffer cells and hepatocytes, unlike in acquired iron overload states, where iron only accumulates in Kupffer cells. In special circumstances with normal liver enzyme results, no hepatomegaly, and positive HFE homozygosity with a ferritin level less than 1000, liver biopsy may not be necessary. Family members of an HHC patient should be screened for the disease with iron studies and HFE gene testing.

Treatment • Phlebotomy to remove excess iron is the definitive treatment for HHC. Since 1 unit of blood contains only about 250 mg of iron, phlebotomies should be done weekly until anemia develops or iron and ferritin levels normalize. Iron chelators are usually not effective in reducing the iron stores to sufficient levels. Treatment early in disease can improve pigmentation, cardiac disease, and life expectancy but usually does not improve secondary sex characteristics. Patients should be instructed to avoid raw shellfish to prevent infection from *Vibrio* spp. Liver transplantation should be considered for cirrhotic patients.

Answers • 1-E   2-E   3-D   4-C

● CASE PRESENTATION

A 52-year-old white man with a history of chronic alcohol abuse, previous alcohol withdrawal seizures, and cirrhosis is taken by ambulance to the emergency room with altered mental status. He is somnolent and lethargic, but arousable. On arousal, the patient has diffuse abdominal pain. He is unable to offer further history. On exam, blood pressure is 96/51 with a pulse of 92/min. Temperature is 99.7 F. The patient is mildly jaundiced and physically wasted. Scleral icterus is noted. Multiple blanching red lesions are noted on his upper chest. Bilateral gynecomastia is noted. The abdomen is diffusely tender and distended with guarding and mild rebound. Shifting dullness is noted along with hepatosplenomegaly. Extremities have 3+ pitting edema. Kernig's and Brudzinski's signs are negative. The patient does have asterixis. Computed tomography (CT) of the head is unrevealing.

1. Which of the following can precipitate a bout of hepatic encephalopathy in a cirrhotic patient?

   A. Hepatocellular carcinoma
   B. Spontaneous bacterial peritonitis
   C. Dietary or medical noncompliance
   D. Gastrointestinal (GI) bleeding
   E. All of the above

2. Which of the following is likely true regarding this patient's ascites?

   A. The serum albumin gradient (SAG) is likely greater than 1.1.
   B. The high protein character of the ascites predisposes to spontaneous bacterial peritonitis (SBP).
   C. Initial treatment of ascites involves portosystemic shunting.
   D. Ascites is largely a cosmetic problem.
   E. All of the above

3. You suspect SBP. Which of the following should the patient receive on admission?

   A. Paracentesis
   B. Lactulose therapy
   C. Benzodiazepine therapy
   D. Intravenous antibiotics after obtaining appropriate cultures
   E. All of the above

4. A review of the patient's records reveals evidence of esophageal varices on prior endoscopy. Which of the following is useful in preventing bleeding from esophageal varices?

   A. Beta-blockers
   B. Spironolactone
   C. Loop diuretics
   D. Lactulose
   E. All of the above

● COMMENT

Hepatic encephalopathy • New-onset hepatic encephalopathy or acute decompensation of chronic hepatic encephalopathy should always prompt a search for precipitating causes. In addition to providing therapy specific to hepatic encephalopathy, the physician should attempt to correct the precipitating causes. These common causes include electrolyte disturbances, malignancy, infection, constipation, medical noncompliance, dietary noncompliance, gastrointestinal bleeding, and new-onset renal insufficiency. Therapy is directed at altering the colonic bacterial milieu because many of the responsible neurotoxins are produced by the intestinal flora. Lactulose is first-line therapy and is titrated to two to three soft stools per day.

Ascites • This patient's ascites is likely due to portal hypertension and is a serious complication of chronic liver disease. The serum albumin gradient (SAG) is the difference between the serum albumin and the albumin in the ascitic fluid and allows one to identify when ascites is due to portal hypertension. If this difference is greater than or equal to 1.1, then ascites is due to portal hypertension. This low-protein ascites is a risk factor for SBP. Treatment of ascites includes paracentesis, loop diuretics, and spironolactone. Refractory ascites can be treated with a transjugular intrahepatic portosystemic shunting procedure (TIPS).

Evaluation of the patient • The patient definitely should have diagnostic paracentesis to rule out SBP and consideration should also be given to lactulose therapy for encephalopathy, benzodiazepine therapy (delirium tremens [DT] prophylaxis), and antibiotic therapy. SBP is defined as growth of a single organism in ascitic fluid with a neutrophil count greater than 250 cells/μL without a surgically remediable intra-abdominal cause. For practical purposes, SBP occurs in the setting of liver disease and ascites is a prerequisite. *Escherichia coli*, *Klebsiella pneumoniae*, and *Pneumococcus* spp. are the most common isolates in SBP. Most patients have fever, abdominal pain, and altered mental status. Antibiotics should be started when the absolute neutrophil count of the ascitic fluid is greater than 250 cells/μL. The most common antibiotic treatment for SBP is the third-generation cephalosporin cefotaxime.

Esophageal varices • Another complication of portal hypertension are esophageal varices. Varices can lead to massive, life-threatening gastrointestinal (GI) bleeding. In patients with known esophageal varices, nonselective beta-blockers (propanolol or nadolol) can be given to help prevent initial bleeding or to decrease the chances of rebleeding. Endoscopic band ligation (preferred) or sclerotherapy can be useful for acute bleeding and prevention of recurrent bleeding. TIPS can be performed on refractory patients.

Answers • 1-E 2-A 3-E 4-A

● CASE PRESENTATION

A 32-year-old man enters your office after he notices that his eyes and skin have turned yellow over the previous 2 days. He reports that he has had poor appetite and nausea and has felt more tired than usual for approximately the last week. He denies excessive alcohol intake and intravenous (IV) drug use but does admit to frequent episodes of unprotected sex since his divorce 1 year ago. He has otherwise been in good health. Pertinent physical exam findings include scleral icterus, mild jaundice, and mildly tender hepatomegaly with liver edge palpable 2 cm below the costal margin. Initial lab results reveal normal complete blood count (CBC) and serum chemistries. Liver testing shows elevated alanine aminotransferase and aspartate aminotransferase (AST) levels of 1100 Iu/L and 900 Iu/L, respectively. Total bilirubin is elevated at 5.1 mg/dL, with direct bilirubin of 3.2 mg/dL. Albumin, prothrombin time (PT), and partial thromboplastin time (PTT) are normal. Viral hepatitis panels yield the following findings:

Hep A Ab (total)-negative

Hep B surface Ab (anti-HBs)-negative

Hep B surface Ag (HBsAg)-positive

Hep B core Ab (IgM)-positive

Hep B core Ab (IgG)-negative

Hep Be Ag-positive

Hep C Ab (total)-negative

1. You determine that the patient has:

    A. Acute hepatitis B Virus (HBV) infection
    B. Chronic active HBV infection
    C. Asymptomatic carrier state with HBV
    D. Past vaccination against HBV and no HBV infection
    E. None of the above

2. What percentage of patients infected with HBV as adults become chronically infected?

    A. None
    B. Less than 5%
    C. 20%
    D. 50%
    E. 90%

3. Which of the following is a possible consequence of HBV infection?

    A. Subsequent infection with the delta agent
    B. Hepatocellular carcinoma
    C. Fulminant liver failure
    D. Asymptomatic carrier state
    E. All of the above

4. Your recommendations for this patient would not include which of the following?

    A. Combination interferon and lamivudine antiviral therapy
    B. Follow-up with frequent office visits and laboratories
    C. Vaccination against HAV
    D. Avoidance of alcohol
    E. Avoidance of unprotected sexual intercourse

● COMMENT

Hepatitis B serologic evaluation • Hepatitis B surface antigen HBsAg appears in serum 1 to 10 weeks after an acute exposure to HBV, before the onset of symptoms or elevation of serum alanine aminotransferase (ALT) level. HBsAg usually becomes undetectable after 4 to 6 months and persistence of HBsAg for more than 6 months implies chronic infection. The disappearance of HBsAg is followed by the appearance of anti-HBs. In most patients, Hepatitis B surface antibody (anti-HBs) persists for life, thereby conferring long-term immunity. However, anti-HBs may not be detectable until after a window period of several weeks to months during which neither HBsAg nor anti-HBs can be detected. At this time, the serologic diagnosis may be made by the detection of immunoglobulin M (IgM) antibodies against hepatitis B core antigen (HBcAg). The detection of IgM hepatitis B core antibody (anti-HBc) is an indication of acute HBV infection. Hepatitis B e antigen (HBeAg) is generally considered to be a marker of HBV replication and infectivity. Seroconversion from HBeAg to anti-HBe is usually associated with the disappearance of HBV deoxyribonucleic acid (DNA) in serum and remission of liver disease.

Likelihood of chronicity • The patient's age at exposure greatly affects the course of the disease. Ninety-five percent of adolescents and adults have clearance of the infection in 3 to 4 months and development of protective HBV surface antibodies. On the other hand, exposure at younger ages and perinatal exposure result in a greater than 90% probability of chronic infection.

Outcomes • HBV infection in developed countries is usually the result of sexual transmission or percutaneous exposure. Seventy percent of patients with acute hepatitis B have subclinical or anicteric hepatitis, and in 30% icteric hepatitis develops. Less than 0.5% of patients progress to fulminant hepatic failure. Patients with chronic infection may be asymptomatic carriers or progress to cirrhosis. Chronic infection is associated with an increased risk of hepatocellular carcinoma. The delta agent is a defective ribonucleic acid (RNA) virus, which requires chronic infection or coinfection with HBV replication.

Treatment • Patients with newly diagnosed acute or chronic infection should be tested for immunity to HAV and vaccinated if necessary. Concurrent infection with both viruses produces a higher incidence of fulminant hepatic failure. Even though antiviral therapy has shown benefit in chronic hepatitis B, there is no indication for antiviral treatment in acute cases (as more than 95% spontaneously clear the infection). In the case discussed, frequent visits and laboratory testing are warranted. Normal coagulation parameters are the best indication of uneventful recovery. Avoidance of hepatotoxins, such as alcohol, and safe-sex practices are obviously indicated.

Answers • 1-A 2-B 3-E 4-A

● CASE PRESENTATION

A 58-year-old man enters your office after being told that he had an "abnormal liver test" while being evaluated for a new insurance policy. He denies any illnesses and has never used alcohol or illegal drugs. He has been married to the same woman for 20 years, though he did have multiple sexual partners before marriage. He works as a bank executive. Seventeen years ago he was involved in an auto accident and required a blood transfusion secondary to injuries sustained. Physical exam reveals hepatomegaly with the liver edge palpable 3 cm. below the costal margin. Additionally, the patient does have a number of tattoos that he obtained while serving in the military in his early 20s. Lab test results reveal normal bilirubin with mildly elevated aspartate aminotransferase (AST) and alanine aminotransferase levels at 65 mg/dL and 76 mg/dL, respectively. Hepatitis A Ab (total) and hepatitis B surface Antigen (HepBsAg), hepatitis B surface Ab, and hepatitis B core Ab results are negative. The hepatitis C Ab result is positive.

1. Which of the following is the likely cause of the patient's hepatitis C infection?
   A. Sexual transmission
   B. Blood transfusions
   C. Fecal-oral transmission during his military travels
   D. Tattoos
   E. B and D

2. Which statement best describes the natural history of HCV infection?
   A. The majority of exposures to HCV result in antibody production, clearance of the virus, and development of immunity.
   B. HCV causes acute but not chronic hepatitis and is usually self-limited.
   C. Fulminant hepatitis is rare. In up to 85% chronic disease develops. One third of cases progress to development of cirrhosis.
   D. Fulminant hepatitis is common. Cirrhosis develops in almost 100% of chronic cases.
   E. Diagnosis during acute infection is common, though there is no good treatment.

3. Chronic HCV infection is associated with which of the following?
   A. Polyclonal gammopathy
   B. Cirrhosis
   C. Hepatocellular carcinoma
   D. Mixed cryoglobulinemia
   E. All of the above

4. Reasonable therapy for chronic HCV infection consists of:
   A. There is no known effective treatment for chronic HCV infection.
   B. Ribavirin monotherapy for 1 year
   C. Lamivudine orally for 1 year
   D. Interferon-alpha and ribavirin for 6 to 12 months
   E. B, C, and D

● COMMENT

Risk factors • Before 1983 HCV was known as non-A, non-B hepatitis and no test was available for screening blood products before transfusion. Consequently, many people were infected secondary to blood transfusions. Other risk factors for HCV are injection drug abuse, tattoos, and accidental needle sticks in health care workers. Risk of transmission from pregnant mother to newborn is 3% to 6%. Sexual transmission is rare.

Diagnosis and natural history • HCV is diagnosed by the presence of HCV antibody by enzyme-linked immunosorbent assay test and confirmed by radioimmune blot assay (RIBA). In order to differentiate chronic infection from previous exposure and clearance (approximately 15% of those initially infected), a polymerase chain reaction assay for viral ribonucleic acid (RNA) is used; it can provide information about viral load and genotype. After exposure to HCV, chronic disease develops in up to 85%. This usually manifests as abnormal transaminase levels, although levels fluctuate in many between normal and abnormal values. The absolute elevation of the transaminase level is not necessarily indicative of the severity of disease. Fulminant hepatitis is rare.

Complications of chronic HCV • Many chronic HCV (33%) patients have disease progression to cirrhosis after an average of 20 years. Chronic HCV infection is also associated with systemic fatigue, polyclonal gammopathy, hepatocellular carcinoma, mixed cryoglobulinemia, and arthritis.

Treatment • Current treatment for chronic HCV infection consists of interferon-alpha and ribavirin for a period of 6 months to 1 year, depending on HCV viral genotype. A response rate of approximately 40% is achieved and results in viral clearance and normalization of transaminase levels. Interferon alone can be used; however, response rate is much lower. Ribavirin has no effect on viral load when used alone. Liver biopsy results are often obtained before initiating therapy.

Answers • 1-E 2-C 3-E 4-D

● CASE PRESENTATION

A 66-year-old man enters your office reporting increasing weakness and fatigue. Blood tests reveal a hematocrit of 27%. His past history includes mild hypertension and an artificial aortic valve replacement 3 years ago. On physical exam, vital signs are normal. A mechanical S_2 with a grade II/VI systolic murmur, which radiates to the neck, is heard. Lungs are clear to auscultation. The liver and spleen are not palpable. The remainder of the physical exam findings are unremarkable. The result of stool guaiac testing for occult blood is negative and the screening colonoscopy result was unremarkable 3 years ago.

Laboratory study results:
  Hematocrit   27% (42.0–52.0)
  Platelet count   400/μL (140–440)
  White blood cell (WBC) count   8,900/μL (4.8–10.8)
  Reticulocyte count   68,000/μL (22k–161k)
  Serum iron   15 μg/dL (50–170)
  Serum TIBC   415 μg/dL (245–425)
  Serum ferritin   14 μg/L (15–150)
  LDH   380 μ/L (90–180)
  Blood urea nitrogen (BUN)   9 mg/dL (8–20)
  Schistocytes seen on peripheral blood smear

1. The most appropriate next step in managing this patient is:
   A. Testing for gastrointestinal blood loss with mesenteric arteriogram and labeled erythrocytes
   B. Bone marrow biopsy and aspiration to determine other causes of anemia
   C. Replacement of the aortic valve
   D. Additional testing and a trial of oral iron
   E. Measurement of erythropoietin level and initiation of erythropoietin therapy

2. Iron deficiency anemia is commonly associated with which of the following?
   A. Amenorrhea
   B. Ileal malabsorption
   C. Colonic polyps
   D. Decreased production of erythropoietin
   E. All of the above

3. Which of the following is a common lab result abnormality noted in iron deficiency?
   A. Decreased red blood cell distribution width
   B. Elevated mean corpuscular volume (MCV)
   C. Hyperchromia (elevated mean corpuscular hemoglobin)
   D. Decreased transferrin saturation
   E. Elevated ferritin level

4. What is the most common side effect of oral iron replacement therapy?
   A. Anaphylaxis
   B. Iron overload
   C. Gastrointestinal intolerance
   D. Dysuria
   E. Headache

● COMMENT

Recognition of intravascular hemolysis causing iron deficiency anemia • Aortic valve replacement can lead to intravascular hemolysis, causing the release of free hemoglobin. Free hemoglobin binds to haptoglobin until haptoglobin is consumed. Once this occurs, free hemoglobin passes through the glomeruli. Some of the free hemoglobin is reabsorbed, but free hemoglobin begins to appear in the urine. Serum ferritin level is low, indicating a profound loss of total body iron. Serum haptoglobin level is low and examination of the urine for hemosiderin is positive. Once one is certain that the valve is functioning properly by echocardiogram, iron replacement should begin. Folic acid requirements may be increased as a result of hemolysis, as well. Additional gastrointestinal (GI) evaluation is unnecessary.

Causes of iron deficiency anemia • Iron deficiency anemia can be related to decreased absorption (primarily in the duodenum and proximal jejunum), blood loss, or, rarely, increased demand (pregnancy, adolescence, frequent blood donors). Blood loss can be due to GI losses (peptic ulcer disease, gastritis, polyps, malignancy, arteriovenous malformations [AVMs], etc.) or genitourinary losses such as menstruation. As noted, intravascular hemolysis can lead to renal loss of hemoglobin.

Laboratory result abnormalities in iron deficiency anemia • Iron deficiency anemia is typically a microcytic (low MCV), hypochromic (low mean corpuscular hemoglobin) anemia. The red blood cell distribution width (RDW) is increased in iron deficiency anemia. Serum iron (SI) level is low and the total iron binding capacity (TIBC) is elevated in iron deficiency. The SI and TIBC are used to calculate the percent saturation of transferrin with iron (SI/TIBC), which is low in iron deficiency. Serum ferritin level is used to evaluate total body iron stores and is quite low in iron deficiency anemia. A low serum ferritin level can help differentiate iron deficiency anemia from other microcytic anemias, such as thalassemia or chronic inflammation.

Side effects of iron replacement therapy • Patients with severe anemia should receive transfusion therapy. If iron deficiency is due to GI malabsorption, then parenteral iron therapy may be necessary, though parenteral therapy can be associated with anaphylaxis. However, most patients are treated with oral iron replacement therapy. Patients should have multiple daily doses (three to four) of oral iron. This should be given between meals. The main side effect of oral iron therapy is GI distress including abdominal pain, nausea, vomiting, constipation, or diarrhea. If these side effects occur, the dosage needs to be reduced.

Answers • 1-D 2-C 3-D 4-C

● CASE PRESENTATION

A 71-year-old woman with mild diabetes mellitus and hypothyroidism arrives at your office. Physical exam findings are unremarkable. Routine lab test results reveal anemia with hemoglobin of 11 g/dL, mean corpuscular volume (MCV) of 102, leukocyte count of 9,800/μL, and platelets of 400,000/μL. Peripheral blood smear reveals macrocytosis and hypersegmentation of neutrophils. On a return visit, her hemoglobin has dropped to 9.8 g/dL and she has increasing paresthesias of both lower extremities. On physical exam the only new finding is a lack of reflexes in the lower extremities.

1. Which of the following is *not* associated with macrocytic anemia?
   A. Vitamin B_{12} (cobalamin) deficiency
   B. Hypothyroidism
   C. Anemia of chronic disease
   D. Alcoholic cirrhosis
   E. Myelodysplastic syndromes

2. How would you initially approach this patient?
   A. Initiate therapy with daily folic acid.
   B. Perform a Schilling test.
   C. Order serum B_{12} level testing and begin treatment with vitamin B_{12}.
   D. Refer to an endocrinologist to treat diabetic neuropathy.
   E. Perform bone marrow aspiration to determine other possible causes of anemia.

3. Which of the following findings are noted in vitamin B_{12} deficiency?
   A. Macrocytic anemia
   B. Generalized fatigue
   C. Peripheral neuropathy
   D. Hypersegmented neutrophils
   E. All of the above

4. Which of the following best characterizes the pathophysiologic characteristics of pernicious anemia?
   A. Inflammation of the jejunum
   B. Autoimmunity-related intrinsic factor deficiency
   C. Inability to utilize vitamin B_{12} stores
   D. Increased excretion of vitamin B_{12}
   E. Serum folate deficiency

● COMMENT

Differential diagnosis of macrocytic anemia • Vitamin B_{12} deficiency and folate deficiency are common causes of macrocytic anemia. Other causes include medications (chemotherapeutic agents, phenytoin, zidovudine, etc.), hypothyroidism, chronic liver disease (including cirrhosis), and myelodysplastic syndromes. The reticulocytosis associated with hemolytic anemias can also cause MCV elevation. Macrocytosis can also rarely be due to an artifact of automatic cell counter technique.

Approach to the patient with suspected B_{12} deficiency • The combination of neuropathy and macrocytic anemia is most suggestive of vitamin B_{12} deficiency. A serum B_{12} level should be drawn and B_{12} supplementation should be initiated before results return to prevent further irreversible nerve damage. History and laboratory testing should be used to rule out any of the causes of macrocytosis noted. Schilling test is useful to differentiate intrinsic factor deficiency from other causes of B_{12} deficiency, but testing is lengthy and costly, requiring accurate urine collection and ingestion of radioactive material. Antibody titers to parietal cells and intrinsic factor can also be measured when pernicious anemia is suspected, but vitamin B_{12} treatment should be initiated regardless. Bone marrow examination would only be necessary if the less invasive tests failed to reveal the cause of anemia.

Clinical findings in vitamin B_{12} deficiency • Patients generally have symptoms of marked fatigue related to anemia. Neurologic symptoms are the result of demyelination of neurons in the spinal column and cerebral cortex. This can lead to paresthesias of the hands and feet, unsteady gait, personality changes, and memory loss. Neurologic exam can reveal decreased vibratory and position sense in the lower extremities, diminished deep tendon reflexes, and ataxia with a positive Romberg's sign finding. Eventually, spastic paralysis can ensue. Other exam findings can include a beefy-red tongue and vitiligo (associated with pernicious anemia). Lab testing reveals decreased B_{12} levels, hypersegmented neutrophils, and elevated levels of serum methylmalonic acid and homocysteine.

Cause of pernicious anemia • Pernicious anemia is an autoimmune disorder that results in vitamin B_{12} deficiency due to a lack of intrinsic factor. Autoantibodies to intrinsic factor and parietal cells are generally present. Vitamin B_{12} deficiency can also be caused by gastrectomy, gastric bypass, impaired absorption in the ileum, and atrophic gastritis with achlorhydria. Though possible in strict vegetarians, diet-related lack of vitamin B_{12} is quite rare in the United States.

Answers • 1-C   2-C   3-E   4-B

● CASE PRESENTATION

A 25-year-old man is referred to you for evaluation for thrombo-cytopenia. This was found incidentally on blood testing done for life insurance enrollment. A complete blood count (CBC) revealed white blood cell (WBC) count of 7 K/cumm (normal: 4.8-10.8), hemoglobin of 13 g/dL, and a platelet count of 11,000/μL (normal: 140,000–440,000). He is in his usual state of health but does note a rash on his lower extremities for the last 2 weeks. He is on no medications and does not drink alcohol. The blood chemical panel and urinalysis results are normal. Human immunodeficiency virus (HIV) finding is negative. The peripheral blood smear is normal except for marked thrombocytopenia. Physical exam is notable for small petechiae on the palate and petechiae on both lower extremities. There is no hepatosplenomegaly and the remainder of the exam findings are normal. Your tentative diagnosis is idiopathic thrombocytopenic purpura (ITP).

1. Which of the following statements best characterizes ITP?
   A. Abnormal distribution of platelets due to splenomegaly
   B. Decreased platelet production due to alcohol or other toxins
   C. Platelet consumption due to intravascular coagulation
   D. Autoimmune destruction of platelets without identifiable predisposing factors
   E. All of the above

2. Which statement about platelet counts and bleeding risk is most accurate?
   A. Patients should have platelet counts higher than 100,000/μL before lumbar puncture.
   B. ITP patients are at substantial risk of intracranial hemorrhage at counts between 20,000 and 50,000/μL.
   C. ITP patients with platelet counts as low as 5000 are not usually at substantial risk for major organ bleeding.
   D. Patients with leukemia or sepsis are not at risk for spontaneous bleeding at counts of less than 10,000/μL.
   E. All of the above

3. What is the natural history of ITP?
   A. Most patients die of severe hemorrhage in acute conditions.
   B. Most patients proceed to a chronic form of ITP.
   C. Patients often have a leukemia of platelet lineage.
   D. ITP is usually self-limited and resolves spontaneously.
   E. Aplastic anemia often follows ITP.

4. The treatment of ITP can include which of the following?
   A. High-dose corticosteroids
   B. Intravenous immunoglobulin
   C. Splenectomy
   D. Intravenous cyclophosphamide
   E. All of the above

● COMMENT

ITP • The differential diagnosis of thrombocytopenia is extensive; it can be loosely divided into decreased platelet production (marrow damage, congenital defects, or ineffective production), abnormal distribution (splenomegaly), or increased destruction. The diagnosis of destruction-related thrombocytopenia can be further divided into non–immune-related (disseminated intravascular coagulation [DIC] or thrombotic thrombocytopenic purpura [TTP]) versus immune-related thrombocytopenia. Immune destruction of platelets can be related to drug ingestion (quinidine, heparin, etc.), autoimmune diseases (systemic lupus erythematosus [SLE], lymphatic malignancies, trauma, and acquired immunodeficiency syndrome), and human immunodeficiency virus [AIDS and HIV] infection. ITP is the autoimmune destruction of platelets due to autoantibodies in the absence of any of the other causes of thrombocytopenia.

Bleeding risk with thrombocytopenia • ITP patients with platelet counts as low as 5000/μL are usually not at a great risk for major hemorrhage. This may be because the platelets in ITP patients demonstrate better than normal function. Any patient who is to undergo major surgery should have a platelet count of greater than 100,000/μL, but minor surgery and other procedures (such as lumbar puncture) can be performed when the platelet count is above 50,000/μL. Normal individuals tolerate platelet counts of around 10,000/μL without difficulty. However, patients with leukemia, other malignancies, or sepsis are at significant risk of bleeding at platelet counts of less than 20,000/μL.

Natural History of ITP • ITP can be a self-limited acute disease, but most cases proceed to chronic ITP with a persistent shortened platelet life span. Patients with chronic ITP often have less severe thrombocytopenia with platelet counts up to 100,000/μL. Children with ITP generally have complete resolution.

Treatment • First-line treatment for ITP is high-dose corticosteroids. Platelet transfusions are given for active bleeding, though the patient may not have a significant response to transfusion because of destruction of the transfused platelets. If patients do not respond to high-dose corticosteroids, they are treated with intravenous immunoglobulin (IV Ig). Patients who do not respond or relapse after IV Ig therapy are often treated with splenectomy. Up to 80% of patients achieve a permanent remission after splenectomy. Refractory thrombocytopenia is treated with intravenous cyclophosphamide or plasmapheresis with immunoglobulin absorption.

Answers • 1-D 2-C 3-B 4-E

● CASE PRESENTATION

A previously healthy 33-year-old woman is admitted to the hospital with a 1-week history of fatigue and dyspnea. Her only medication is omeprazole for gastroesophageal reflux disease (GERD). Vital signs are normal. Physical exam is remarkable for bilateral lower extremity petechiae and the finding that the patient is somnolent and confused. Laboratory data reveal hemoglobin of 5.2 g/dL, hematocrit of 16%, leukocyte count of 9,900/μL with a normal differential, and platelets of 15,000/μL (normal: 140,000–440,000). Chemical test results are normal except for creatinine of 1.5 mg/dL, lactate dehydrogenase (LDH) of 1422 units/liter (elevated), and a total bilirubin of 3 mg/dL (0.5 mg/dL direct bilirubin). Examination of the blood smear reveals fragmented erythrocytes and polychromasia, with only one to two platelets per high-power field. The direct Coombs' (direct antiglobulin) test result is negative. Coagulation studies (prothrombin time [PT], partial thromboplastin time [PTT], fibrinogen, fibrin split products) yield normal findings.

1. Which of the following is part of the classic pentad of thrombotic thrombocytopenic purpura (TTP)?

   A. Hypothermia
   B. Thrombocytosis
   C. Coombs' test—positive hemolytic anemia
   D. Hematologic malignancy
   E. Renal dysfunction

2. Which of the following findings on blood smear is essential to the diagnosis of TTP?

   A. Suppressed reticulocyte count
   B. Schistocytes
   C. Spherocytes
   D. Granulocytopenia
   E. Plasmacytosis

3. What is the most appropriate management for this patient?

   A. Suspect drug-induced thrombocytopenia and hemolytic anemia. Discontinue omeprazole.
   B. Initiate plasma exchange therapy for TTP.
   C. Transfuse platelets immediately.
   D. Institute IV Ig therapy.
   E. Monitor the patient carefully over the next several weeks for any new neurologic findings.

4. Which of the following statements related to the development of TTP is true?

   A. Most cases of TTP occur sporadically.
   B. TTP can be related to certain drug therapies.
   C. The syndrome of TTP overlaps with hemolytic uremic syndrome (HUS).
   D. TTP can be a postpartum complication.
   E. All of the above

● COMMENT

TTP • The classic pentad of TTP includes thrombocytopenia, microangiopathic hemolytic anemia, acute renal failure, neurologic disorders, and fever. It is rare to see all five characteristics. The minimal criteria for initiating plasma exchange are thrombocytopenia and microangiopathic hemolytic anemia without another clinical cause noted by history, physical, or initial laboratory studies. Diagnosis often requires a high level of suspicion. Neurologic findings can vary greatly and include mental status changes, seizures, focal neurologic deficits, and coma. Laboratory testing in TTP reveals anemia, thrombocytopenia, and altered renal function along with an elevated LDH level (due to hemolysis) and relatively normal PT, PTT, fibrinogen, and fibrin split products findings. Coombs' testing typically yields a negative result in TTP as opposed to autoimmune hemolytic anemia with thrombocytopenia (Evan's syndrome).

Peripheral smear in TTP • The presence of schistocytes on peripheral smear is considered to be essential to diagnosis of TTP. Schistocytes are red blood cell fragments, which occur in TTP as a result of intraarteriolar platelet thrombi and fibrin deposition. Helmet cells may be present as well. The reticulocyte count is markedly elevated in response to hemolysis. Spherocytes are generally seen on peripheral blood smear in immune-mediated hemolysis rather than in TTP.

Treatment of TTP • Plasmapheresis with plasma exchange is the recommended treatment for TTP and has resulted in a greater than 90% survival rate. Therapy should be initiated as soon as possible to improve response and minimize complications. High-dose corticosteroids are typically given, but their efficacy is unproved. Antiplatelet agents (aspirin, dipyridamole, etc.) are often given as unproven adjuncts as well. Vincristine, cyclophosphamide, and splenectomy have been used in refractory cases. Up to 10% to 20% of patients experience relapse. Platelet transfusions should be prevented because they can precipitate thrombosis. Patients who have progressed to coma or severe renal failure have a worse prognosis. The severity of the anemia, thrombocytopenia, and LDH elevation also negatively impact prognosis.

Risk factors for TTP • Most cases of TTP occur sporadically with no clear cause. TTP has occurred with ticlopidine therapy, after chemotherapy, and after bone marrow transplantation. It also rarely occurs in the postpartum period. Hemolytic uremic syndrome HUS is more common in children and findings overlap with those of TTP. Common findings include hemolytic anemia and renal failure. HUS has been related to hemorrhagic colitis caused by eating undercooked meat contaminated with *Escherichia coli* serotype O157:H7.

Answers • 1-E 2-B 3-B 4-E

● CASE PRESENTATION

A 22-year-old woman enters the emergency room because of a 2-day history of swelling in the left leg and pleuritic chest pain. Her only medication has been oral contraceptives for the past 4 years. She does not smoke. There is no history of venous thrombosis in her parents or siblings. Physical exam reveals a tall slender tachypneic woman. Crackles are heard at the left lung base and she has a swollen, tender left lower extremity from calf to thigh. Lab data reveal a hematocrit of 42%, leukocyte count of 11,200/μL, and platelet count of 365,000/μL. The international normalized ratio (INR) and activated partial thromboplastin time results are normal. The duplex ultrasound result is consistent with an ileofemoral thrombosis and the V/Q scan indicates a high probability of pulmonary embolus. She is admitted and heparin therapy is instituted. She is started on warfarin within 24 hours after a negative pregnancy test result. Oral contraceptives are discontinued.

1. You are asked to evaluate the patient on the third hospital day. Which of the following is the most reasonable approach to further evaluation of this patient?

   A. Test for factor V Leiden mutation and anticardiolipin antibodies now and for other primary hypercoagulable states after warfarin sodium (Coumadin) is discontinued.

   B. Test for protein C, antithrombin III, and protein S deficiency before hospital discharge.

   C. Do not test for a hypercoagulable state because the patient was taking oral contraceptives.

   D. Test only for an acquired condition such as antiphospholipid antibody syndrome.

   E. Resume oral contraceptives as they may be protective .

2. Which of the following is the most common primary hypercoagulable state?

   A. Protein C deficiency

   B. Protein S deficiency

   C. Antithrombin III deficiency

   D. Activated protein C resistance (factor V Leiden mutation)

   E. Approximately equal incidence of all

3. True statements regarding the treatment of venous thromboembolism (VTE) include which of the following?

   A. Six weeks of warfarin therapy is equivalent to 6 months for an initial idiopathic VTE.

   B. Heparin therapy should be initiated and should overlap with warfarin therapy for at least 4 to 5 days.

   C. The target INR for VTE therapy is 3.0 to 4.0.

   D. Oral warfarin therapy is the treatment of choice for the pregnant patient with a VTE.

   E. All of the above

4. Which of the following is an indication for placement of an inferior vena caval (IVC) filter?

   A. Recurrent VTE with a therapeutic INR

   B. Initial VTE in a patient with factor V Leiden mutation

   C. Recurrent idiopathic VTE

   D. VTE related to knee or hip surgery

   E. All of the above

● COMMENT

Evaluation for primary hypercoagulable states • Age below 50, family history of VTE, recurrent VTE, or life-threatening VTE should trigger an evaluation for primary hypercoagulable states. Pregnancy and oral contraceptive use do increase the risk of VTE somewhat, but this risk is markedly increased if there is a superimposed hypercoagulable state. This patient should be tested for primary and acquired conditions (antiphospholipid antibody syndrome), but a number of the tests are affected by heparin or warfarin therapy. Heparin or warfarin can affect the results of tests for lupus anticoagulant and activated protein C resistance. Heparin decreases levels of antithrombin III (ATIII), and protein C and S levels decrease in patients on warfarin. Thus the best time to evaluate for these conditions accurately is after anticoagulation has been stopped. Heparin and warfarin do not affect anticardiolipin antibodies, clotting assays for lupus anticoagulant, and polymerase chain reaction testing for factor V Leiden mutation and testing need not be delayed.

Factor V Leiden mutation • Activated protein C resistance due to the factor V Leiden mutation has been detected in 12% to 40% of idiopathic VTE patients. It is more common than the combination of ATIII, protein C, and protein S deficiencies. Other primary hypercoagulable states include prothrombin gene mutations, and hyperhomocysteinemia.

Treatment of VTE • Intravenous heparin or low-molecular-weight heparin (LMWH) should be initiated in VTE patients and should overlap with warfarin therapy for at least 4 to 5 days. This therapy prevents warfarin sodium–induced skin necrosis if the patient has protein C or S deficiency. Warfarin therapy should be titrated to an INR of 2.5 (2.0:3.0) to maximize benefit and minimize risk of bleeding complications. The duration of warfarin therapy varies, depending on the individual patient. Patients with reversible risk factors (postorthopedic surgery, immobility) should be treated for a minimum of 3 months, and patients with an initial idiopathic VTE should likely receive at least 6 months of therapy. Recurrent VTE or persistent risk factors (cancer, antiphospholipid antibodies) should be treated with therapeutic doses of warfarin for an indefinite period (at least 12 months).

Indications for IVC filters • If there is an absolute contraindication to anticoagulant therapy (i.e., active bleeding), an IVC filter should be placed. Further, most sources recommend IVC filter placement for recurrent VTE on adequate anticoagulant therapy. Finally, pulmonary hypertension due to recurrent VTE or treatment with pulmonary embolectomy or thromboendarterectomy is an indication for an IVC filter.

Answers • 1-A 2-D 3-B 4-A

● CASE PRESENTATION

The patient is a 58-year-old black man who arrives at your office reporting marked fatigue and worsening low back pain. Past medical history, social history, and family history are unremarkable. Physical examination findings are within normal limits. Laboratory data are remarkable for a normocytic anemia with hemoglobin of 8.0 g/dL. Rouleaux formation is noted on the differential. Additionally, serum calcium is elevated at 12.3 mg/dL (normal: 8.4–10 mg/dL) with an albumin level of 3.0 gm/dL (normal: 3.5–4.8). Serum protein is elevated at 9.2 g/dL. Serum creatinine is within normal limits. Lumbosacral x-rays reveal significant osteopenia with a number of "punched out" vertebral lesions.

1. Your tentative diagnosis is multiple myeloma. This is a malignant proliferation of which type of cell?

   A. T lymphocytes
   B. Platelets
   C. Plasma cells
   D. Osteocytes
   E. Granulocytes

2. Which of the following is *least* helpful in completing this patient's work-up?

   A. Bone scan
   B. Bone marrow biopsy
   C. Skeletal survey with skull films
   D. Serum protein electrophoresis
   E. Urine protein electrophoresis

3. Important negative prognostic factors include which of the following?

   A. Serum calcium of less than 12 mg/dL
   B. Hemoglobin greater than 8.5 g/dL
   C. Low M protein levels
   D. Serum creatinine of less than 2 mg/dL
   E. Advanced lytic bone lesions

4. Which of the following is a potential complication of multiple myeloma?

   A. Renal failure
   B. Increased susceptibility to infection
   C. Pathologic fractures
   D. Hyperviscosity syndrome
   E. All of the above

● COMMENT

Pathogenesis • Multiple myeloma is a malignant proliferation of plasma cells in the bone marrow. Most patients have bone pain, which is often worse with movement. This pain is caused by lytic bone lesions, which are caused by activation of osteoclasts by cytokines produced by the tumor. This condition also results in marked hypercalcemia. Myeloma is more common in black patients.

Diagnosis • Myeloma is characterized by more than 10% plasma cells indicated by bone marrow biopsy, the demonstration of lytic bone lesions, and a characteristic monoclonal protein elevation (M spike) on serum protein electrophoresis and/or urine electrophoresis. Lytic bone lesions are best demonstrated on plain x-rays (skeletal survey). Bone scans are less useful because uptake is limited by the rarity of an osteoblastic response. Other common laboratory abnormalities include hypercalcemia, anemia, hypogammaglobulinemia, elevated total serum protein, elevated erythrocyte sedimentation rate (ESR), and elevated β_2-microglobulin level. Alkaline phosphatase is relatively normal. Rouleaux formation is noted on the peripheral smear.

Prognosis • Anemia (hemoglobin <8.5 g/dL), marked hypercalcemia (>12 mg/dL), advanced lytic bone lesions, and higher levels of monoclonal proteins are associated with advanced staging and poorer prognosis. A serum creatinine of greater than 2 mg/dL is also associated with a poorer outcome in myeloma patients. Finally, multiple myeloma patients with higher levels of β_2-microglobulin fare worse than patients with lower levels.

Complications • The lytic bone lesions and generalized osteopenia in multiple myeloma increase the risk for pathologic fractures. Renal failure frequently occurs and is often due to the nephrotoxicity of the monoclonal light chain proteins (Bence Jones proteins) in the urine. Other contributors to renal insufficiency include hypercalcemia, dehydration, and enhanced toxicity of radiocontrast medium or antibiotics. Patients can also have symptoms related to their anemia or hypercalcemia. Recurrent bacterial infections, particularly pneumonia and urinary tract infections (UTIs), are very common because of the low levels of normal immunoglobulin and poor host response to antigens. Patients with markedly elevated M protein levels can experience hyperviscosity syndrome with mental status changes, headaches, visual disturbances, and excess bleeding. Other neurologic symptoms can be related to amyloid deposition or cryoglobulins.

Answers • 1-C 2-A 3-E 4-E

● CASE PRESENTATION

A 71-year-old man has a routine physical exam. His only symptom is minor fatigue over the last 2 months. Otherwise, his review of systems is unremarkable. Physical examination findings are essentially normal. Lab results reveal hemoglobin of 15 g/dL, a leukocyte count of 26,000/uL, with 85% lymphocytes, and a platelet count of 180,000/μL. Serum immunoglobulin levels are somewhat reduced. Bone marrow biopsy is performed and reveals diffuse infiltration with normal-appearing leuhemia. The tentative diagnosis is chronic lymphocytic leukemia (CLL).

1. Which of the following is the most likely physical finding in patients with CLL?
   A. Gingival hyperplasia
   B. Leukemic skin infiltrate
   C. Diffuse adenopathy
   D. Gynecomastia
   E. Subungual (splinter) hemorrhages

2. Which of the following is the worst prognostic factor in CLL?
   A. Degree of lymphocytosis
   B. Splenomegaly
   C. Central nervous system (CNS) involvement
   D. Age greater than 60
   E. Thrombocytopenia

3. Relatively common complications of CLL include which of the following?
   A. Pathologic fractures
   B. Coombs' test—positive hemolytic anemia finding
   C. Defects in T-cell immunity
   D. Renal failure
   E. All of the above

4. Which statement summarizes the best treatment plan for the patient?
   A. The patient should be observed and given supportive care.
   B. Chemotherapy with chlorambucil or fludarabine should be initiated.
   C. Intravenous gamma globulin should be given monthly to prevent infection.
   D. Glucocorticoids should be initiated to prevent autoimmune hemolytic anemia and thrombocytopenia.
   E. B, C, and D are true.

● COMMENT

Chronic lymphocytic leukemia (CLL) • CLL is a clonal proliferation of CD5+ B-cell lymphocytes that look like normal small lymphocytes. Patients are often asymptomatic and come to medical attention as a result of adenopathy or an abnormal complete blood count (CBC). When symptoms are present, they are nonspecific, including fatigue, weight loss, anorexia, and night sweats. Common lab findings include lymphocytosis (often marked), anemia, thrombocytopenia, and reduced serum immunoglobulins. Physical exam often reveals splenomegaly and generalized adenopathy. The incidence of CLL increases with age, and most cases occur in patients older than 60 years of age. Diagnosis is based on typical clinical findings along with a suggestive CBC. Confirmation requires immunophenotyping and gene rearrangement studies along with a finding of low levels of serum immunoglobulin.

Prognosis • Prognosis in CLL is largely related to staging; advanced stages display a worse prognosis. Patients with lymphocytosis and little or no adenopathy have an average survival duration of 10 or more years. Significant adenopathy and splenomegaly adversely affect prognosis somewhat (survival duration of 7 to 9 years), but anemia and thrombocytopenia confer an advanced stage of disease and a much worse prognosis (1- to 2-year survival duration). The most common genetic abnormality is trisomy 12, which is also associated with a poorer prognosis. Finally, it appears that CD38+ tumors have a worse prognosis.

Complications • Complications of CLL include infections related to hypogammaglobulinemia (encapsulated organisms such as *Streptococcus pneumoniae* and *Haemophilus* influenzae), autoimmune hemolytic anemia, immune thrombocytopenia, marrow infiltration (resulting in anemia and thrombocytopenia), and rarely evolution into an aggressive lymphoma (Richter's syndrome) or prolymphocytic leukemia. Massive adenopathy or splenomegaly can cause mechanical complications as well. Death is generally due to infections or marrow failure.

Pharmacologic treatment • Pharmacologic treatment of CLL is not curative and should be deferred until the patient has symptoms or complications (usually anemia and thrombocytopenia). If anemia and thrombocytopenia are autoimmune in nature, glucocorticoids (or even splenectomy) may be helpful. For anemia and thrombocytopenia related to marrow replacement, cytotoxic therapy is given with fludarabine or chlorambucil. Though monthly intravenous immunoglobulin infusions do decrease the rate of infections, this therapy is expensive and is usually reserved for patients with recurrent bacterial infections.

Answers • 1-C 2-E 3-B 4-A

● CASE PRESENTATION

A 35-year-old woman reports fatigue over the past "couple of months." Physical exam findings are normal except for an enlarged spleen, three finger breadths below the left costal margin. The hematocrit is 42%, leukocyte count is 80,000/μL, with 51% neutrophils, 18% band forms, 10% metamyelocytes, 7% myelocytes, 6% promyelocytes, 3% monocytes, and 5% lymphocytes. The platelet count is 525,000/μL. Bone marrow biopsy and cytogenetic results are pending.

1. Your tentative diagnosis is chronic myelogenous leukemia (CML). Which of the following statements about CML is true?
   A. Thrombocytopenia is typical at presentation.
   B. The peripheral smear resembles the myeloid maturation sequence in the marrow.
   C. The leukocyte alkaline phosphatase level is increased.
   D. Basophil count is decreased.
   E. Marked anemia is typical at presentation.

2. What is the most likely cytogenetic finding in this patient?
   A. t(9;22)
   B. t(15;17)
   C. t(9;11)
   D. t(8;14)
   E. All of the above

3. Which of the following best characterizes the natural history of CML?
   A. CML often has a prolonged chronic phase, which can be relatively asymptomatic.
   B. After 3 to 5 years, an accelerated phase often appears.
   C. An acute leukemia–like condition is the final stage of evolution.
   D. Massive splenomegaly can result in abdominal discomfort.
   E. All of the above

4. Which of the following is accurate regarding therapy for CML?
   A. Because of an excessive mortality rate, bone marrow transplantation (BMT) should only be considered in blast crisis.
   B. Prolonged interferon-alpha therapy is associated with better results in subsequent BMT.
   C. Early treatment with interferon or hydroxyurea results in an increased mortality rate.
   D. Interferon therapy and allogeneic BMT can result in prolonged disease-free survival.
   E. All of the above

● COMMENT

Laboratory findings in CML • The most notable laboratory abnormality in CML is a markedly elevated white blood cell count (50,000 to 200,000μL). The peripheral smear closely resembles the myeloid maturation sequence of the bone marrow with increased numbers of metamyelocytes, myelocytes, and promyelocytes, and even a few blasts. Patients often have significant numbers of basophils, as well. At presentation, thrombocytosis is actually characteristic and the hemoglobin is relatively normal. Leukocyte alkaline phosphatase is decreased.

Philadelphia chromosome • The Philadelphia chromosome translocation, t(9;22), is the hallmark of CML and over 90% of patients demonstrate this finding. The translocation forms the BCR-ABL hybrid gene that results in the formation of a p210 protein. This protein interacts with the RAS protein, a protein responsible for cell proliferation and differentiation. The t(8;14) is associated with Burkitt's lymphoma. The translocations t(15;17) and t(9;11) are associated with M3 and M5 acute myelogenous leukemia, respectively.

Natural history of CML • The peak incidence of CML is around the age of 50. Patients may be asymptomatic or may have nonspecific symptoms, such as fatigue, weight loss, or abdominal fullness. CML often has a prolonged chronic phase, during which the patient is relatively asymptomatic, as long as granulocyte counts are kept under control. After an average of several years, an accelerated phase, which is marked by increasing splenomegaly and increased proliferation of white cells and platelets, appears. Fatigue, weight loss, and abdominal discomfort may worsen. After approximately 1 year in the accelerated phase, patients generally have an acute leukemia–like picture, known as *blast crisis*. Blast crisis has an extremely poor prognosis.

Treatment • Younger patients who have a human leukocyte antigen (HLA) matched sibling or an unrelated HLA match donor should probably have allogeneic bone marrow transplantation relatively early in the chronic phase of the disease. Interferon-alpha therapy can also result in prolonged disease-free survival, though the success rate of subsequent bone marrow transplantation may be significantly reduced when this therapy is given for more than 6 months. Hydroxyurea has often been used to achieve control of the hematologic abnormalities of patients in the chronic phase of disease. A new therapy for CML, Gleevec, is a specific inhibitor of the tyrosine kinase produced by the Philadelphia chromosome abnormality. This therapy has shown significant activity in the chronic and blast phases of CML. Its overall role in therapy is yet to be defined.

Answers • 1-B 2-A 3-E 4-D

● CASE PRESENTATION

A 22-year-old woman reports bleeding from her gums. She has also noted extreme fatigue and weakness over the last 5 days as well as increased bruising. Physical examination is remarkable for palatal and distal lower extremity petechiae. Laboratory studies reveal a leukocyte count of 3500/μL, with 50% granulated blasts. The hemoglobin is 7 g/dL and the platelet count is 18,000/μL. Prothrombin time is elevated at 20 seconds, fibrinogen is 120 mg/dL (normal: 231–486 mg/dL), and D-dimers are greater than 10 FEU (normal: <0.43 FEU) (all suggestive of disseminated intravascular coagulation). Bone marrow biopsy result reveals markedly increased cellularity with more than 50% blast cells. The patient is diagnosed with acute myelogenous leukemia (AML).

1. Which of the following findings characterizes AML?

   A. Presence of Auer rods
   B. Prolonged chronic phase in most patients
   C. Marked adenopathy and mediastinal mass
   D. Thrombocytosis
   E. All of the above

2. What is the most likely French-American-British (FAB) classification of this patient's AML?

   A. M1
   B. M3
   C. M5
   D. M6
   E. M7

3. Which of the following statements regarding prognosis in AML is correct?

   A. Older patients actually fare better with AML.
   B. AML secondary to prior alkylating agents has a better prognosis.
   C. AML secondary to myelodysplastic syndromes has a poor prognosis.
   D. Multiple chromosomal mutations confer a better prognosis.
   E. All of the above are true.

4. The patient has a temperature of 102.4 F. The absolute neutrophil count (ANC) is calculated at approximately 250. Initial empirical antibiotic therapy should definitely cover which of these organisms?

   A. *Pseudomonas aeruginosa*
   B. *Candida albicans*
   A. *Aspergillus* spp.
   D. Herpes simplex virus
   E. All of the above

● COMMENT

AML • AML is generally characterized by the sudden appearance of fatigue, fever, bleeding, bacterial infections, and bone pain. Older patients can experience slower onset of disease, though this is not typical. Results of laboratory studies reveal marked anemia, thrombocytopenia, and granulocytopenia. Patients may have marked leukocytosis or leukopenia. Diagnosis requires at least 30% blasts indicated on bone marrow biopsy. Abnormal rod-shaped granules known as *Auer rods* are diagnostic for AML when they are present.

FAB classification of AML • The FAB system classifies AML into seven M types: M1 (undifferentiated), M2 (myeloblastic), M3 (promyelocytic), M4 (myelomonocytic), M5 (monocytic), M6 (erythroleukemia), and M7 (megakaryocytic). This patient likely has AML M3, which often causes disseminated intravascular coagulation (DIC). This is associated with a 15:17 translocation. The use of all-*trans*-retinoic acid (tretinoin) as part of the chemotherapeutic regimen improves the overall outcome in AML M3. AML M5 (monocytic) leukemia is frequently associated with leukemic infiltrates in the skin, gingiva, and central nervous system (CNS).

Prognosis in AML • Younger patients tend to fare better with AML. Certain mutations, such as t(15;17) or t(8;21), are associated with a favorable prognosis, but multiple mutations in the same patient are associated with an unfavorable prognosis. AML that develops secondary to previous chemotherapy or myelodysplasia has a very poor prognosis. Likewise, the AML associated with chronic myelogenous leukemia (CML) blast crisis has an unfavorable prognosis.

Infections in AML • After a thorough physical examination, appropriate x-rays, and cultures, empirical antibiotics should be started for the febrile (≥100.5 F) neutropenic (<500 ANC) patient. These antibiotics should be broad-spectrum to cover for gram-negative and gram-positive organisms. Particular attention should be given to the coverage of *Pseudomonas aeruginosa*. If the patient does not respond adequately after 2 days, vancomycin should be added for enhanced staphylococcal coverage. Antifungal therapy is not typically part of the initial empirical antibiotic regimen. However, amphotericin should be started if the patient has 4 to 6 days of uncontrolled or relapsing fevers on broad-spectrum antibiotic coverage.

● CASE PRESENTATION

A 26-year-old man reports a several-week history of a right supra-clavicular mass. He also reports night sweats and a 10-pound weight loss. The night sweats occur several times per week and require changing of his clothing or sheets. Past medical history, family history, and social history are unremarkable. Physical exam is remarkable for a 3-cm fixed, nontender lymph node in the right supraclavicular area as noted. He also has a palpable spleen tip. Lab testing reveals a normal white blood cell count, but the patient is anemic with hemoglobin of 9 g/dL. The chest x-ray result is suggestive of mediastinal adenopathy. A biopsy of the lymph node reveals nodular sclerosing Hodgkin's disease.

1. The presence on biopsy of which of the following characterizes Hodgkin's disease?
   A. Clonal proliferation of plasma cells
   B. Auer rods
   C. Large binucleated cells with prominent nucleoli (Reed-Sternberg cell)
   D. Lymphoblasts
   E. All of the above

2. Which of the following symptoms is *least* likely in patients with Hodgkin's disease?
   A. Unexplained itching
   B. Fever
   C. Weight loss
   D. Seizure
   E. Night sweats

3. Which of the following are appropriate steps in the evaluation and management of this patient?
   A. Referral to an oncologist for consideration of chemotherapy or radiation
   B. Scheduling of bone marrow biopsy and computed tomography (CT) scans of chest, abdomen, and pelvis to determine extent of disease
   C. Ordering of hepatic enzymes (including lactate dehydrogenase) and erythrocyte sedimentation rate (ESR)
   D. Consideration of staging laparotomy if radiation therapy is being considered for primary therapy
   E. All of the above

4. True statements regarding therapy for Hodgkin's disease include which of the following?
   A. Advanced stage disease is initially treated with radiation therapy.
   B. Radiation therapy has less risk of secondary carcinomas than chemotherapy.
   C. Infertility is a major concern for patients undergoing chemotherapy.
   D. Chemotherapy is contraindicated for patients with early stages of disease.
   E. All of the above

● COMMENT

Pathogenesis • The characteristic finding in Hodgkin's disease is the Reed-Sternberg cell, a large cell with bilobed nuclei and prominent nucleoli. There does seem to be some genetic susceptibility, though the cause is unknown. The histologic types of Hodgkin's include nodular sclerosing (most common in the United States), mixed cellularity (more common in older patients), lymphocyte-predominant (uncommon), and lymphocyte-depleted (worst prognosis). Multiple myeloma is a malignancy of plasma cells, and lymphocytic leukemias manifest lymphoblasts. Auer rods are characteristic of acute myelogenous leukemia (AML).

Clinical presentation • Hodgkin's disease is relatively rare overall. It is slightly more common in men with a peak incidence in the 20s and a second peak late in life. Many patients have nontender cervical or axillary adenopathy and no symptoms. Fever, night sweats, and weight loss (B symptoms) are present one third of the time and are associated with a poorer prognosis. Other symptoms can include generalized pruritus, cough (from mediastinal adenopathy), and lymph node pain with alcohol ingestion. Nephrotic syndrome and cerebellar degeneration are relatively rare complications. Impaired cellular immunity is generally evident and does not improve with successful therapy.

Staging and management • Staging is crucial in determining treatment. A complete staging work-up includes lab evaluation (including liver function tests, LDH, and ESR) and CT scans of the chest, abdomen, and pelvis, as well as a bone marrow biopsy. Stage I disease represents one node, stage II disease represents two or more nodal regions on the same side of the diaphragm, stage III represents nodal regions on both sides of the diaphragm, and stage IV indicates diffuse or disseminated involvement of one or more extranodal sites. Stages are also designated as A or B on the basis of the presence or absence of B symptoms. Staging laparotomy is rarely performed, but it would be considered if radiation therapy alone were contemplated. Oncology referral is needed for definitive therapy. Lymph node excision and monitoring is an unacceptable strategy.

Outcomes • Though patients with advanced stage disease and with B symptoms at presentation do not fare as well, overall prognosis is very good with appropriate therapy. This has led to increased focus on minimizing toxicity from therapy. Radiation therapy to the chest has been associated with an increased risk of secondary carcinomas, accelerated coronary artery disease, hypothyroidism, and other complications. Therefore, there is a trend toward initial treatment with chemotherapy (Adriamicin, bleomycin, vinblastine, dacarbazine [ABVD] or mechlorethamine, Oncovin, procarbazine, dacarbazine [MOPP]) for all stages of Hodgkin's disease. Chemotherapy (particularly MOPP) is associated with an increased risk of infertility and with an increased risk of secondary leukemia.

Answers • 1-C 2-D 3-E 4-C

● CASE PRESENTATION

Ms. C. is a 54-year-old woman who goes to your office for a routine physical examination. She admits to some slight fatigue, but she feels well overall. Past medical history is completely unremarkable. The only pertinent findings on physical examination are some painless supraclavicular, cervical, and axillary lymphadenopathy along with a palpable spleen tip. Findings of complete blood count (CBC), liver function tests, and a basic metabolic panel are unremarkable. Computed tomography (CT) scans of the chest and abdomen reveal mediastinal and retroperitoneal adenopathy. Splenomegaly is confirmed as well.

1. You have a strong clinical suspicion of lymphoma. Which diagnostic test would you perform next?

   A. Excisional biopsy of a cervical or supraclavicular lymph node
   B. Fine-needle biopsy of the spleen
   C. Staging laparotomy and retroperitoneal lymph node dissection
   D. Fine-needle aspiration of an accessible lymph node
   E. Follow-up in 3 to 4 months for reassessment

2. Low-grade non-Hodgkin's lymphoma (NHL) is confirmed as the diagnosis. Which of the following statements about NHL is true?

   A. NHL is decreasing in prevalence.
   B. The cure rate is superior for low-grade lymphomas.
   C. High-grade lymphomas are more likely than low-grade lymphomas to be widespread at diagnosis.
   D. High-grade lymphomas are generally very aggressive, but long-term disease-free survival is possible.
   E. Elevated lactate dehydrogenase (LDH) level is a good prognostic indicator in NHL.

3. Which of the following statements regarding the cell lineage of NHL is most accurate?

   A. T-cell lymphomas are much more common than B-cell lymphomas.
   B. Significant skin involvement is suggestive of B-cell lymphomas.
   C. B-cell lymphomas typically have a wider overall tissue distribution.
   D. The majority of lymphomas are of B-cell lineage.
   E. B- and T-cell lymphomas occur with approximately equal frequency.

4. Which statement regarding specific causes of NHL is accurate?

   A. Human immunodeficiency virus (HIV) infection places patients at a higher risk of primary central nervous system lymphomas.
   B. Gastric *Helicobacter pylori* infection is a risk factor for certain types of NHL.
   C. Certain autoimmune illnesses increase the risk for NHL.
   D. Human T-lymphotropic virus type I (HTLV-I) infection increases the risk for T-cell lymphomas.
   E. All of the above are accurate.

● COMMENT

Diagnosis • The diagnosis of NHL requires adequate tissue for histologic, immunologic, and cytogenetic studies. Excisional biopsy of an affected lymph node is the best diagnostic test and needle aspiration is not generally adequate. Staging in NHL should include a careful physical examination, CBC, metabolic panel, serum protein electrophoresis, bilateral bone marrow biopsies, and CT scans (chest, abdomen, and pelvis). Further evaluation should be guided by the characteristics of the patient's particular type of NHL and any symptoms the patient is experiencing.

Natural history of NHL • The prevalence of NHL is increasing for unknown reasons. There are a number of classification systems, but it is useful to group NHLs by the clinical behavior of the tumor. Low-grade lymphomas such as follicular lymphoma are often very indolent, with survival duration up to 10 years or more. These lymphomas can be responsive to chemotherapy or immunotherapy, but there is no evidence that they are curable. They are almost always widely disseminated at diagnosis. High-grade lymphomas such as large-cell lymphoma are very aggressive and death ensues quickly without treatment. However, high-dose multidrug chemotherapy (i.e., cyclophosphamide, hydroxydaunomycin, Oncovin, prednisone [CHOP]) can lead to long-term disease-free survival. Age greater than 60, elevated LDH level, poor performance status, advanced stage of disease, and extranodal involvement are poor prognostic indicators in NHL.

B-cell versus T-cell NHL • The majority (around 80%) of NHLs are of B-cell origin. B-cell lymphomas tend to occur in an anatomic distribution within the lymphatic system, and T-cell lymphomas tend to have a wider tissue distribution. T-cell lymphomas can have skin involvement as the major clinical manifestation (mycosis fungoides).

Conditions associated with NHL • A number of infectious agents have been associated with particular types of NHL. The incidence of NHL, particularly primary central nervous system (CNS) lymphomas, is significantly increased in human immunodeficiency virus (HIV) patients. Epstein-Barr virus is definitely linked to African Burkitt's lymphoma and has been associated with other lymphomas as well. HTLV-I can lead to adult T-cell leukemia and lymphoma. Gastric *Helicobacter pylori* infection is associated with mucosa-associated lymphoid tissue (MALT) tumors. In fact, eradication of *H. pylori* can result in significant regression of the tumor. Other immunodeficiencies also predispose patients to NHL. Additionally, autoimmune disorders, such as Sjögren's syndrome and rheumatoid arthritis, are associated with an increased risk for lymphoma.

Answers • 1-A 2-D 3-D 4-E

● CASE PRESENTATION

A 40-year-old woman has a change in color of a mole on her right shoulder. Approximately 2 months ago, the mole was the size of a pencil head; it has since doubled in size. She denies pruritis or bleeding at the site. She admits to extensive sunbathing in the past. She has a history of blistering sunburns as a child. There is a family history of melanoma in her father and paternal aunt. On physical exam, she is a healthy appearing fair-skinned woman in no distress. She has multiple dysplastic nevi. The mole on the shoulder is 1 cm by 2 cm, with irregular borders and multiple coloration, and is slightly raised. Her right axilla has no adenopathy. The results of laboratory tests including complete blood count (CBC) and liver panel are normal. The patient underwent wide local excision of the right shoulder lesion. Pathologic findings are consistent with malignant melanoma with a depth of invasion of 1.1 mm.

1. Risk factors for malignant melanoma include which of the following?
   A. History of blistering sunburns
   B. Living in a southern latitude
   C. Fair complexion and high incidence of freckling
   D. A positive family history of melanoma
   E. All of the above

2. Of the following, which is the most suspicious skin change for malignant melanoma?
   A. A mole with regular borders
   B. A mole with marked color variation
   C. An unpigmented, scaling lesion in a sun-exposed area
   D. A flesh-colored, pearly appearing lesion in a sun-exposed area
   E. A small, flat skin lesion

3. For melanoma patients without evidence of metastasis, what is the most important prognostic factor?
   A. The location of the lesion
   B. The skill of the surgeon
   C. The thickness of the tumor
   D. The absence of pigmentation
   E. Sensitivity of the tumor to chemotherapy

4. Primary treatment for melanoma without evidence of metastasis includes which of the following?
   A. Local excision with 1- to 2-cm margins
   B. Immunotherapy with interferon and/or interleukin 2
   C. Systemic chemotherapy
   D. Early regional lymph node dissection
   E. All of the above

● COMMENT

Risk factors • The amount of time spent in the sun, living in southern latitude, fair complexion, ease of freckling, history of blistering sunburns, and family history of melanoma are all important risk factors for the development of malignant melanoma. This patient most likely has the familial atypical mole and melanoma syndrome. This is characterized by one or more first- or second-degree relatives with a history of malignant melanoma together with large numbers of typical moles and dysplastic nevi. Affected patients have a very high risk of development of malignant melanoma. The familial syndrome is inherited in an autosomal dominant manner and requires careful monitoring by a dermatologist. The use of sunscreens has not been proved to alter risk.

Characteristic appearance • The mnemonic ABCDE (A, asymmetry; B, irregular border; C, color is mottled; D, large diameter; E, elevation and enlargement) helps one remember the signs of melanoma. Any change in the size, color, shape, or consistency of a nevus is reason for concern. Larger lesions with asymmetrical, irregular borders should raise concern. Melanomas are generally pigmented with some color variation (brown, black, red, blue, and white) as well. Any area can be affected, but the back and lower extremities are the most common sites. The four clinical types of melanoma are superficial spreading (the most common type), lentigo maligna (occurs commonly in the elderly), nodular (rapid vertical growth), and acrolentiginous (palmar, plantar, or subungual). Pearly, translucent papules with rolled edges are most consistent with basal cell carcinoma, the most common form of skin cancer.

Prognosis • The two major prognostic indicators in malignant melanoma are the presence or absence of metastasis and the thickness of the tumor. Thin tumors are associated with a much better prognosis. Melanoma often metastasizes to regional lymph nodes relatively early in the course. Liver, lung, bone, and brain are other common sites of metastasis. Cure is extremely unlikely after the tumor has metastasized. Sensitivity to chemotherapy is irrelevant for patients without evidence of metastasis.

Treatment • Local excision with 1- to 2-cm margins is the definitive treatment for localized melanoma. Early lymph node dissection is not indicated if there is no evidence of metastasis, though this conclusion is somewhat controversial. Immunotherapy (interferon-alpha and/or interleukin 2) or systemic chemotherapy is utilized in patients with metastatic disease.

● CASE PRESENTATION

A 33-year-old man was recently diagnosed with stage II (cancer extending into the serosa) colon cancer. He was in good health until he was found to have occult blood in his stools on routine employment physical. He underwent surgical resection without complications 6 weeks ago. He is taking no medications and neither drinks nor smokes. His family history is notable: his father had colon cancer at age 43, and two paternal aunts had colon cancer as well.

1. Which of the following is considered to be a risk factor for the development of colon cancer?

   A. Daily aspirin therapy
   B. Long-term oral calcium supplementation
   C. Family history of breast or gynecologic malignancies
   D. High-fiber diets
   E. All of the above

2. Which one of the following statements regarding this patient's colon cancer is true?

   A. If a new primary colon cancer develops, he should undergo a complete colectomy.
   B. Surveillance sigmoidoscopies should be performed every 5 years.
   C. His family history is coincidental and the patient should have routine screening at age 50.
   D. Routine radiographic evaluation with chest films and computed tomography (CT) scans for the next year will increase his survival.
   E. He should start aspirin therapy to protect against polyp formation.

3. Which of the following statements regarding colon cancer screening is true?

   A. Colonoscopy every 10 years beginning at age 50 is an acceptable screening technique for average-risk patients.
   B. Annual fecal occult blood testing is an ineffective screen because of poor sensitivity and specificity.
   C. Flexible sigmoidoscopy alone is an adequate screening test for patients with a known familial polyposis syndrome.
   D. Annual digital rectal examination definitively improves overall survival rate from colon cancer.
   E. Carcinoembryonic antigen (CEA) testing should begin at age 50 for most patients.

4. True statements regarding prognosis of colon cancer include which of the following?

   A. Low CEA levels at diagnosis portend a poor prognosis.
   B. Prognosis is excellent even with distant metastasis.
   C. Though immediately dangerous, bowel perforation is a good prognostic sign.
   D. Tumors limited to the mucosa and submucosa have a greater than 90% 5-year survival rate.
   E. All of the above

● COMMENT

Risk factors for colon cancer • Adenocarcinoma of the colon trails only lung cancer as a cause of cancer deaths in the United States. A strong family history is thought to be the single most important risk factor. In fact, a family history of breast cancer or gynecologic malignancies in a first-degree relative also confers increased risk. Most colon cancers arise from polyps, and a number of hereditary syndromes are associated with markedly increased risk (familial polyposis coli, Gardener's syndrome, Turcot's syndrome, hereditary nonpolyposis syndrome). A long history of inflammatory bowel syndrome, particularly ulcerative colitis, markedly increases the risk of colon cancer as well. Other risk factors seem to include a high-fat/low-fiber diet, living in developed countries, and hypercholesterolemia. Long-term dietary calcium supplementation and daily aspirin ingestion seem to decrease the risk of polyp formation.

Hereditary nonpolyposis colon cancer • This patient likely has hereditary nonpolyposis colon cancer (HNPCC), or Lynch syndrome. Diagnosis requires that at least three family members in at least two generations were diagnosed with colon cancer. Patients with this disorder have a high risk of development of colon cancer at an early age, often in the right colon. HPNCC occurs as a result of mutations in the deoxyribonucleic acid (DNA) mismatch repair genes on chromosomes 2 and 3. Many experts recommend total colectomy with the first diagnosis of colon cancer. A second primary colon cancer would certainly prompt colectomy.

Screening • Though fecal occult blood testing (FOBT) does have a low sensitivity and specificity for detecting colon cancer, screening with FOBT does result in an overall survival benefit for average-risk patients. Either periodic flexible sigmoidoscopies (every 3 to 5 years) or colonoscopies (every 10 years) beginning at age 50 are also good screening techniques. Patients with familial colon cancer syndromes should have colonoscopic screening approximately 10 years before the first familial diagnosis. Digital rectal exam affords no proven survival benefit. CEA testing is not a useful screening tool. Most colon cancer occurs in the left colon, but colon cancer resulting from familial polyposis syndromes tends to occur in the right colon. Flexible sigmoidoscopy is not an adequate screening test in these patients.

Prognosis • Overall prognosis in colon cancer closely parallels the degree of invasion at diagnosis, as surgical resection is the best treatment. Patients with distant metastases have a very poor prognosis, but cancer limited to the mucosa or submucosa is associated with an over 90% 5-year survival rate. Other poor prognostic indicators include high CEA levels, bowel perforation, and specific chromosomal deletions or mutations.

Answers • 1-C 2-A 3-A 4-D

● CASE PRESENTATION

A 70-year-old man reports weight loss and a nonproductive cough over the last several weeks. He and his family report some increasing lethargy as well. The patient is known to be a long-term smoker and has no significant past medical history. He takes no medications. On physical exam, he is a thin man in no acute distress. Vital signs are stable without orthostatic changes. A 3-cm mass is noted in the right supraclavicular fossa. There are decreased breath sounds throughout. Laboratory study results are remarkable for elevated serum calcium of 12 mg/dL. Chest radiograph reveals a right hilar mass. A chest computed tomography (CT) scan reveals the right hilar mass and paratracheal adenopathy.

1. In addition to tobacco abuse, which of the following is a known risk factor for lung cancer?
   A. Asthma
   B. Radon gas
   C. Bronchiectasis
   D. Allergic bronchopulmonary aspergillosis
   E. Wegener's granulomatosis

2. Which of these histologic types of lung cancer tends to be centrally located?
   A. Bronchoalveolar carcinoma
   B. Adenocarcinoma
   C. Small cell lung cancer
   D. Large cell lung cancer
   E. All of the above

3. Which histologic type of lung cancer is most commonly associated with a paraneoplastic process that causes hypercalcemia?
   A. Bronchoalveolar carcinoma
   B. Small cell carcinoma
   C. Adenocarcinoma
   D. Squamous cell carcinoma
   E. All equally associated with hypercalcemia

4. The highest cure rates in non–small cell lung cancer are associated with which of the following treatments?
   A. Surgical resection
   B. Primary radiation therapy
   C. Combination chemotherapy
   D. Chemotherapy and radiation therapy
   E. Immunotherapy

● COMMENT

Risk factors for lung cancer • The most common cause of lung cancer by far is tobacco abuse, particularly cigarette smoking. There are a number of recognized carcinogens in cigarette smoke, and even passive exposure to cigarette smoke has been associated with an increased risk of lung cancer. Other risk factors include asbestos exposure and radon gas (a product of uranium decay) exposure. The cancer potential of these exposures is multiplied by concomitant smoking. There seems to be a familial predisposition to lung cancer as well.

Tumor location • Adenocarcinoma (including bronchoalveolar) and large cell carcinoma usually produce peripheral nodules or masses. Small cell (oat cell) and squamous cell carcinoma (epidermoid) tend to cause central masses. Small cell carcinoma is usually widely metastatic at presentation and is thus staged as limited disease (tumor confined to one hemithorax and regional nodes) or extensive disease (any additional evidence of metastasis). Non–small cell cancers are somewhat less likely to have metastasized. These tumors are staged on the basis of the tumor size, node, and metastasis (TNM) system. Chest and abdomen CT scans can help identify the extent of disease, though any question of mediastinal adenopathy must be confirmed histologically. Bone scans and head CT scans should be ordered if symptoms are suggestive of tumor involvement in these areas.

Hypercalcemia of malignancy • Hypercalcemia of malignancy is the most common paraneoplastic syndrome and is usually mediated by parathyroid hormone–related peptide (PTHrP). PTHrP production is most common with squamous cell carcinoma. This can be treated with hydration and long-acting bisphosphonates (such as pamidronate disodium) along with therapy for the underlying malignancy. Other endocrine paraneoplastic syndromes in lung cancer include syndrome of inappropriate antidiuretic hormone (SIADH) (small cell), Cushing's syndrome (small cell), and gynecomastia (large cell).

Treatment of non–small cell lung cancer • Cure rates in non–small cell lung cancer correlate with TNM staging. This is largely because earlier stages of disease are surgically resectable in patients who can tolerate the surgery. Any tumor invasion of the mediastinum, evidence of tumor metastasis, contralateral mediastinal or hilar nodes, or supraclavicular nodal involvement (as seen in our patient) makes the tumor unresectable and survival rate is limited. Combination chemotherapy and radiation therapy is associated with some prolongation of life and improved quality of life, but long-term survival is extremely rare.

Answers • 1-B 2-C 3-D 4-A

● CASE PRESENTATION

A 55-year-old black man enters the office for a routine physical examination. The patient's only symptom is some diminution of his urine stream and two episodes of nocturia each night. Past medical history is unremarkable. Family history is remarkable for prostate cancer in his 80-year-old father. Physical exam is remarkable for a smoothly enlarged prostate with no discrete nodules. Laboratory evaluation reveals a PSA level at 12 ng/ml.

1. What is the most logical next step in evaluating your patient?
   A. Repeat the PSA and digital rectal exam in 1 year.
   B. Order a bone scan to look for bony metastases.
   C. Reassure the patient that he has no palpable mass and is at minimal risk for prostate cancer.
   D. Refer the patient for transrectal ultrasound and biopsy.
   E. Order CT scans of the chest, abdomen, and pelvis .

2. True statements regarding prostate cancer include which of the following?
   A. Prostate cancer is more common in blacks.
   B. Higher Gleason scores (histologic grades) are associated with a higher risk of metastases.
   C. Bone is the most common site of distant metastases.
   D. Not all patients with prostate cancer have an elevated PSA level.
   E. All of the above

3. Which of the following is the most logical treatment for localized prostate cancer?
   A. Alpha-blocker therapy
   B. Radical prostatectomy
   C. Testosterone replacement therapy
   D. Castration
   E. Chemotherapy

4. Which of the following is *not* a reasonable treatment for metastatic prostate cancer?
   A. Surgical castration
   B. Androgen deprivation with leuprolide acetate and flutamide
   C. Palliative radiation therapy for bony metastases
   D. Estrogen therapy
   E. Testosterone therapy

● COMMENT

Evaluation of elevated PSA level • Screening for prostate cancer with digital rectal examination (DRE) and annual PSA testing is somewhat controversial, but most authorities recommend annual screening for patients 50 and older. The PSA level can be elevated in patients with benign hypertrophy (BPH), but the levels are virtually always less than or equal to 10 ng/ml. Patients with abnormalities on DRE or with a PSA level greater than 10 ng/ml should undergo transrectal ultrasound-guided needle biopsy. Patients with PSA levels between 4 and 10 and a normal DRE result can either be referred for transrectal ultrasound (and possible biopsy) or monitored to assess any increase in the PSA level over time.

Prostate cancer • Adenocarcinoma of the prostate is the most common cancer in men and one of the leading causes of cancer deaths in men. Advancing age and a family history in a first-degree relative increase the risk of prostate cancer. Additionally, prostate cancer is more common in blacks than in whites. Patients have symptoms similar to those of benign prosthetic hypertrophy (urgency, hesitancy, nocturia), symptoms from bony metastases, or no symptoms at all. The histologic grade or Gleason score (range of 2 to 10) does seem to predict biologic behavior, as there are much higher rates of metastasis in patients with higher scores. PSA level is also somewhat predictive of tumor spread. Bone is the most common site of distant metastasis. PSA levels are generally elevated in prostate cancer, but up to one-third of prostate cancer patients have a normal PSA level.

Treatment of localized disease • Patients with disease localized to the prostate can be treated with radical prostatectomy or radiation therapy (external beam radiation or radiation seed implants). Incontinence and erectile dysfunction are common side effects of both therapies.

Treatment of metastatic disease • Prostate cancer is androgen-sensitive so androgen deprivation is the treatment of choice for patients with metastatic disease. This can be accomplished with surgical castration, but most patients prefer medical therapy. This generally consists of monthly injections of leuprolide acetate, which inhibits pituitary gonadotropin production coupled with the androgen receptor blocker flutamide. Testosterone therapy is contraindicated.

Answers • 1-D 2-E 3-B 4-E

● CASE PRESENTATION

A postmenopausal 52-year-old white woman without significant medical history has routine follow-up. Family history is remarkable for breast cancer in the patient's mother, who was diagnosed at age 50. Physical exam is remarkable for a 1-cm, firm nodule at 2 o'clock in the right breast. A recent mammogram was read as unremarkable.

1. What is your next step in the management of this patient?
   A. Reassure the patient that her mammogram is normal.
   B. Repeat the mammogram in 6 months.
   C. Refer the patient for breast biopsy.
   D. Urge the patient to avoid chocolate and caffeine.
   E. Instruct the patient to return for repeat exam in 2 to 4 weeks.

2. Which of the following is associated with an increased risk of breast cancer?
   A. Early onset of menses
   B. Family history of breast cancer in a first-degree relative
   C. Female sex
   D. Delayed menopause
   E. All of the above

3. Which of the following is associated with a favorable prognosis?
   A. Presence of tumor in axillary nodes
   B. Presence of distant metastases
   C. Large primary tumor
   D. Expression of estrogen receptors
   E. High growth fraction of the tumor

4. Common sites of metastasis for breast cancer include:
   A. Bone
   B. Liver
   C. Lung
   D. Brain
   E. All of the above

● COMMENT

Diagnosis • Postmenopausal women with a solid breast mass (like our patient) should have mammography and excisional breast biopsy, regardless of the mammogram results. Premenopausal women with a nonsuspicious small mass should undergo repeat examination in 2 to 4 weeks and persistent masses should be aspirated. For patients between the ages of 50 and 69, screening with annual mammography and physician breast exam has been shown to improve survival rate for women of average risk. The benefits of screening mammography for younger patients are less clear, but many authorities recommend initiating screening at 35 or 40 years of age.

Risk factors • The average American woman has about a 1:9 lifetime risk of development of breast cancer, which is a 150 times greater incidence than in men. The incidence of breast cancer increases with advancing age. Patients with a first-degree relative with breast cancer are at increased risk; approximately 8% to 10% of breast cancer is familial. Breast cancer is hormone-dependent, so early onset of menses and delayed menopause increase the risk of breast cancer as well. Estrogen replacement therapy seems to increase the risk somewhat, but the overall benefits of hormone replacement therapy may outweigh the risks. Dietary fat and excess alcohol intake are controversial risk factors. BRCA-1 and BRCA-2 mutations are associated with an increased risk of breast cancer.

Factors affecting prognosis • Prognosis is dictated by the size of the primary tumor, the involvement of regional lymph nodes, and the presence or absence of distant metastases. These factors are used to stage the tumor, and advanced stages are associated with a worse prognosis. Tumors expressing estrogen receptors have an improved prognosis, but overexpression of HER-2/neu, p53 mutations, high growth fraction, and aneuploidy are associated with a worse prognosis.

Sites of metastasis • Common sites of breast cancer metastasis include bone, lungs, liver, skin, and brain. However, breast cancer can spread almost anywhere.

Answers • 1-C   2-E   3-D   4-E

● CASE PRESENTATION

A 69-year-old gentleman with recently diagnosed stage 3b non–small cell lung carcinoma returns to your office after several rounds of radiation therapy without apparent complications. He is feeling well, without symptoms, and this bears out on his physical exam and a recent chest x-ray he gives you from his radiation oncologist, which shows some regression of his tumor. His wife is accompanying him as usual, and after reporting your encouraging findings, you ask whether now would be a good time to discuss advanced directives. They appear perplexed by this turn in the conversation but agree that they probably should.

1. He volunteers that that he feels that when he has clearly reached "the end of the road," he does not want cardiopulmonary resuscitation, "breathing machines," food by "the tube," and wants to be allowed to go in peace. You inform him that:

   A. It is unethical and violates the Hippocratic oath to withhold food from any patient.
   B. In "Do not resuscitate" (DNR) patients, it is standard practice to withhold all medical therapy, including nutrition.
   C. He should be certain of his wish, since once documented it is irreversible.
   D. If some medical personnel unknowingly place a feeding tube during an acute deterioration in his condition, it is illegal to remove it.
   E. None of the above

2. His wife asks you whether he is likely to have much pain near the end of life. When you tell her that it is likely, she asks you how doctors usually treat this pain. You inform her:

   A. Frequently, opiates need to be prescribed, but addiction is a concern.
   B. To gain effective pain relief, it is likely that you need to give him such large doses of narcotics that he will be somnolent near the end.
   C. You will be able to control his pain with narcotics, but pain medicine should be cut back at the end to prevent hastening death.
   D. Large-dose narcotics may be necessary, but it is usually possible to titrate these medications to pain relief, without compromising a patient's level of consciousness.
   E. None of the above

3. He asks you about some cases reported in the media of doctors who "helped" their terminally ill patients commit suicide. He talks about one such case in considerable detail and then waits for you to respond.

   A. You tell him that euthanasia involves providing the means for a patient to commit suicide, and "physician-assisted suicide" entails the physician's actively participating in the patient's death.
   B. You tell him that it is illegal to discuss such actions, let alone perform them.
   C. You discuss the reasons why this case had such significance for him and subtly check for signs of suicidal ideation and depression.
   D. You reason that he is obviously frightened and depressed by what the future holds and prescribe an antidepressant.
   E. None of the above

4. His wife asks you whether they need to get an attorney to draw up a living will. You tell her:

   A. A living will is a document that explicitly defines a patient's wishes in the event he or she is unable to make informed health care decisions. It does not require an attorney.

   B. It is unnecessary to have a living will, since family members usually know what patients would want done.
   C. A living will is unnecessary, since the physician can decide the appropriate end of life care.
   D. It is appropriate to have a living will drawn up now, but it may be better to wait until he becomes ill, since his wishes may change, and no doctor will oppose a living will.
   E. Living wills are a good idea but need to be drawn up and notarized, with a copy for the patient and a copy to the chart; otherwise, they will be disregarded.

● COMMENT

Terminal nutrition and hydration • Terminal nutrition and hydration are often considered therapies that address basic needs and therefore require application of different standards than other treatments. Physicians and families often equate these needs with their own basic sensations of hunger and thirst. However, in incapacitated terminally ill patients, these sensations are largely blunted. Furthermore, there is no historical or legal precedent that distinguishes these levels of care from other modalities. It is more important to understand that a patient (or surrogate) has autonomy to choose his or her level of support as the end of life approaches.

Palliative care • Palliative care addresses the needs of terminally ill patients, focusing on care over cure. Terminal patients frequently suffer from severe pain and require large doses of narcotics to relieve their suffering. Physicians have historically been reluctant to address these needs for fear of creating a state of addiction to the medications or creating such tolerance that medications lose their efficacy. These fears are unfounded, as legitimate use of strong narcotics is unlikely to create a state of addiction (regardless of whether this is germane to a terminally ill patient) and can continue to be effective with titration to sufficient dosages. The skilled provider can titrate medication to effect pain relief without compromising a patient's level of consciousness. When a patient is near death, it is ethically imperative to continue serving the patient's needs, including appropriate analgesia, which in many circumstances may actually hasten death in exchange for pain relief.

Euthanasia • Euthanasia entails causing death, at a patient's request, through direct participation by the physician. Physician-assisted suicide is less direct, in that a physician provides the means (medications, etc.) for the patient to commit suicide. These practices are highly debatable on ethical and legal grounds, and most physician organizations oppose them. When patients, regardless of their level of illness, choose to discuss the issue of suicide, it is the provider's obligation to explore these thoughts in more detail, paying particular attention to signs of depression or suicidal ideation.

Living wills • Living wills are directed documents specifically stating the patient's preferences in the event that he or she becomes too incapacitated to make decisions concerning health care. Though legally binding in all 50 states, they need not be drawn up by an attorney nor notarized. A *durable power of attorney* is a document that is drawn up in the legal setting, where legal authority is appointed to a surrogate of the patient's choosing to make health care decisions in the event of incapacitation. Living wills are binding but can be changed at any time by the patient. The importance of living wills stems from studies showing that providers and families seldom know patients' preferences regarding end of life issues.

Answers • 1-E 2-D 3-C 4-A

● CASE PRESENTATION

A new finger-stick blood test is developed to check rapidly for the presence of a deep vein thrombosis (DVT) at the bedside. The manufacturer claims 80% sensitivity and 80% specificity on the basis of a preliminary study conducted in a large teaching hospital's emergency room. All patients reported new-onset unilateral leg pain, edema, and tenderness. The presence or absence of DVT was ultimately determined by venography, the gold standard. The data is as follows:

TABLE 4 · Deep Vein Thrombosis

	Present	Absent	Totals
Test result positive	32	12	44
Test result negative	8	48	56
Totals	40	60	100

1. The positive predictive value, in terms of the data specified, is closest to:
   A. 86%
   B. 80%
   C. 73%
   D. 40%
   E. 14%

2. Of the patients who had a negative test result, 85.7% (48 of 56) did not have a DVT. The term used to describe this probability is:
   A. Incidence
   B. Negative predictive value
   C. Odds ratio
   D. Negative confounder
   E. Hazard ratio

3. The prevalence of DVT in this group of patients is:
   A. 100%
   B. 60%
   C. 44%
   D. 40%
   E. None of the above

4. The staff at a large emergency room (ER) is considering the study described in designing triage protocols for patients who have similar symptoms. They note a significant difference in their patient population from that of the study in that only about 20 in 100 of their patients who have the symptom actually have a DVT. They anticipate the effect of this is:
   A. No change in the sensitivity of the test in their ER
   B. A decrease in the positive predictive value of the test in their ER
   C. An increase in the negative predictive value
   D. None of the above
   E. A, B, or C

● COMMENT

Positive predictive value · Positive predictive value (or predictive value positive) is the measure (proportion or percentage) of the patients who actually have the disease, if they have a positive test result. For the DVT exercise, the calculation is $32/(32 + 12) = 0.727$ or 72.7%. *Sensitivity* represents the proportion or percentage of patients with the disease in question who have a positive test result. Similarly, the *specificity* of a test is the proportion of patients without the given disease, who have a negative test result. In our exercise, these are not given but can easily be calculated as well: $32/(32 + 8) = 0.8$ and $48/(12 + 48) = 0.8$ (respectively).

Negative predictive value · Negative predictive value (or predictive value negative) is analogously the percentage or proportion of those who have a negative test result who actually do not have the disease in question. In our exercise, this is calculated as follows: $48/(8 + 48) = 0.857$ or 85.7%. We say that a given individual has an 85.7% probability of not having a DVT when he experiences new-onset unilateral pain, tenderness, and edema, *if* the test result is negative.

Prevalence · Prevalence is the proportion of a given population with the disease in question. In our exercise, this is $40/(40 + 60) = 0.40$ (or 40%). It is important to understand that this means 40% of patients who have unilateral leg pain, tenderness, and edema actually have a DVT. The prevalence for those who have fewer symptoms is likely to be lower, and the prevalence of DVT in the general population (regardless of symptoms) is much lower still.

Changes in test characteristics based on prevalence · Commonly, we talk of the merit or strength of a test in terms of its sensitivity or specificity; however, predictive values (positive or negative) convey more meaning to the value of a given test. Furthermore, we use (or estimate) the prevalence to gauge whether that particular test would be helpful in a setting (or with a patient). In our exercise, the prevalence of DVT for those patients with the symptoms specified in the ER that is considering implementing the test is only 20%, or half of what it was in the study. The sensitivity and specificity do not change for the two settings; however, now $16/(16 + 16) = 50\%$ of patients who have a positive test result actually have a DVT. For those with a negative result, $64/(64 + 4) = 94\%$ do not have a DVT. A decrease in the prevalence increases our negative predictive value (we can be more confident when we tell patients who had negative test results that they do not have a DVT) but lowers our positive predictive value (a greater proportion of those who have a positive test result actually do not have a DVT; this is called a false-positive result).

• Index